On Becoming
a Leader

Also by Warren Bennis

More praise for *On Becoming a Leader*

"Warren Bennis—master practitioner, researcher, and theoretician all in one—has managed to create a practical primer for leaders without sacrificing an iota of necessary subtlety and complexity. No topic is more important; no more able and caring person has attacked it."

—TOM PETERS

"The lessons here are crisp and persuasive."

—FORTUNE

"This is Warren Bennis's most important book."

—PETER DRUCKER

"A joy to read. . . studded with gems of insight."

—DALLAS TIMES-HERALD

"Bennis identifies the key ingredients of leadership success and offers a game plan for cultivating those qualities."

—SUCCESS

"Clearly Bennis's best work in a long line of impressive, significant contributions."

—BUSINESS FORUM

"Totally intriguing, thought-stretching insights into the clockworks of leaders. Bennis has masterfully peeled the onion to reveal the heartseed of leadership. Read it and reap."

—HARVEY B. McKAY

"Warren Bennis gets to the heart of leadership, to the essence of integrity, authenticity, and vision that can never be pinned down to a manipulative formula. This book can help any of us select the new leaders we so urgently need."

—BETTY FRIEDAN

"Warren Bennis's insight and his gift with words make these lessons, from some of America's most interesting leaders, compelling reading for every executive."

—CHARLES HANDY

On Becoming
a Leader

Warren Bennis

BASIC
BOOKS

A MEMBER OF THE PERSEUS BOOKS GROUP
NEW YORK

Library of Congress Control Number: 2003100205
ISBN: 978-0-465-01408-8; 0-7382-0817-5

Basic Books is a member of the Perseus Books Group.
Find us on the World Wide Web at www.basicbooks.com.
Books published by Basic Books are available at special
discounts for bulk purchases in the U.S. by corporations,
institutions, and other organizations. For more information,
please contact the Special Markets Department at the
Perseus Books Group, 2300 Chestnut Street, Suite 200,
Philadelphia, PA 19103, or call (800) 810-4145, ext. 5000,
or e-mail special.markets@perseusbooks.com.

Text design by Lisa Kreinbrink
Set in 11-point Janson Text by the Perseus Books Group

LSC-C

21   20   19

To David Cannom, MD,
David Gergen, and
Stephen Sample
for their unsparing efforts to make
our world healthier and saner.

Contents

Acknowledgments

Although mine is the only name on this book, it has been a collaboration, as all books are. I discovered long ago that the way I learn most effectively is in conversation with other people. It is in the playful, exhilarating, joyous thrashing out of ideas with brilliant colleagues that my own ideas are brought to life, refined and vetted. In previous editions of *On Becoming a Leader*, I tried to acknowledge all the people who originally helped to shape this book, and I remain enormously grateful to all those original collaborators and other colleagues and friends who so generously shared their counsel, expertise, and time.

For this twenty-first-century edition, collaborators deserve special mention. First is my assistant at the University of Southern California, Marie Christian. Tirelessly, and with great tact and intelligence, Marie keeps my professional life in order. In ways great and small, she frees me to think and write, for which I am grateful on a daily basis. Next is Nick Philipson, my editor at Perseus Books. In preparing the 2003 edition of *On Becoming a Leader*, Nick did far more than an editor is expected to do. He began by re-reading the book with an affectionate but critical eye, noting the places where it continued to speak to today's reality and, even more important, identifying those passages that were no longer resonant. He gave me a map for revising the book that made the task far less daunting. And, throughout the process, he was a friend and colleague of the best sort, offering sharp insights as well as praise, alert for errors but protective of my voice and ideas, and both involved in the work and unobtrusive. In short, he was a joy to work with. For the anniversary edition, Eric Paul Biederman contributed valuable insight, able editing, and a critical eye. Finally, I must thank my longtime friend and collaborator Patricia Ward Biederman. Pat and I have the kind of working relationship people dream about. For decades now, she has stimulated my ideas and helped them soar. Each time we work together, I am reminded that the best collaborations are those in which there is much thought, much passion, and much laughter.

Introduction
to the Revised
Edition, 2003

The introduction is a snapshot of the world as it was when a book was written. When I wrote the original introduction to *On Becoming a Leader*, just before its publication in 1989, the world was on the brink of extraordinary change. Although few of us could have predicted it, the Berlin Wall would fall in November, to the joyous clamor of rock music, effectively ending the partition of Germany that dated back to the end of World War II. But when the book came out earlier in the year, Germany was still divided, the Soviet Union was intact, and another, older George Bush was president of the United States. Not far from Berlin was the relatively peaceful, unified nation of Yugoslavia. The man who would later be hailed as the George Washington of Africa, Nelson Mandela, remained a prisoner of apartheid in a South African jail. The only people familiar with the Internet were 400 users at a handful of universities and government agencies, and even those visionaries were unaware how utterly it would transform everything from the global economy to the way terrorists do their awful business. In

1989, Americans had cordless phones and VCRs, but the cell phone and the DVD existed only in the human imagination.

Fast forward thirteen years to 2002. As I write this in Cambridge, Massachusetts, much of the world is consumed with the question of whether the United States will go to war with Iraq. Former President Jimmy Carter recently won the Nobel Peace Prize, and, days later, North Korea revealed that it has nuclear weapons after all. The possibility of nuclear catastrophe looms over the planet as it has not done since the early 1960s, at the height of the Cold War, when every American school child knew to duck and cover in case of a Soviet attack. When I wrote that original introduction, the United States was still recovering from the stock market crash of October 1987. Since then, the nation has undergone a period of unprecedented prosperity— only to become mired, in the last year or two, in the most painful recession most people under 50 have ever seen. In 1989, the Democrats, eager to take back the White House, had high hopes for the charismatic young governor of Arkansas. Bill Clinton would serve two terms as president, only to be impeached (and ultimately acquitted) after a tacky scandal involving a young White House intern with an infamous blue dress. George W. Bush is now in the Oval Office, after losing the popular vote in 2000 and having the presidential election decided, for the first time ever, by the Supreme Court of the United States. The human genome has been decoded and the secrets of the human brain revealed as never before, thanks to extraordinary imaging technology. And AIDS is no longer an automatic death sentence in America, although it is killing more people in sub-Saharan Africa than any disease since the great plagues of the Middle Ages and rapidly spreading throughout Asia.

The opening chapter of *On Becoming a Leader* urges readers to "master the context," and that is both more important than ever and more difficult. In some ways, everything is different from how it was in 1989. Indeed in his 1999 best-seller, *The Lexus and the Olive Tree*, Pulitzer Prize–winning journalist Thomas L. Friedman writes: "the world is only ten years old."

The World Wide Web provides the most dramatic example of how the last decade has transformed the world. In 1989, the Internet's 400 early adopters were predicting that it would revolutionize how people communicate, but even they could not imagine how pervasive it would become. As I write this, there are more than 580 million Internet users worldwide, and usage doubles every 100 days. Even if the Berlin Wall had not fallen on November 9, 1989, the ability of people around the world to effectively communicate electronically brought down *all* the walls that previously separated and ghettoized nations.

Since 1989, technology has done what ideology could not and created a worldwide community of the wired. The web allows revolutionary minorities to make their case to the outside world, even when they are under siege, as rebels did several years ago in the Mexican state of Chiapas. But even as technology has facilitated the global exchange of ideas and made the world a smaller place, it has failed to make it a peaceful one. The last time I had the heart to check, the world was torn by twenty-five border disputes, involving some forty nations. And instant communication—that most modern of inventions—has facilitated, rather than impeded, the rise of religious fundamentalism around the world, in a form that demonizes nonbelievers and gleefully puts the most up-to-date technology to medieval use. As a result, we now live in a world where a woman can still be stoned to death for adultery, and everyone can watch it on satellite TV.

The world has undergone economic transformation as well. China has embraced entrepreneurism and other forms of capitalism. And the European Union, once dismissed as a Utopian pipe dream, is now a reality—so real it has eliminated the franc and the deutsche mark and replaced them with the Esperanto of currencies, the euro. In the United States during the last dozen years, the New Economy emerged, soared, and crashed. During the 1990s, it seemed as if every bright twenty-something started his or her own e-business and saw its stock boom even before products were marketed or profits turned. Given that this was an economy based almost entirely on promise, the dot bomb should have come as no surprise. But certain elements of the New Economy are still valid in spite of the woeful state of the Nasdaq.

The New Economy was fueled by intellectual capital, as the economy of the twenty-first century will be. The days when a company's most important assets are buildings and equipment are gone forever. Ideas are now the acknowledged engine and currency of the global economy. For leaders, and would-be leaders, the take-home lesson of the New Economy is that power follows ideas, not position. Right now, the business media are filled with stories on how dispirited workers have abandoned the dream of early retirement as they watch their 401(k) balances shrink quarter after quarter. In the last half of 2002, workers are happy to have jobs, and are doing what they have to do to keep them. But that will change. And when it does, leaders who want their organizations to succeed will once again have to reward, even cosset, those employees who have the best ideas. Bad economic times allow second-rate leaders to exercise power recklessly and with impunity. Good times will come again, and when they do, the leaders who survive and flourish will be those who treat the people around them, not as underlings, but as invaluable colleagues and collaborators.

Just as the New Economy rose and fell, so has the imperial leader. One of the truly dreadful trends of the 1990s was the emergence of the celebrity CEO. Chrysler's Lee Iacocca was probably the first modern business leader whose face became as recognizable as a film or rock star's. Americans have always tended to see their institutions as the lengthened shadows of great men—a tendency that drove a genuinely collaborative leader like John Adams to near madness—and we have tended to reward such charismatic leaders out of proportion to their contribution. But that tendency got completely out of hand in the last years of the twentieth century.

The principal indicator of how out of sync the image and reality of the typical corporate leader had become was executive compensation. No one expects successful entrepreneurs or hardworking heads of successful companies to take a vow of poverty, but executive compensation spun out of control in the 1990s. In 1970, a CEO in America made forty-four times as much as the average worker. By the year 2000, the average CEO was making more than 300 times the average worker's salary, according to the AFL-CIO. *BusinessWeek* reported in 2002 that America's top executives had median annual compensation of $11 million, in a nation where the median income is around $30,000 a year.

The most disturbing aspect of this grotesque disparity is that it underlines the dangerous and growing gap between the 1 percent of Americans who control 50 percent of the wealth and everyone else—namely, the vanishing middle class and a burgeoning underclass that lacks hope and health insurance. The rise of the middle class was the great economic success story of the second half of the twentieth century. The disappearance of that middle class, made up of people who had come to believe that loyalty and hard work would bring security and a comfortable standard of living, may well turn out to be the most important economic story of the new century. And unless the current trend toward more and more wealth in fewer and fewer hands is reversed, it could be a very grim story indeed.

When CEOs began to make as much as tsars, they should have known they would eventually reap the whirlwind. Instead, many became increasingly arrogant. In 2001 and 2002, one high-flying company after another crashed, in a spreading scandal about accounting irregularities, illegal loans, and insider trading. The march of shame included Enron, WorldCom, Adelphia, Global Crossing, and ImClone—some of their top executives were indicted and led off in handcuffs. Most shocking of all may have been the prospect of domestic goddess Martha Stewart facing criminal charges for selling her ImClone stock shortly before it was announced that its much anticipated new cancer drug would not get FDA approval. Her downfall was anticipated with unseemly glee by people who joked about prison-striped wallpaper and stenciling her cell, a case of taking-pleasure-in-the-pain-of-others that one wag termed *Marthafreude*.

Philosopher Ralph Waldo Emerson used to hail friends he had not seen for a long time with the greeting: "What's become clear to you since we last met?" One thing that has become clearer than ever to me is that integrity is the most important characteristic of a leader, and one that he or she must be prepared to demonstrate again and again. Too many leaders—corporate heads but church officials and leaders in countless other fields as well—forgot that they were under scrutiny and that they could be called to account at any time. They forgot that something's being legal doesn't mean it's right. And they forgot that what the public giveth, it can take away. Just ask Martha Stewart.

The corporate scandals have had a devastating effect on the stock market, one that is liable to persist long after the headlines about Enron and other rogue companies have been forgotten. Trillions of dollars of wealth were destroyed by men who themselves walked away with princely severance packages. So pervasive was the cloud over American business that Intel's former CEO Andy Grove declared: "These days I'm ashamed I'm part of corporate America."

Where does this leave today's leaders? One likely outcome of the recent tumult is that, eventually, executive compensation will become more modest, although CEOs are still likely to make more in a year than the average worker will make in a lifetime. Because workers are now stockholders, thanks largely to those now shrunken 401(k)s, they are likely to demand more genuine performance of their leaders in the future and to pay them less lavishly for it. Heads of nonprofits and other large organizations will likely receive less money and more scrutiny as well. That will probably be a good thing. Everything we learn about creativity suggests that money is more often an obstacle to creative work than an incentive. More modestly paid leaders might be able concentrate more fully on the intrinsic rewards of doing good work. And they might be more likely to recognize that their role has a moral dimension that is just as important, in its way, as fattening the bottom line.

My hope is that the furor will die down enough for people to look, deeply and critically, at such vital questions as, What are the purposes of the corporation and other organizations in today's world? The metaphor of the organization as a machine that creates value for stakeholders is too simplistic, everyone agrees. But what metaphors are more illuminating? I am intrigued by the notion of the organization as a changing, responsive organism and by Charles Handy's ideas about the organization as community. The case for viewing a company or other organization as a community is especially compelling in a world where we spend more and more of our lives in the workplace and grow ever hungrier for greater balance between work and personal life. Even as we are shackled by our pagers and cell phones to the workplace, we long for work that seems meaningful enough to justify missing out on great chunks of our children's lives. Leaders of every kind of organization need to be thinking long and hard about such issues as meaningful rewards for workers and humanizing the downsized workplace. It would be tragic if the recent scandals so distracted and preoccupied leaders that they failed to address these moral and philosophical concerns. And it would be even more tragic if the scandals were to cause business to be perceived as an unworthy calling, just as political scandals have so often tainted public service in the past.

As ugly as the recent headlines have been, I think it is important to remember that our attitudes toward leaders are cyclical. We tend to lavish disproportionate attention and praise on them for a time, to treat them like royalty, only to turn on them at some point and treat them like devils. Neither extreme is true. It is worth remembering that for every Dennis Kozlowski (the ousted CEO of Tyco), there are hundreds, even thousands of able, honorable business leaders. And there are good men and women at the top in non-government organizations, community-action groups, colleges and universities, cultural institutions, and other nonprofit organizations. These are the people would-be leaders need to seek out and emulate.

Let me give you just one example. I recently published a book comparing and contrasting young and old leaders, titled *Geeks and Geezers*. One of the impressive senior leaders co-author Bob Thomas and I interviewed was Sidney Harman, CEO of Harman International Industries. Not long ago, when every day seemed to bring a new revelation of corporate mischief, Sidney sent a message to the company's stakeholders in its quarterly report. He told them that the company does no business with its mostly independent board members and outlined the mechanisms that are in place to ensure the integrity of the board and the firm itself. He assured the stakeholders that he would know if something were amiss because, he wrote, "I am fully engaged in this company. I pay attention and I know what goes on throughout it." There is a name for that kind of responsive, responsible behavior. It's called leadership.

One of the most important things that Sidney, like all great leaders, does is to cultivate a culture of candor. I had been writing about leadership for many years before it struck me that there was a vital aspect of any organization's success that had been overlooked—not great leadership, but great followership. Sidney keeps a plaque on his desk that reads: "In every business there is always someone who knows exactly what is going on. That person should be fired." Sidney's plaque is ironic, of course, and he is committed to listening to, even inviting, informed dissent. But, in too many organizations, those who speak unwelcome truths *are* fired or at least marginalized.

One tragic example involves the Challenger explosion. On January 28, 1989, the Space Shuttle Challenger exploded shortly after launch, killing all on board—six astronauts and the first teacher in space, Christa McAuliffe. It was the worst space disaster in American history, made even more heartbreaking by the presence of the crew's families, and it need not have happened. Only the day before, Roger Boisjoly, an engineer with NASA supplier Morton Thiokol, had warned his superiors that there was a serious flaw in the spaceship's O-rings. Boisjoly's fate was that of so many modern-day Cassandras whose well-informed alarms are ignored. Boisjoly's reward for his courageous efforts to prevent the disaster was the end of his career. Since then, he has made his living lecturing on whistle blowing and other ethical issues, in large part, because he was unable to get another job in aerospace. One hard-won bit of advice he gives would-be whistle blowers—make sure you have another job lined up first.

However honorable, dissenters are rarely embraced by their organizations. I am reminded of a recent cartoon showing an industrial titan, surrounded by his suited minions, who is barking: "All those opposed, signify by saying, 'I quit.'" Organizations tend to deal harshly with those who insist upon speaking embarrassing truths, as Enron's Sherron Watkins learned, as did FBI agent and critic Colleen Rowley. And yet no one is more valuable to the organization than the subordinate willing to speak truth to power. Organizations sometimes go to absurd, even immoral lengths to ignore bad news—the auto industry's silence on dangerous car and truck models is an egregious example. But authentic leaders embrace those who speak valuable truths, however hard they are to hear. Nothing will sink a leader faster than surrounding him- or herself with yes-men and women. Even when principled nay-sayers are wrong, they force leaders to reevaluate their positions and to poke and prod their assumptions for weaknesses. Good ideas are only made stronger by being challenged. The subordinate who speaks truth to power needs courage, and may pay the price for candor. But, by doing so, he or she evinces nothing less than leadership. The willingness to stand up to the bosses may not save the candid individual's job, but it will serve him or her well in another, better organization.

That brings me to another thing I've learned since writing *On Becoming a Leader*. Great leaders and followers are always engaged in a creative collaboration. We still tend to think of leaders, like artists, as solitary geniuses. In fact, the days when a single individual, however gifted, can solve our problems are long gone. The problems we face today come at us so fast and are so complex, that we need groups of talented people to tackle them, led by gifted leaders, or even teams of leaders. As co-author Patricia Ward Biederman and I write in our book, *Organizing Genius: The*

Secrets of Creative Collaboration, "The Lone Ranger is dead." In order to lead a Great Group, a leader need not possess all the individual skills of the group members. What he or she must have are vision, the ability to rally the others, and integrity. Such leaders also need superb curatorial and coaching skills—an eye for talent, the ability to recognize correct choices, contagious optimism, a gift for bringing out the best in others, the ability to facilitate communication and mediate conflict, a sense of fairness, and, as always, the kind of authenticity and integrity that creates trust. Nothing about the world today is simpler than it was or slower than it was, which makes the ability to collaborate and facilitate great collaboration more vital than ever.

Two recent events seem especially relevant to leadership today. The first is 9/11. The terrorist attacks on the World Trade Center and the Pentagon on September 11, 2001, changed American life as profoundly as the attack on Pearl Harbor. Those of us who think fulltime about leadership and change have long argued that the pace of change continues to accelerate and that we must find ways to embrace and celebrate it. But some change is hard to love, and 9/11 is a prime example. Since the Great Depression, the United States has been a place of growing security. No war has been fought on American soil since the Civil War. For all its inequality and racism, the nation has been a place of remarkable freedom and acceptance of diversity. The attacks of 9/11 made the United States seem far less safe. In 2002, the terrorist bombing of a night club in Bali, clearly aimed at Westerners, and a series of sniper attacks in the Washington, D.C., suburbs, further eroded America's sense of itself as a secure nation. We are still coming to terms with 9/11, trying to find meaning in the thousands of casualties, digging in its rubble for lessons that will transform it into something more than a senseless catastrophe.

One thing we know is that a more dangerous world makes the need for leadership, in every organization, in every institution, more pressing than ever. In 2002, in the course of studying how geeks and geezers became leaders, Bob Thomas and I discovered that their leadership always emerged after some rite of passage, often a stressful one. We call the experience that produces leaders a crucible. I once told an interviewer who asked how I became interested in leadership, that it was impossible to live through the 1930s and '40s without thinking about leadership. There *were* giants on the earth in those days—leaders of the stature of FDR, Churchill, and Gandhi. And there were also men who wielded enormous power in the most horrific ways—Hitler and Stalin—men who perverted the very essence of leadership and killed millions of innocent people in the process. The Great Depression and the battlefields of World War II were my crucible, as they were for so many people my age.

The crucible is an essential element in the process of becoming a leader that I didn't fully appreciate in 1989. Some magic takes place in the crucible of leadership, whether the transformational experience is an ordeal like Mandela's years in prison or a relatively painless experience such as being mentored. The individual brings certain attributes into the crucible and emerges with new, improved leadership skills. Whatever is thrown at them, leaders emerge from their crucibles stronger and unbroken. No matter how cruel the testing, they become more optimistic and more open to experience. They don't lose hope or succumb to bitterness. In a moment, I'll describe some of the qualities that I now realize are essential for leadership, although not sufficient to ensure it. But first let me say something more about crucibles. Leadership guru Abigail Adams was right on the mark (as she so often was) when she wrote to son John Quincy Adams in 1780 that hard times are the crucible in which character and leadership are forged: "It is not in the still calm of life or the repose of a pacific station that great characters are formed," she counseled. "The habits of a vigorous mind are formed in contending with difficulty. Great necessities call out great virtues." Just as World War II forged the leaders of the second half of the twentieth century, I predict that 9/11 and the dot-com implosion will be the crucibles that create a whole new generation of leaders. If so, we will have reason to celebrate as well as to mourn.

In addition to the qualities I describe in *On Becoming a Leader*, all leaders have four essential competencies. First, they are able to engage others by creating shared meaning. They have a vision, and they can persuade others to make that vision their own. Hitler is a ghastly example of this ability, and a reminder of the under-appreciated role that rhetoric and performance play in leadership. One reason that leaders are able to promulgate their vision is because they are exquisitely attuned to their followers and feel their pain, their wants, their needs. Leaders, in every field, are richly endowed with empathy.

Second, all authentic leaders have a distinctive voice. By voice, I mean a cluster of things—a purpose, self-confidence, and a sense of self, and the whole gestalt of abilities that, thanks to Daniel Goleman, we now call Emotional Intelligence. Voice is hard to define but terribly important. One of the reasons cited for Al Gore's loss of the 2000 presidential election was his lack of voice. Those of us who know Gore are struck by his intelligence, his decency, his vision, and his wry sense of humor. Yet, during his campaign, the public was never able to hear his true voice. President George W. Bush, on the other hand, has a distinctive voice that projects a likeable, low-key persona that even people who reject his politics respond to. And voice matters more than ever because modern media broadcast it everywhere.

The third quality that all true leaders have is integrity. Recently, we have been reminded how important integrity is because we have perceived its lack in so many corporate leaders—the corporate weasels, as they have been called. One component of integrity is a strong moral compass. It need not be religious faith, but it is a powerful belief in something outside one's self. Ralph Nader's commitment to consumerism is a good example. Leadership is always about character. One of my favorite observations about the centrality of character to leadership is something David McCullough said about Harry Truman, in an essay collected in the book *Character Above All*. "Character counts in the presidency more than any other single quality," McCullough writes. "It is more important than how much the President knows of foreign policy or economics, or even of politics. When the chips are down—and the chips are almost always down in the presidency—how do you decide? Which way do you go? What kind of courage is called upon? Talking of his hero Andrew Jackson, Truman once said, 'It takes one kind of courage to face a duelist, but it's nothing like the courage it takes to tell a friend, No.'"

But the one competence that I now realize is absolutely essential for leaders—the key competence—is adaptive capacity. Adaptive capacity is what allows leaders to respond quickly and intelligently to relentless change. A whole new decision-making process has evolved in the last thirteen years in response to a changed context. As psychologist Karl Weick so eloquently writes, leaders of the old school could rely on maps. The leaders of today's digital age, whose world is never still or quite in focus, must depend on compasses. Weick explains: "Maps, by definition, can help only in known worlds—worlds that have been charted before. Compasses are helpful when you are not sure where you are and can get only a general sense of direction." Adaptive capacity allows today's leaders to act, and then to evaluate the results of their actions, instead of relying on the traditional decision-making model, which calls for collecting and analyzing the data, then acting. Today's leaders know that speed is of the essence, and that they must often act before all the data are in. They must assess the results of their actions, correct their course, and quickly act again.

Adaptive capacity is made up of many things, including resilience or what psychologists call "hardiness." People who are able to act quickly and appropriately are all "first-class noticers," as novelist Saul Bellow describes one of his characters. Adaptive capacity is a kind of creativity. And adaptive capacity also encompasses the ability to identify and seize opportunities. As I have watched hundreds of people become leaders over the years, I have been struck again and again by how effectively some people are able to recruit the mentors they need. I realize that one of my own gifts as a younger man was the ability to find and somehow woo great teachers. This ability is more complex and more important than mere networking. It is nothing less than the ability to spot the handful of people who can make all the difference in your life and to get them on your side. I have seen the process from the mentor's side over the last few decades, and I am always struck by the art with which some talented younger people draw me into their lives, make me care about them, and make me want to help them in any way I can. That ability is essential to becoming a leader. And it is a success strategy that other primates seem to adopt as well as people. In studying male baboons, Stanford University neuroscientist Robert Sapolsky found that the difference between living a long life and dying early often came down to the ability of some older males to recruit younger, stronger males to protect them. Mentoring is much more than a career strategy. It is a reciprocal dance that benefits both parties.

In talking to successful geezers, I am always dazzled by their adaptive capacity. I am surer now than ever that the process of becoming a leader is the same process that makes a person a healthy, fully integrated human being. And it is the same process that allows one to age successfully. When I think of adaptive capacity I think of such serial leaders as Arthur Levitt, Jr., former head of the Securities and Exchange Commission. Arthur's adaptive capacity has allowed him to reinvent himself time after time. As I write this, he has a book about Wall Street and corporate America on the best-seller list, and he is much sought after as a critic of the way America has done business in recent years. Time has only made him a more distinguished leader and burnished his remarkable ability to adapt and grow.

Timeless leadership is always about character, and it is always about authenticity. Let me underscore the observation made by pioneering psychologist William James about authenticity. "I have often thought," he wrote, "that the best way to define a man's character is to seek out the particular mental or moral attitude in which, when it came upon him, he felt himself most deeply and intensively active and alive. At such moments, there is a voice inside which speaks and says, 'This is the real me.'"

In 1989 I urged you to discover and cultivate that authentic self, the part of you that is most alive, the part that is most you. Now, as then, finding and nurturing that authentic self is the one sure way of becoming a leader.

Introduction
to the Original
Edition, 1989

For decades, I've devoted the bulk of my time to the study of leadership. An integral part of that study was observation of and interviews with some of this country's leading men and women. My first report on the subject was published as *Leaders* (Harper & Row, 1985, co-authored with Burt Nanus). Suddenly, I was a ranking authority. When anyone anywhere had a question about leadership, he or she inevitably wound up on my doorstep. I say this with as much chagrin as pride, since I didn't by any means have all the answers.

The study of leadership isn't nearly as exact as, say, the study of chemistry. For one thing, the social world isn't nearly as orderly as the physical world, nor is it as susceptible to rules. For another, people, unlike solids, fluids, and gases, are anything but uniform and anything but predictable. Having been a teacher and student all of my adult life, I am as leery as anyone of the idea of leaping to conclusions, or making more of evidence than is demonstrably true. So I have been forced, again and again, to qualify my answers. People wanted The Truth, and I was giving them opinions. To an extent, leadership is like beauty: it's hard to define, but you know it when you see it.

I still don't have all the answers, but in the years since the publication of *Leaders*, I've learned much more about leadership. So here is my second report. *Leaders* covered the *whats*. *On Becoming a Leader* is the *hows:* how people become leaders, how they lead, and how organizations encourage or stifle potential leaders.

But since leadership, by definition, cannot take place in a vacuum, I've begun with the current context—the myriad forces that conspire against would-be leaders. Everyone deplores the alleged lack of leadership in America today, and the blame usually lands at the feet of the individual who hasn't made the grade. Greed, timidity, and lack of vision are rampant among the current crop of pseudo-leaders. Certainly, no matter how many genuine leaders there are in this country—and I know there are many, because I've met them and talked with them—we could use more, particularly at the national level. But our shortcomings as individuals are symptomatic of a much larger problem.

If it is fair to say that all too often our leading citizens seem incapable of taking control of their various domains, it is even fairer to add that the world itself is out of control. The changes in the last generation have been so radical that it seems even in business as if the world plays soccer while America plays football. It's not just that the rules changed—it's a different game.

For this reason, before people can learn to lead, they must learn something about this strange new world. Indeed, anyone who does not master this mercurial context will be mastered by it. Plenty of people have prevailed, including the leaders you will meet in these pages. They range all over the map in background, experience, and vocation, but they have in common a passion for the promises of life and the ability to express themselves fully and freely. As you will see, full, free self-expression is the essence of leadership. As Ralph Waldo Emerson said, "The man is only half himself, the other half is his expression."

On Becoming a Leader is based on the assumption that leaders are people who are able to express themselves fully. By this I mean that they know who they are, what their strengths and weaknesses are, and how to fully deploy their strengths and compensate for their weaknesses. They also know what they want, why they want it, and how to communicate what they want to others, in order to gain their cooperation and support. Finally, they know how to achieve their goals. The key to full self-expression is understanding one's self and the world, and the key to understanding is learning—from one's own life and experience.

Becoming a leader isn't easy, just as becoming a doctor or a poet isn't easy, and those who claim otherwise are fooling themselves. But learning to lead is a lot easier than most of us think it is, because each of us contains the capacity for leadership. In fact, almost every one of us can point to some leadership experience. Maybe the experience wasn't running a company, or governing a state, but as Harlan Cleveland wrote in *The Knowledge Executive*,

> The aristocracy of achievement is numerous and pervasive. . . .
> They may be leaders in politics or business or agriculture or labor
> or law or education or journalism or religion or affirmative action
> or community housing, or any policy issue from abortion to the
> municipal zoo. . . . Their writ may run to community affairs, to
> national decisions or global issues, to a whole multinational

industry or profession or to a narrower but deeper slice of life and work: a single firm, a local agency, or a neighborhood.

He might have added a classroom to that list. Whatever your leadership experience, it's a good place to start.

In fact, the process of becoming a leader is much the same as the process of becoming an integrated human being. For the leader, as for any integrated person, life itself is the career. Discussing the process in terms of "leaders" is merely a way of making it concrete.

Braque, the French painter, once said, "The only thing that matters in art can't be explained." The same might be said of leadership. But leadership, like art, can be demonstrated. And I am still as fascinated by observing and listening to some of this country's most distinguished leaders as I was when I started studying leadership decades ago. Like everyone else, these particular men and women are the sum of all their experiences. Unlike most people, however, each of them amounts to more than the sum, because they have made more of their experiences. These are originals, not copies.

My paradigm, then, is leaders, not theories about leaders, and leaders functioning in the real world, rather than in some artificial setting. I deliberately chose people who are not only accomplished, but multitalented: a writer who's a CEO, a scientist who heads a foundation, a lawyer who served in the cabinet, a young man who's on his third career. They are all people whose lives have made a difference—thoughtful, articulate, and reflective.

Because I would argue that our culture is currently dominated and shaped by business, almost a third of this group of leaders are in business. (To those of you who would argue that it is shaped by the media I would answer—as legendary television producer Norman Lear does—that even television is shaped by business.) Some head leading American companies, others run their own companies. There are also leaders in the media and the arts here, people who've traded business careers for nonprofit enterprises, a sports figure, academics, a writer-psychoanalyst, lawyers, the aforementioned scientist, and Betty Friedan, the housewife-turned-author-and-feminist-leader who inspired a revolution. As you may have noticed, I've excluded politicians, because candid politicians are in very short supply, and I was more interested in ideas than in ideology.

These leaders are by no means ordinary people. They work out there on the frontier where tomorrow is taking shape, and they serve here as guides—guides to things as they are and as they will be, or scouts reporting back with word from the front. As diverse as they are in terms of background, age, occupations, and accomplishments, they are in accord on two basic points.

First, they all agree that leaders are made, not born, and made more by themselves than by any external means. Second, they agree that no leader sets out to be a leader per se, but rather to express him- or herself freely and fully. That is, leaders have no interest in proving themselves, but an abiding interest in expressing themselves. The difference is crucial, for it's the difference between being driven, as too many people are today, and leading, as too few people do.

Something else they have in common is that each of these individuals has continued to grow and develop throughout life. This is in the best tradition of leadership—people such as George Bernard Shaw, Charles Darwin, Katharine Hepburn, Martin Luther, Mahatma Gandhi, and Jean Piaget are a few examples that spring immediately to mind. Winston Churchill is said to have jaywalked through life until he was 66.

So one of the things this book is about is adult learning. Most psychologists have virtually nothing to say about mental life, learning and growing, in our adult years. For whatever reasons, we tend to associate creative behavior and learning with the young. I think it's a matter of socialization that we don't think of the old (post–45, perhaps) as learners. Certainly, if we look at enough examples of "grown-up" learning, from Churchill to Picasso to Beethoven—to Freud, even—we must think again about our assumptions.

Because we are still questioning the assumptions, there are no theories. But the best information we have suggests that adults learn best when they take charge of their own learning. Taking charge of your own learning is a part of taking charge of your life, which is sine qua non in becoming an integrated person.

But of all the characteristics that distinguished the individuals in this book, the most pivotal was a concern with a guiding purpose, an overarching vision. They were more than goal-directed. As Karl Wallenda said, "Walking the tightwire is living; everything else is waiting." Along with the vision, the compelling goal, is the importance of the metaphor that embodies and implements the vision. For Darwin, the fecund metaphor was a branching tree of evolution on which he could trace the rise and fate of various species. William James viewed mental processes as a stream, or river. John Locke focused on the falconer, whose release of a bird symbolized his "own emerging view of the creative process"—that is, the quest for human knowledge. None of the metaphors from this group may be quite that profound, but they serve the same purpose.

Thomas Carlyle said, "The ideal is in thyself; the impediment, too, is in thyself." As we learned from Socrates and Plato, such impediments can be dissolved by close scrutiny and the right questions at the right time. Each of these leaders seems to have overcome whatever impediments he or she contained, and in my dialogues with them (they were not interviews in the ordinary sense) we searched not for pat answers to standard questions, but for some truths about leadership. In a sense, we did together what each of them had already done individually in the process of finding his or her own means of full self-expression.

Plato argued that learning is basically recovery or recollection—that in the same way bears and lions instinctively know everything they need to know to live and merely do it, each of us does, too. But in our case, what we need to know gets lost in what we are told we should know. So learning is simply a matter of remembering what is important. As Jung said, psychoanalysis is less a form of healing than a form of learning.

So we already know what we need to know, but each of us must recover that basic knowledge, and such recovery inevitably begins with questions. I had some questions in mind as I started each dialogue:

- What do you believe are the qualities of leadership?
- What experiences were vital to your development?
- What were the turning points in your life?
- What role has failure played in your life?
- How do you learn?
- Are there people in your life, or in general, whom you particularly admire?
- What can organizations do to encourage or stifle leaders?

Basic as these questions are, they generated wide-ranging, free-wheeling answers, which, in turn, led to an exploration of my fundamental concerns: how people learn, how they learn to lead, and how organizations help or hinder the process— or, to put it succinctly, how people become leaders.

We like to think that if someone has the right stuff, he or she will naturally rise to the top, in the way that cream rises to the top of the milk bottle—or used to when we had milk bottles, and before we removed the cream. But it isn't true. The late Stella Adler, once a famous actress and later a famous acting teacher, refused to discuss her former students who had become stars. She said that she had so many equally talented students who didn't become stars for one reason or another, whether lack of motivation or bad luck, and she didn't want to risk hurting them by her comments. In the same way that acting talent doesn't guarantee stardom, the capacity for leadership doesn't guarantee that one will run a corporation or a government. In fact, in the current win-or-die context, people of extraordinary promise often have more difficulty fulfilling their promise than people of more docile character, because, at least in our time, genuine achievement can be less valued than simplistic success, and those who are skilled at achieving prominence are not necessarily those who are ready to lead once they arrive.

Although I have said that everyone has the capacity for leadership, I do not believe that everyone will become a leader, especially in the confusing and often antagonistic context in which we now live. Too many people are mere products of their context, lacking the will to change, to develop their potential. I also believe, however, that everyone, of whatever age and circumstance, is capable of self-transformation. Becoming the kind of person who is a leader is the ultimate act of free will, and if you have the will, this is the way.

Since the transformation is a process, *On Becoming a Leader* is a story of that process rather than a series of discrete lessons. As a modern story, it has no beginning, middle, or end. But it has many recurring themes—the need for education, both formal and informal; the need to unlearn so that you can learn (or, as Satchel Paige is supposed to have said, "It's not what you don't know that hurts you, it's what you know that just ain't so"); the need for reflecting on learning, so that the meaning of the lesson is understood; the need to take risks, make mistakes; and the need for competence, for mastery of the task at hand.

I know—this book has more leitmotifs than a Wagnerian opera. But I warned you this was a complex business. And not only do the themes recur, but they overlap. For example, the story Sydney Pollack tells about directing Barbra Streisand that appears in chapter five, "Operating on Instinct," also illustrates risk taking and reflection. After you've finished reading the book the first time, you may want to browse through it again. At least, I hope you will.

At bottom, becoming a leader is synonymous with becoming yourself. It's precisely that simple, and it's also that difficult. So let's get started.

Cast of Characters

I've always liked the Russian novelists' custom of listing their characters in advance of the story. Herewith, then, the cast of characters in *On Becoming a Leader*, in alphabetical order. Their updated biographies appear at the end of the book.

> ***Herb Alpert and Gil Freisen,*** longtime partners in A&M Records
>
> ***Gloria Anderson,*** newspaper editor and executive

Anne Bryant, former executive director of the American Association of University Women, now executive director of the National School Boards Association

James Burke, former chairman and CEO, Johnson & Johnson

Barbara Corday, former television executive, now chair of the division of film and TV production in the University of Southern California's School of Cinema-Television

Horace Deets, retired executive director, AARP, now an advisor to the organization

Robert Dockson, former chairman and CEO, CalFed

Richard Ferry, former president and co-founder, Korn/Ferry International

Betty Friedan, author and co-founder of the National Organization for Women

Alfred Gottschalk, president emeritus, Hebrew Union College

Roger Gould, psychoanalyst and author

Frances Hesselbein, former executive director, Girl Scouts of America, and author

Shirley Hufstedler, lawyer, former judge, and former U.S. secretary of education

Edward C. Johnson III, CEO, Fidelity Investments

Martin Kaplan, former Walt Disney executive, now a research professor at the USC Annenberg School for Communication

Brooke Knapp, record-setting aviator and entrepreneur

Mathilde Krim, scientist and AIDS activist

Norman Lear, television writer-producer and first-amendment activist

Michael McGee, former athletic director, University of Southern California and the University of South Carolina

Sydney Pollack, Oscar-winning motion picture director and producer

Jamie Raskin, former Massachuetts assistant attorney general, now law professor and Maryland state senator

Don Ritchey, former CEO, Lucky Stores

Richard Schubert, former CEO, American Red Cross

John Sculley, former CEO, Apple Computers, now a venture capitalist

Gloria Steinem, writer, activist, founding editor, *Ms.*

Clifton R. Wharton, Jr., former chairman and CEO, Teachers Insurance and Annuity Association, College Retirement Equities Fund

Larry Wilson, entrepreneur, founder and former CEO, Wilson Learning Corporation

Renn Zaphiropoulos, founder, Versatec, and former Xerox executive

1
Mastering the Context

Leaders have a significant role in creating the state of mind that is the society. They can serve as symbols of the moral unity of the society. They can express the values that hold the society together. Most important, they can conceive and articulate goals that lift people out of their petty preoccupations, carry them above the conflicts that tear a society apart, and unite them in pursuit of objectives worthy of their best efforts.

—JOHN W. GARDNER
No Easy Victories

In November 1987, *Time* asked in a cover story, "Who's in Charge?" and answered its own question, saying, "The nation calls for leadership, and there is no one home." A recent Google search on "lack of leadership" produced more than 53.3 million hits (up from 27,000 five years ago), many laments on the dearth of leaders in world organizations, nations, states, religious organizations, corporations, nonprofit organizations, professions, education, health care, sports, and virtually every other human endeavor.

The world's hunger for leadership has been growing for years. There is no doubt that a charismatic new leader took the world stage on November 4, 2008, with the election of Barack Obama as president of the United States. On the night of his victory, millions of Americans wept with pride in their country and relief that he had triumphed over old prejudices. Watching on television, children cheered in the Indonesian grade school the president-elect had attended as a child. Brits raised pints in countless pubs, and Kenyans danced with Obama's relatives in the village where his father was born. But Barack Obama's presidency is in its earliest days, and what we have now is the hope that he will become one of the giants.

One result of Barack Obama's extraordinary election is to remind us of just how thin our leadership bench is. Most of the leaders we once revered are gone. FDR, who challenged a nation to rise above fear, is gone. Churchill, who demanded and got blood, sweat, and tears, is gone. Schweitzer, who inspired mankind with a reverence for life from the jungles of Lambaréné, is gone. Einstein, who gave us a sense of unity in infinity, of cosmic harmony, is gone. Gandhi, the Kennedys, Martin Luther King, Jr.—all were slain.

The stage is littered with flawed and disappointing leaders. Ronald Reagan, the "Teflon president," was stained by the Iran-contra disaster and other scandals. Bill Clinton was dogged by rumors of personal indiscretion even before he took office and was impeached (and acquitted), the first elected U.S. President to be censured in so spectacular a fashion.

Unlike the 2008 election, the 2000 presidential contest was notable less for the contrast of the candidates than for the roller-coaster ride of the process, which ended in George W. Bush being declared the winner, in spite of his trailing Al Gore by a half-million popular votes. The election was decided, for the first time in American history, by the Supreme Court, leading to an unprecedented diminution, in the minds of many, of a body once thought to be above partisan politics. And while President Bush responded forcefully, if belatedly, to the terrorist attacks of 9/11, his administration quickly devolved into a string of disasters—the unwarranted, protracted war in Iraq; the shameful symbolism of Guantanamo and Abu Ghraib prisons; the bungled rescue of hurricane-battered New Orleans; the outing of C.I.A. agent Valerie Plame; the unprecedented politicization of the Justice Department; and not one but two economic crises. The 2008 meltdown was the worst since the Great Depression. Stocks plunged almost 1,000 points in a single day, and 1.2 million American jobs vanished in the first ten months of the year.

If political leaders disappointed us, corporate leaders proved even worse. As evidence emerged of greed and wrongdoing at such once-esteemed institutions as Lehman Brothers and major banks, the public and the media called for new leadership and greater regulation. Without drawing much attention to themselves, capable people continued to keep our institutions afloat—able university presidents, city managers, state governors, heads of non-government organizations, and others. But we increasingly perceived authentic leaders to be an endangered species, buffeted by events and circumstances over which they seemed to have little or no control.

A scientist at the University of Michigan once listed what he considered to be the ten basic dangers to our society. First and most significant is the possibility of some kind of nuclear war or accident that would destroy the human race. The second danger is the prospect of a worldwide epidemic, disease, famine, or depression. The third of the scientist's key problems that could bring about the destruction of society is the quality of the management and leadership of our institutions.

Today we must add global warming, the widening gap between rich and poor, and international terrorism to that list of major dangers. But the relative lack of leadership continues to be an enormous threat. The simple truth is that 304 million people cannot long abide together without leaders, any more than 304 million people can drive on our roads and highways without certain rules, or eleven men can play football without a quarterback, or four people can hike from X to Y unless at least one knows where Y is.

One person can live on a desert island without leadership. Two people, if they're totally compatible, could probably get along and even progress. If there are three or more, someone has to take the lead. Today we have a more nuanced view of leadership. We no longer think in terms of the Lone Ranger or the Great Man. But no matter how collaborative our organizations, someone still needs to choreograph the players and make final decisions. Leadership might rotate among the three inhabitants on a desert island, as it does in three-engineer teams at Google, but leadership is needed nonetheless.

So let's admit it: in a nation, in a world, as complex and fluid as ours, we cannot function without leaders. Our quality of life depends on the quality of our leaders (as the sorry economy of 2008 reminded us so painfully). And we need more than one. As never before, we need leaders in all our organizations and all our institutions. We need leaders in every community, corporation, and country. That leadership vacuum creates an enormous opportunity. If you've ever had dreams of leadership, this is the place, now is the time.

There are three basic reasons why leaders are important. First, they are responsible for the effectiveness of organizations. The success or failure of all organizations, whether basketball teams, community-action groups, moviemakers, makers of video games, auto manufacturers, or lending institutions, rests on the quality of their decision makers. Stock prices rise and fall according to the public perception of how good the leader is. But, just as important, the leader is responsible for who is hired, the organization's goals and aspirations, working conditions, who has authority over whom, morale, allocation of resources, transparency, and ethical standards.

Second, the change and upheaval of the past years has left us with no place to hide. We need anchors and guides. The very best of our leaders serve in that way. They inspire us and restore our hope.

Third, there is a pervasive national concern about the integrity of our institutions. It is hard to imagine that there was once a time when Wall Street was a place where a man's word was his bond (until Muriel Siebert bought a seat on the New York Stock Exchange, there were few women on Wall Street). Its reputation tarnished in the 1980s by the white-collar crimes of Ivan Boesky, Michael Milken, and others, Wall Street was gravely damaged in the first years of the twenty-first century by the greed and double-dealing of a series of CEOs who received imperial compensation even as they bilked both shareholders and their own employees.

Starting with the discovery that the energy firm Enron endorsed bookkeeping practices that would have embarrassed Al Capone, the nation watched as once trumpeted corporate leaders did the perp walk, led in handcuffs from their homes as TV cameras rolled. In quick succession, criminal charges were brought against top executives at Tyco International, ImClone Systems, and Adelphia Communications. WorldCom, Global Crossing, and other former stars of the New Economy tumbled into bankruptcy amidst allegations of fiscal improprieties. A cry immediately went up for the wholesale reform of corporate boards, accounting practices, executive recruitment, and employee retirement plans, a call for sweeping change in how America does business unlike any since the Great Depression.

These scandals were especially troubling to all of us who have been engaged for decades now in training future leaders. Business schools responded quickly to the debacle by adding cautionary case studies of Enron and ImClone to their curricula and beefing up ethics courses. But, clearly, not everyone learned the lessons on transparency, accountability, and fair play contained in these case studies and reform-minded courses. If they had, there would have been no subprime mortgage crisis of 2008, which shook world markets and left the American public with a $700-billion tab.

And American business was not the only institution that showed itself to be gravely flawed. The Roman Catholic Church in the United States experienced an unprecedented series of scandals involving the molestation of children and young adults by priests. The revelation that some priests betrayed and abused children was shocking in its own right. But almost as disturbing was the revelation that members of the Catholic hierarchy had known of the abuse and covered it up, often by reassigning dangerous priests to new parishes where they molested anew. No major American institution seemed unblemished, including the prestigious Ivy League. In 2002, Princeton University staff hacked into admissions records at

Yale, apparently to gain information that would help it steal top applicants away from its rival.

Scandal also touched government agencies. Where was the Central Intelligence Agency, the public demanded to know, when terrorists with expired visas were taking lessons at American flight schools in order to crash into the World Trade Center and the Pentagon? Where was the C.I.A., for that matter, when two of its agents spied for years for Moscow? And the Federal Bureau of Investigation didn't fare any better. It, too, failed to prevent the terrorist attacks of 2001 and the deadly mailing of anthrax-laden letters that followed. Perhaps most shocking was the failure of the Federal Emergency Management Agency, or FEMA, to provide services for the mostly poor minority residents who remained in New Orleans after Hurricane Katrina. Bodies floated in the flooded streets for days, while clueless public officials congratulated each other on a job well done.

We see these things, and we lament them, but what do we do about them? What *can* we do about them, caught up as we are in the context of our own professional and personal lives? For the most part, our lives are busier and more demanding than those of any generation in recent history. Thanks to ubiquitous cell phones and other forms of instant communication, we are tied to our workplaces as never before, immersed in a context that is volatile, turbulent, ambiguous, and all but impossible to escape. That we often feel oppressed by that context is evident from the desperation with which so many people dream of simplifying their lives. But we must master that context if we are to solve our own problems, let alone societal ones, and to do that we must first examine it. Unfortunately, looking at our own context is as difficult for us as it is for fish to look at water.

Everything's in motion. Digital technology and international competition are altering the shape and thrust of American business. Changing demographics and the ability to use new technology to identify and serve slices of the population are altering the marketplace where, increasingly, the niche is all. Certain venerable industries, such as print journalism, teeter on the verge of extinction, while new "green" businesses open every day. We now live and work in the global village that Marshall McLuhan predicted. In the European Union, national borders no longer confine workers. In recent years, Eastern Europeans poured into newly wealthy, high-tech Ireland. When the Irish economy sagged, Poles working in Ireland returned to their own reinvigorated economy. The economy of the United States is also in flux. Just as millions of blue-collar jobs went overseas in recent decades, more and more white-collar jobs are being exported. Using the Internet, a couple can save money on their nuptials in Des Moines by hiring a wedding planner in Bangalore. Aided by their fluency in English, now the universal language of business, professionals in Southeast Asia read American X-rays and vet American contracts. Instant communication and digitally enabled social networking are changing the political as well as the economic map. Markets are freer everywhere, and so are people, as the Internet magnifies voices of dissent in such authoritarian nations as Myanmar and Iran.

While mergers and acquisitions continue to create international megacorporations, small, agile companies now generate more new jobs than big traditional industries. Today, Google, Pixar, and other idea-driven firms that know the worth of their creative talent get first pick of top-notch new graduates. The once-dominant Big Three television networks are now owned or controlled by large corporations, and all three are scrambling to keep market share in a growing field of rivals. Cable networks such as HBO and Showtime produce much of the best original programming. And more and more viewers get their news from such alternative sources as CNN, Fox (on the right), MSNBC (on the left), and Comedy Central, home of two of today's most trusted and unlikely newscasters, Jon Stewart and Stephen Colbert. Thanks to Tivo and other means of recording programs for later viewing, people watch their favorite shows whenever they choose, and only the masochistic need to sit through commercials, a development that threatens the very economic basis of commercial TV.

Deregulation changed the airline industry forever, giving birth to new cut-rate airlines and driving Pan Am and other venerable carriers out of business. But the use of airplanes as flying megabombs in the 2001 terrorists attacks was a devastating blow to the airline industry, and the Draconian tightening of security procedures afterward made flying less attractive than ever. In 2008, soaring gas prices caused airlines to raise ticket prices, trim schedules, and impose fuel surcharges and bag-checking fees. To avoid burgeoning travel costs, more and more companies turned to new videoconferencing technology, putting even more financial pressure on the troubled airline industry.

America's aging population is changing its economy—indeed its culture—in ways that are only beginning to be felt. American demographics are shifting in other ways. Latinos have an increasingly powerful voice in American life, as evidenced by the significant role Latino voters played in the election of Barack Obama. Globalization is shaping American life at every turn. American business once owned the American market and much of the European market as well. Today publishing and other sectors of the American economy are largely European-owned, a trend that is likely to continue as the European Union begins to exercise its true collective clout. European nations will increasingly do business with each other, thanks to the elimination of internal trade barriers and the increased use of an almost universal currency, the euro. China would have a major impact on the United States if only because it holds trillions of dollars of American debt. But China impacts us in many ways. Once primarily an exporting nation, China is now a billion-person market for the rest of the world's goods. Its rapid modernization has caused global shortages of concrete and steel. And China, India, and other ascendant giants are the great unknowns in the life-and-death question of whether the world will find a way to balance the conflicting needs for growth and limiting greenhouses gasses. One result of these global changes is that Wall Street, once the only player, is now one among many financial centers, one subject to such unpredictable forces as overseas investors, currency fluctuations, and an American public that increasingly mistrusts what the Street says and does.

The new order is so insane that it's hard to satirize, but former Salomon Smith Barney analyst Julius Maldutis captured the madness some years ago when he said: "I have it on good authority that Delta is buying Eastern, Eastern is buying Pan Am. Pan Am is really going after United now that it has all of United's cash, and American's Bob Crandall, who has been devilishly silent all along, is getting ready to make a tender offer for the whole industry once he reaches an agreement with his pilots. Furthermore, I spoke to Frank Lorenzo this morning, and he assured me that his next targets are Peru and Bolivia, which he plans to merge into the first low-cost country." That two of those airlines are long gone only underscores the point.

The business world has undergone a series of sea changes in recent decades. Remember the futurist speculation that was all the rage forty years ago? Despite the flurry of prognostication, no one foresaw the profound impact Japan would have, for a time, on the American economy. For much of the 1980s, Japan—a clutch of distant, overcrowded islands with no basic resources, devastated by World War II and once renowned for producing junk—caused America to have an economic identity crisis. We began to question our vaunted know-how, our conviction that we are the most creative nation on earth—birthplace of such practical geniuses as Edison and Ford—and our claim to the most robust and successful business practices. There were days when we felt that the Japanese did everything better than we did, from designing appealing new automobiles to finding new ways to guarantee quality. Japan soon bested us in manufacturing and marketing what we used to think of as basic American goods, not just cars, but TV sets, even steel. It was only a vicious recession in Japan, and the wholesale adoption of the best Japanese practices by our own firms, that allowed us to forget the sense we once had of being humiliated by Japanese economic superiority.

In the twenty-first century it is impossible to predict where the next great economic shift will come from. China, India, Russia, even tiny but wealthy Dubai are emerging forces. Most economists believe we are entering a period of slower growth throughout the developed world. And what of the Middle East? Americans are hopeful that our troops will leave Iraq in the near future. But the whole world is nervously watching Iran, a vocal enemy of Israel with nuclear ambitions. The emergence of a particularly violent form of Islamic fundamentalism that uses modern technology to cause chaos in the westernized world continues to shape global politics, and peace in the Middle East is as elusive as ever.

As the late John Gardner pointed out, when the Founding Fathers gathered in Philadelphia to write the Constitution, America had a population of only 3 million, yet six world-class leaders were among the authors of that extraordinary document. Washington, Jefferson, Hamilton, Madison, Adams, and Franklin created America. Today, there are 304 million Americans and we wonder, every four years, why we can't find at least two superb candidates for the nation's highest office.

What happened?

As eighteenth-century America was notable for its geniuses, nineteenth-century America was notable for its adventurers, entrepreneurs, inventors, scientists, and writers, the titans who made the industrial revolution, the explorers who opened up the West, the writers who defined us as a nation and a people. Thomas Edison, Eli Whitney, Alexander Graham Bell, Lewis and Clark, Hawthorne, Melville, Dickinson, Whitman, and Twain. These men and women whose vision matched their audacity built America.

Twentieth-century America started to build on the promise of the nineteenth, but something went terribly wrong. After World War II, America was chiefly notable for its bureaucrats and managers, its organization men, its wheeler-dealers who remade, and in some cases unmade, the institutions and organizations of America, in both the public and private sectors.

There have been bright spots, including the rise of the civil rights movement and extraordinary American accomplishments in science and technology. But even though we emerged from World War II as the richest and most powerful nation on earth, by the mid–1970s, America had lost its edge. America lost its edge because it lost its way. We forgot what we were here for.

The rebellion of the 1960s, the Me Decade that followed, the yuppies of the 1980s, and the subsequent rise of Wall Street's Gordon Gekkos with their philosophy that greed is good are all consequences of the mistakes and crudities of the organization men. Unable to find America's head or heart, many of its citizens seem to have declared their independence from it and from each other.

While the 1960s saw the birth of such important contributions to our country as the civil rights movement and the women's movement, too many of its so-called breakthroughs became breakdowns. We talked about freedom and democracy, but we sometimes practiced license and anarchy. People were often not as interested in new ideas as they were in recipes and slogans. Gurus Abraham Maslow and Carl Rogers told us we could create our own reality, and we did, with everyone insisting on having it his or her way.

There has always been a tension in the American character between individual rights and the common good. While we've loved and admired John Wayne striking out on his own with just a horse and a rifle, we've also known that the wagon train couldn't make it across the plains unless we all stuck together. That tension is as fierce today as it has ever been. Whenever upward mobility and good citizenship diverge, we have less and less in common, and less and less that is good.

Our Founding Fathers based the Constitution on the assumption that there was such a thing as public virtue. James Madison wrote, "The public good . . . the real welfare of the great body of people . . . is the supreme object to be pursued."

But in the early 1920s, when Calvin Coolidge said, "The business of America is business," hardly anyone disagreed. The idea of public virtue had been overtaken by special interests, which today are often replaced by individual concerns. Some in America have devolved into what Robert Bellah and his co-authors describe in their book, *Habits of the Heart*, as "a permissive, therapeutic culture . . . which urges a strenuous effort to make our particular segment of life a small world of its own."

Battered by the economic uncertainty of the last decade, many people have retreated into their electronic castles, working at home and communicating with the world via computers and cell phones. They mediate their human contacts through their personal digital assistants, ordering movies from Netflix and reheating take-out Thai in the microwave. Some would rather Instant Message than speak. Some prefer virtual reality to what lies outside the front door. A few spend so much time romancing other people's avatars in Second Life that their spouses call their divorce lawyers. Many have two kinds of friends—the ones they actually know and the ones ostentatiously listed on their Facebook page. Cocooning has entered the digital age.

The United States stock market has imploded twice in this young century, erasing trillions of dollars of wealth in the process. But the gap between the rich and the poor in the United States remains dangerously wide. The American middle class, which once trusted in its future because of swollen 401(k)s and soaring home equity, has been devastated by the recent crash. Growing numbers of have-nots and have-too-littles worry daily about the skyrocketing cost of health care, ignoring symptoms and splitting pills. Afraid of another Great Depression, some Americans cling to jobs they hate, fearful that their children won't be able to afford college. Meanwhile, certain social and environmental problems continue to haunt us. Poverty and drug addiction perpetuate an American underclass that fills our prisons to overflowing, and the oceans continue to rise.

For a time, our economic worries were overshadowed by the national trauma of 9/11, which caused virtually all Americans to look at their lives and reconsider their priorities. The wrenching accounts of doomed men and women calling their loved ones from the Twin Towers to say good-bye were seared into the nation's consciousness. So were the images of ordinary people whose control over their lives had been reduced, through no fault of their own, to the decision of whether to be immolated or jump a hundred stories to an equally certain death.

For the first time in decades, Americans seemed to see themselves as one nation, a single people united in their commitment to democratic principles. Unfortunately, the genuine sense of unity that emerged after the attacks did not lessen the nation's sense of alienation from many of its institutions. There was mistrust, in many quarters, of a government increasingly martial in tone and eager to eliminate, at whatever cost, "an axis of evil" embodied in Iraq's Saddam Hussein. Many Americans were increasingly estranged from national leaders who seemed to use terrorism as an excuse for hacking away at Constitutional protections. As Abigail Adams said, great suffering often engenders great leadership, but pain does not guarantee it. And, after 9/11, many Americans were left longing for leadership, as well as for a time, not so long ago, when terrorism was as rare in America as hunger. Yes, the nation had shared a tragedy, but that suffering did not produce a common vision of what the United States should be and how to achieve it. And we seemed to lack leaders of sufficient stature to give us that vision.

This, then, was the context, at least until the election in 2008 of a young president promising change and renewed hope. What those geniuses created in Philadelphia in the eighteenth century and their rowdy successors embellished in the nineteenth century, uninspired leaders and passive followers, in both government and business, too often turned into a giant machine, its wheels spinning frantically in the mud, going nowhere.

Like the outsized American cars of the Eisenhower era, America often seems too big and too awkward to work very well, much less respond quickly and wisely to events. This became painfully evident in the wake of 9/11 when Americans discovered, to their shock and dismay, that our security apparatus was vast but dangerously inefficient. It seems that the F.B.I. had been collecting information as assiduously as ever but hadn't bothered to update its computer networks so that information could be shared, analyzed, and acted upon quickly and effectively. The C.I.A. had failed to reinvent itself after the fall of the Soviet Union and had failed to anticipate new threats that would require new foreign language skills and other capabilities. The security agencies had a history of turf wars, not cooperation. And even when crucial information was flowing, it could be blocked by a single preoccupied supervisor or one with his or her own agenda. Combine those systemic flaws with an arrogant belief that the unimaginable couldn't happen here, and disaster was inevitable.

But authentic leaders are able to analyze the context and transcend it. Always an innovator, television producer/writer Norman Lear has enjoyed astonishing success—financially as well as creatively. When I talked with him, we discussed not only his life and his work, but also his concern with what he described as "the societal disease of our time"—short-term thinking: "It's asking what the poll is saying, not what's great for the country and what's best for the future, but what do I say in the short term to get me from here to there." And that national obsession with the short term has come directly from business. Lear continued, "Joseph Campbell once said that in medieval times, as you approached the city, your eye was taken by the cathedral. Today it's the towers of commerce. It's business, business, business, and in an escalating fashion it has gotten more short-term oriented. . . . You know, they're not funding the real iconoclasts today, not funding the innovators, because that's risky—that's long-term investment."

I think Lear is absolutely right. American business has become the principal shaper and mover in contemporary America—even more so than television—and has, in an odd irony, by zealously practicing what it preaches, sandbagged itself. Having captured the heart and mind of the nation with its siren songs of instant gratification, it has locked itself into obsolete practices. Before the flameout of the New Economy and the equally spectacular fall from grace of the American CEO, corporate leaders had achieved a popularity such as they had never experienced before in history. But even as we fawned over these corporate superstars, we failed to ask a crucial question: How much genuine leadership was being practiced inside even the most successful companies?

How many of those we believed to be leaders were really corporate Wizards of Oz, their perceived abilities as illusory as their cooked books?

Richard Ferry, former president and co-founder of the recruiting firm of Korn/Ferry International, spoke to the problem of short-term thinking two decades ago and his observations are just as relevant today: "Corporate America may talk, on an intellectual level, about what it'll take to succeed in the twenty-first century, but when it gets right down to decision making, all that matters is the next quarterly earnings report. That's what's driving much of the system. With that mind-set, everything else becomes secondary to the ability to deliver the next quarterly earnings push-up. We're on a treadmill. The reward system in this country is geared to the short term."

Our addiction to the short term gave us freeze-frame shots of a changing world, preventing us from seeing that it was shrinking, heating up, growing rancorous and ambitious—not just politically, but socially and economically. Just as our forebears challenged British rule, China, Japan, and Korea, virtually all of Europe, Scandinavia, and Australia have challenged American corporate rule—even as the Arab nations began to take back their oil. These upstarts are beating us at our own game, manufacturing and marketing. Japan, above all, saw that the marketplace was the real battlefield and that trade was not only the ultimate weapon, but the source of true national security. The Soviet Union's recognition that trade trumps ideology led to its inevitable dismantling and accounts for the eager self-interest with which the Czech Republic and other former Soviet countries sought inclusion in the European Union.

Perhaps because they're centuries older than we are, and therefore more sophisticated and wiser, our friends in Asia and Europe know that political regimes come and go, and ideologies wax and wane, but—human nature being what it is—our basic needs are economic, not political.

Some in America are still addicted to the quick fix and the fast buck. They haven't yet realized that the new bottom line is that there is no bottom line—there aren't any lines, much less limits or logic. Life on this turbulent, complex planet is no longer linear and sequential, one thing logically leading to another. It is spontaneous, contrary, unexpected, and ambiguous. Things do not happen according to plan, and they are not reducible to tidy models. We persist in grasping at neat, simple answers, when we should be questioning everything.

Wallace Stevens, a renowned poet who was also vice president of an insurance company, put it nicely in his poem, "Six Significant Landscapes":

> *Rationalists, wearing square hats,*
> *Think, in square rooms,*
> *Looking at the floor,*
> *Looking at the ceiling.*
> *They confine themselves*
> *To right-angled triangles.*
> *If they tried rhomboids,*
> *Cones, waving lines, ellipses—*
> *As, for example, the ellipse of the half-moon—*
> *Rationalists would wear sombreros.*

It's time for America to trade in its square hat on a sombrero, or a beret, and consider this new context.

And as Norman Lear put it, "One person can matter . . . a citizen can matter in this country."

Today, the opportunities for leaders are boundless, but so are the challenges. Our best and brightest are as smart, innovative, and capable as any generation of leaders has ever been, but the route to the top is more arduous and trickier than it has ever been, and the top itself is more slippery and more treacherous than Everest ever was. But reaching the top is not the only goal. Today's leaders often reinvent themselves periodically in order to scale new mountains.

We sometimes feel that we are at least halfway through the looking glass, on our way to utter chaos. And though the context is highly volatile, it's not apt to change in any fundamental way as long as the principal players are driven by it, are swimming through it like fish blind to the water. To put it another way, the current climate is self-perpetuating because it has created an entire generation of managers in its own image.

As we have discovered recently, too many CEOs became bosses, not leaders, and it is the bosses who have gotten America into its current fix. Ironically, they are as much products of the context as today's corporate scandals are. They are perfect expressions of the context, driven, driving, but going nowhere.

The first step in becoming a leader, then, is to recognize the context for what it is—a breaker, not a maker; a trap, not a launching pad; an end, not a beginning—and declare your independence.

SURRENDERING TO THE CONTEXT

Having described the context, I'm tempted to skip a step and go right to the people who beat it. Success is more fun than failure—to write about as well as to live. Besides, everyone knows people who didn't get what they wanted out of life. But learning from failure is one of the most important themes in this book, one that we'll return to again and again, so I think we need to look at one case, one individual who didn't make it out of the quagmire, and some of the reasons why. I'll call him Ed.

Ed was born of working-class parents in Brooklyn, New York. Smart, ambitious, determined to succeed, he went to work in a factory right out of high school and enrolled in night school. Working day and night, he managed to take a degree in accounting. He moved off the factory floor and into management with the same manufacturing firm. In a few short years, he fought his way up the ladder, passing some MBAs on the way. He proved himself to be not only hard-working and aggressive, but a talented nuts-and-bolts man. Efficient, competent, and tough, he eventually was made a vice president.

Ed was a company man. Everyone said so. He not only knew how everything worked, he was capable of making it work better, and when necessary, he didn't mind yanking out the deadwood. He was not an easy man to work for, but he was just the kind of man his bosses liked (that he and most of the other executives in the firm were male surprised no one). He was 100 percent loyal to the company, a workaholic, always willing and eager to go that extra mile, and impatient with anyone who was less devoted than he.

Ed's competence, combined with his drive and toughness, made him an ideal executive in the win-or-die 1980s and '90s. To look at him or see him in action, no one would have ever guessed that he grew up poor on the streets of south Brooklyn, or that he was a night school product.

In fact, he'd nearly forgotten it himself. He looked, dressed, and talked like his bosses. He had an attractive, devoted wife who looked, dressed, and talked like his bosses' wives. He had two handsome, well-behaved sons, a nice house in Westchester, a wicked serve, and great prospects—if he wanted to move. The president of the company was in his early 50s, Ed's age, and apparently happy with his position.

About the time Ed began getting restless, a family-owned firm in the same industry was looking for new blood. The CEO, the grandson of the founder, was thinking of retirement, and there was no one to whom he could hand the reins. He wanted to bring someone in as a vice president, get to know him, and if all went well, turn over the firm to him within two or three years. Although the firm was based in Minneapolis, the executive search firm found Ed in New York. Ed saw the move to Minneapolis as his shortcut to the top.

He handled the job-hop as efficiently as he handled everything else. He moved his family into a bigger and better house in Edina, moved himself into a big corner office with a view of a lake, and seemed to adjust to the slower Midwestern rhythm without missing a beat.

But he was, if anything, tougher than before, coming down harder than ever on people who failed to please him. The more-relaxed Minnesotans in the office made fun of him privately, nicknamed him "the Brooklyn Bomber," but when he said jump, they jumped.

After Ed had been in Minneapolis about a year, Baxter, the CEO, took him to lunch and offered him the COO spot. Ed was pleased, but not surprised. No one worked harder than he did, no one could have learned more about the company than he had, and no one deserved it more. The sky was the limit for the Bomber now. Baxter and Ed were a great team. Baxter, genial and encouraging, steered the company, while Ed, tougher than ever, took care of the nuts and bolts. And the dirty work.

Baxter decided that Ed was indeed the fellow to replace him when he retired, and he announced the decision to the family—who were also the board of directors. For the first time in his life, Ed ran into something he couldn't tough his way through. Some members of the family board told Baxter that Ed was too tough, too rough on his fellow executives. They would not approve his appointment unless he improved his "people skills."

Baxter gave Ed the bad news. If Ed was disturbed—and he was—so was the CEO. Baxter was ready to retire, and, further, he'd chosen Ed as his successor and begun to groom him for the job. Now his orderly plan had fallen apart. At this point Baxter called a friend who recommended that he hire me as a consultant. After outlining his dilemma, he asked me if I'd work with Ed to help him improve his people skills. He said Ed was willing to do whatever it took to secure the CEO slot.

After a lot of conversation and thought, I agreed. Although I had certain reservations, it was an interesting task, and I had enough other business taking me to Minneapolis that it didn't mean rearranging my life drastically. Still, I wondered whether anyone could effect what amounted to a basic personality change in a 55-year-old man.

On my next trip to Minneapolis, I met Ed. I spent a couple of days shadowing him, watching everything he did and how he did it. On the following trip, I interviewed everyone who worked with Ed and asked him to take a series of personality tests.

Everyone was, of course, operating out of self-interest. Anxious to retire, Baxter wanted his successor in place ASAP. The recalcitrant board members wanted a way out of this difficult situation, which I would have to give them, whether I succeeded or failed in working a change in Ed. Ed, who was never anything but cooperative, wanted the job.

After a while, it became clear to me that everything everyone said about Ed was true. He was very competent and very ambitious, but he was also a tyrant. He was impulsive and frequently abusive of people who worked for him. They would actually cower in his presence. He had a desperate need to control both people and events. He was incapable of thanking anyone for a job well done—he couldn't even give a compliment. And, of course, he was a sexist.

Ed tackled his problem the way he tackled everything else—at full speed and with all of his resources. In the course of my work with him, he became easier to get along with. He managed to smooth away his rougher edges. He became less abrasive, more polite, as he fine-tuned himself in the same way he fine-tuned the company. That was the good news.

The bad news was that, for all Ed's effort, the people who worked with him continued to be wary of him. They just didn't trust the "new" Ed. And the board remained divided. The members who liked the "old" Ed and his no-nonsense, bottom-line philosophy were somewhat thrown by his new, milder demeanor, while the ones who had originally blocked Ed's ascendance now found new flaws. They argued that, for all his drive and competence, he lacked both vision and character.

Believing that character is as vital in a leader as drive and competence, I had to agree with them. And character was something I couldn't help Ed find—he would have to do that on his own. As I've said before, it is not enough for a leader to do things right; he must do the right thing. Furthermore, a leader without some vision of where he wants to take his organization is not a leader. I had no doubt that Ed could run the company. I had grave doubts about where he might take it.

After telling Ed that, while I was impressed with his progress, I could not recommend him for CEO, I filed my report with Baxter and the board. Baxter, I discovered, was actually relieved.

While he had needed someone like Ed to help him run the business, he had known that the board was right: the business that had been in the family for three generations was on the line, and they simply couldn't turn it over to Ed. Baxter stayed on and Ed stayed in place until another successor for Baxter was found. Baxter then retired, and Ed resigned.

If this had been a movie, of course, Ed would have turned into Jimmy Stewart by the last reel and gotten the job. But real life doesn't work like the movies, and heroes and villains aren't as easy to spot.

In fact, I don't think Ed was either a hero or a villain. He was a victim, a man who saw himself as self-made, but who in fact had patterned himself after the wrong models in the wrong corporate culture.

He came into the business world as a tough street kid, a boy from the wrong side of the tracks who was determined to make good. He was ambitious and industrious. But ultimately he was just another product of the prevailing climate. Whatever character or vision he might have had atrophied along the way.

Ed might have learned to lead. Certainly, when he started work in the factory, he had a passion for the promises of life. But then he went through the looking glass into a dog-eat-dog world where people were rewarded not for expressing themselves but for proving themselves. In proving himself an ideal servant of the system, Ed never fully deployed himself—he allowed himself to be deployed by his employer. Himself driven, he drove others, becoming the pluperfect boss. He couldn't adjust to a new corporate climate where vision and character were important.

When I sorted it out afterward, I realized that there were actually five things that the board was interested in: technical competence (which Ed had), people skills, conceptual skills (meaning imagination and creativity), judgment and taste, and character. It wasn't just the people skills, as they had originally told me. So even when he worked hard to improve in that area, he simply could not get people on his side. They questioned his judgment and his character. And they felt that they couldn't trust him.

Since this is the era of failing upward, Ed is now chairman and CEO of a prominent Atlanta manufacturing firm. He was credited by its search committee not only with his own nuts-and-bolts successes, but with all of Baxter's achievements, too—including the creation of new products and maintaining a reputation for service and quality that are admired in the industry. Unfortunately, when Ed tightens all the nuts-and-bolts in Atlanta, but fails to generate new products or revenues, he may find the context unforgiving—unless he learns from his failure and he chooses to begin the arduous process of becoming himself. I haven't been able to find out, because he won't return my phone calls.

We all know "Eds"—in fact, they tend to be more the rule than the exception. But as you will see, people can and do overturn the rules and overcome the context and succeed in ways that the Eds can only imagine.

MASTERING THE CONTEXT

The leader I've picked to underscore the reasons why Ed didn't make the grade is Norman Lear.

He broke into TV during its so-called golden age as a comedy writer for such shows as "The Colgate Comedy Hour," "The George Gobel Show," and "The Martha Raye Show," which he also directed. In 1959, Lear and Bud Yorkin founded Tandem Productions, which produced and packaged TV specials with such stars as Fred Astaire, Jack Benny, Danny Kaye, Carol Channing, and Henry Fonda. Tandem produced a number of theatrical feature films, too, including *Come Blow Your Horn*, *The Night They Raided Minsky's*, *Start the Revolution Without Me*, and *Cold Turkey*. Lear's original screenplay *Divorce: American Style* earned an Academy Award nomination in 1967. By any definition, Lear was a success, but in 1971, he and Tandem took a giant step upward with the premiere of the landmark TV series "All in the Family." That series, featuring the unforgettable Archie Bunker, and the various series that followed—"Sanford and Son," "Maude," "The Jeffersons," "One Day at a Time," and "Mary Hartman, Mary Hartman"—revolutionized television and gave America a funny but acute look at itself.

The brilliant writer Paddy Chayefsky said, "Norman Lear took television away from the dopey wives and dumb fathers, from the pimps, hookers, hustlers, private eyes, junkies, cowboys and rustlers that constituted television chaos, and in their place he put the American people . . . he took the audience and put them on the set."

More than anyone else, Lear caused TV to grow up. Not only were his shows hits, they were not afraid to be controversial, focusing on such then taboo issues as abortion and prejudice. But no one wanted "All in the Family" in the beginning. It was turned down by ABC, reluctantly aired by CBS, and hardly watched at all for a while. Fortunately, CBS stuck with it. And Lear not only mastered the context, he revolutionized it.

In each of eleven consecutive seasons, 1971–1982, at least one Lear situation comedy placed in the top ten of all prime-time programs. In 1974–1975, five of the top ten shows were Lear's. In November 1986, five of the top nine off-network sitcoms in syndication were his. Nearly 60 percent of Lear's pilots have sold as series, which is twice the industry average. More than a third of all his network series went on to become hits in syndication, three times the industry average.

Lear's career, consistently characterized by innovation and risk, proves the efficacy of both, for Lear is not only a creative phenomenon but a financial wizard as well. But when the Writers Guild of America went on strike in March 1988, this man who revolutionized an industry, this multimillionaire, this communications pioneer and leader, walked the picket lines with his fellow writers and loved it.

Lear has performed brilliantly as a writer, a producer, a businessman, and a citizen-activist (he is co-founder of People for the American Way, a foundation devoted to civil rights and liberties). His counsel continues to be sought by presidential candidates and other politicians. And he continues to contribute to American public life in other ways. In 2000, he and Internet entrepreneur David Hayden, paid a record $7.4 million for the original copy of the Declaration of Independence and announced plans to make it available to the public. Lear also donated more than $5 million to establish a multidisciplinary center at the University of Southern California for the study of the implications of "the convergence of entertainment, commerce and society." The Norman Lear Center conducts academic research and shapes public policy.

Lear's story is the American Dream made manifest, a plot straight out of Horatio Alger, except that he didn't marry the boss's daughter. Starting with nothing, he has become very, very rich and very, very famous, and very, very powerful. Indeed, his life is the stuff of which TV shows and movies are made. His accomplishments prove, beyond a doubt, the efficacy of full self-expression.

There are four steps in the process behind Norman Lear's success in mastering the context: (1) becoming self-expressive; (2) listening to the inner voice; (3) learning from the right mentors; and (4) giving oneself over to a guiding vision.

These steps are all illustrated in the story he told me of how he was profoundly influenced by Ralph Waldo Emerson's essay "Self-Reliance" in high school: "Emerson talks about listening to that inner voice and going with it, against all voices to the contrary. I don't know when I started to understand that there was something divine about that inner voice. . . . To go with that—which I confess I don't do all of the time—is the purest, truest thing we have. And when we forgo our own thoughts and opinions, they end up coming back to us from the mouths of others. They come back with an alien majesty. . . . So the lesson is, you believe it. *When I've been most effective, I've listened to that inner voice.*"

Listening to the inner voice—trusting the inner voice—is one of the most important lessons of leadership. I think it's so important that I've devoted the bulk of one chapter to it later in this book.

Lear spoke, too, of other influential people in his life. "My grandfather was the person who taught me very early on that you can matter. I lived with him between the ages of 9 and 12. He was an inveterate letter writer. And I was a captive audience for every one of those letters. 'My dearest, darling, Mr. President, don't you listen to them when they say such-and-such and so-and-so.' Or if he disagreed with the President, it was 'My *dearest*, darling, Mr. President, you should never have done such-and-such.' I ran down the four flights of stairs to the brass mailbox to pick up the mail each day. Every once in a while my 9½-, 10-, 11-year-old heart would miss a beat because there was a little white envelope that said White House on it. I couldn't get over it. The White House was writing to him.

"My father was a guy who had bits and pieces of paper in his pockets and in the brim of his hat, and that's how he managed things. He was always into more than he could handle, because he was never organized. So I guess inversely he taught me the need to be prepared and keep both feet on the ground. He was a man who knew he was going to have a million dollars in two weeks, and of course he never made it. But he never stopped believing. He leaned into life, like M. Hulot, bent in with head tilting, the stride strong."

Like his father the rascal, the son has never stopped believing, and he, too, leans into life. He told me, "First and foremost, find out what it is you're about, and be that. Be what you are, and don't lose it. . . . It's very hard to be who we are, because it doesn't seem to be what anyone wants." But, of course, as Lear has demonstrated, it's the only way to truly fly.

Norman Lear had a guiding vision, a belief in himself, a belief that he could make a difference. And that vision allowed him to master the context in television, an arena in which producers traditionally survive by being like everybody else, by coming up with a clone of last season's hit, by playing to the lowest common denominator with the least objectionable programming. Lear not only made it to the top and stayed there for two decades—and this in an industry in which five years is considered a career—he did it by producing original shows, shows that stood out in bright colors next to their pale competitors. He was there for others to point to, when a new show didn't become a hit right away. Thanks to Lear's success, other worthy shows were given a second chance: It is no exaggeration to say that television would not now be airing such highly touted, groundbreaking shows as "30 Rock," "Entourage," and "Dexter," if it were not for Norman Lear and "All in the Family."

Of course, Lear resides at the extreme. He is the creator of his circumstances and surroundings in a way that few of us are able to match. But there are Norman Lears in all walks of life who master the context wherever they are. And leaders have always fought the context. Mathilde Krim, the scientist who has long been a leader in the fight on AIDS, said, "I have little tolerance for institutional restraints. Institutions should serve people, but unfortunately it's often the other way around. People give their allegiance to an institution, and they become prisoners of habits, practices, and rules that make them ultimately ineffectual."

If most of us, like Ed, are creatures of our context, prisoners of the habits, practices, and rules that make us ineffectual, it is from the Norman Lears, the people who not only challenge and conquer the context but who change it in fundamental ways, that we must learn. The first step toward change is to refuse to be deployed by others and to choose to deploy yourself. Thus the process begins.

2
Understanding the Basics

As we survey the path leadership theory has taken, we
spot the wreckage of "trait theory," the "great man" theory,
and the "situationist" critique, leadership styles, functional
leadership, and, finally, leaderless leadership, to say nothing of
bureaucratic leadership, charismatic leadership, group-centered
leadership, reality-centered leadership, leadership by objective,
and so on. The dialectic and reversals of emphases in this
area very nearly rival the tortuous twists and turns of
child-rearing practices, and one can paraphrase Gertrude
Stein by saying, 'a leader is a follower is a leader.'

—*Administrative Science Quarterly*

Leaders come in every size, shape, and disposition—short, tall,
neat, sloppy, young, old, male, and female. Nevertheless, they
all seem to share some, if not all, of the following ingredients:

- The first basic ingredient of leadership is a *guiding vision*.
  The leader has a clear idea of what he or she wants to
  do—professionally and personally—and the strength to
  persist in the face of setbacks, even failures. Unless you

know where you're going, and why, you cannot possibly get there. That guiding purpose, that vision, was well illustrated by Norman Lear.

- The second basic ingredient of leadership is *passion*—the underlying passion for the promises of life, combined with a very particular passion for a vocation, a profession, a course of action. The leader loves what he or she does and loves doing it. Tolstoy said that hopes are the dreams of the waking man. Without hope, we cannot survive, much less progress. The leader who communicates passion gives hope and inspiration to other people. This ingredient tends to come up with different spins on it—sometimes it appears as enthusiasm, especially in chapter eight, "Getting People on Your Side."

- The next basic ingredient of leadership is *integrity*. I think there are three essential parts of integrity: self-knowledge, candor, and maturity.

"Know thyself," was the inscription over the Oracle at Delphi. And it is still the most difficult task any of us faces. But until you truly know yourself, strengths and weaknesses, know what you want to do and why you want to do it, you cannot succeed in any but the most superficial sense of the word. Leaders never lie to themselves, especially about themselves, know their faults as well as their assets, and deal with them directly. You are your own raw material. When you know what you consist of and what you want to make of it, then you can invent yourself.

Candor is the key to self-knowledge. Candor is based in honesty of thought and action, a steadfast devotion to principle, and a fundamental soundness and wholeness. An architect who designs a Bauhaus glass box with a Victorian cupola lacks professional integrity, as does any person who trims his or her principles—or even ideas—to please. Like Lillian Hellman, the leader cannot cut his or her conscience to fit this year's fashions.

Maturity is important to a leader because leading is not simply showing the way or issuing orders. Every leader needs to have experienced and grown through following—learning to be dedicated, observant, capable of working with and learning from others, never servile, always truthful. Having located these qualities in themselves, leaders can encourage them in others.

- Integrity is the basis of *trust*, which is not as much an ingredient of leadership as it is a product. It is the one quality that cannot be acquired, but must be earned. It is given by co-workers and followers, and without it, the leader can't function. I'll talk about trust in greater detail in chapter eight, "Getting People on Your Side."
- Two more basic ingredients of leadership are *curiosity* and *daring*. Leaders wonder about everything, want to learn as much as they can, are willing to take risks, experiment, try new things. They do not worry about failure, but embrace errors, knowing they will learn from them. Learning from adversity is another theme that comes up again and again in this book, often with different spins. In fact, that could be said of each of the basic ingredients.

Even though I talk about basic ingredients, I'm not talking about traits that you're born with and can't change. As countless deposed kings and hapless heirs to great fortunes can attest, true leaders are not born, but made, and usually self-made. Leaders invent themselves. They are not, by the way, made in a single weekend seminar, as many of the leadership-theory spokesmen claim. I've come to think of that one as the microwave theory: pop in Mr. or Ms. Average and out pops McLeader in sixty seconds.

Billions of dollars are spent annually by and on would-be leaders. Many major corporations offer leadership development courses. And corporate America has nevertheless lost its lead in the world market. I would argue that more leaders have been made by accident, circumstance, sheer grit, or will than have been made by all the leadership courses put together. Leadership courses can only teach skills. They can't teach character or vision—and indeed they don't even try. Developing character and vision is the way leaders invent themselves.

The Great Depression was the crucible in which Franklin D. Roosevelt was transformed from politician to leader. Harry Truman became president when FDR died, but it was sheer grit that made him a leader. Dwight Eisenhower, the nation's only five-star general, was underestimated by Republican party bosses who saw only his winning smile. He turned out to be his own man, and a leader. Pols like Chicago's mayor Richard Daley gave John Kennedy a boost into the White House, but he shone there on his own. Like them or not, FDR, Truman, Ike, and JFK were all true leaders.

Truman never saw himself as a leader and was probably as surprised as anyone else when he became president. Eisenhower was a good soldier blessed with a constellation of better soldiers who made both his military and political victories possible. Those charming rich boys Roosevelt and Kennedy were, in the vernacular of the time, traitors to their class, but heroes to the people. Each of these men was his own invention: Truman and Eisenhower, the quintessential small-town boys rising to the top; Roosevelt and Kennedy, driven by ambitious and powerful parents, worldly but conventional, remaking themselves and their worlds.

Being self-made is, of course, not all of it. Lyndon Johnson, Richard Nixon, and Jimmy Carter could be described as self-made men, but they failed to win our hearts or engage our minds, and finally failed as national leaders.

All three were highly competent, but their ambitions overrode their talent. Johnson set out to make a Great Society, but made a bad war instead. Nixon wanted less to lead us than to rule us. It was never clear what Carter wanted, besides the White House. In each case, their minds seemed to be closed—to us, at least, and perhaps to themselves as well. Whatever vision each may have had went unexpressed (or in Johnson's case unfulfilled). Each was given to saying one thing and doing another, and each seemed to look on the American people as adversaries. When we questioned the Vietnam War, Johnson questioned our loyalty. Nixon had an enemies list. And Carter accused us of malingering.

As presidents, Johnson, Nixon, and Carter were all more driven than driving, and each seemed trapped in his own shadows. They were haunted men, shaped more by their early deprivations than by their later successes. They did not, then, invent themselves. They were made—and unmade—by their own histories.

When Henry Kissinger was asked what he had learned from the presidents he had worked with—a list that started with Kennedy, through whom he met Truman—Kissinger replied, "Presidents don't do great things by dwelling on their limitations, but by focusing on their possibilities." They leave the past behind them and turn toward the future.

37

Just as Roosevelt and Kennedy made themselves new, and therefore independent and free, Johnson and Nixon were used goods, no matter how far they got from their pinched beginnings, no matter how high they rose. Roosevelt, Truman, Eisenhower, and Kennedy invented themselves and then invented the future. Johnson and Nixon were made by their pasts. They imposed those mean lessons of their pasts on the present, enshrouding the future. Good leaders engage the world. Bad leaders entrap it, or try.

Jimmy Carter, who never managed to put a distinctive stamp on his one-term presidency, was able to reinvent himself as an international peace-maker. His 1980 re-election doomed as long as American hostages remained in Iran, he continued to be shaped out of office by his passionate Christianity. But his unshakeable convictions were a far better fit with a career as an almost saintly ambassador of peace than with the office of president of the United States. Carter became an inspiring symbol of what a former president, or any person who has attained and lost great power, can achieve. With wife Rosalynn ever at his side, Carter builds homes for the poor with Habitat for Humanity. And whenever Carter feels he is needed, he jets off to far-flung trouble spots to monitor elections and insure human rights. Some see his efforts as naive. Many more see them as evidence of authentic moral leadership, for which he received the Nobel Peace Prize in 2002.

In the years since Carter left office in 1981, we have had self-made men in the White House (Ronald Reagan and Bill Clinton) and American aristocrats (George Herbert Walker Bush and his son George W. Bush). The first Hollywood president, former actor Reagan proved that leadership is, to an extraordinary degree, a performance art. He earned his reputation as "the Teflon president" largely because of his winning manner even when faced with the Iran-contra scandal and a stock market plunge, on October 19, 1987, inevitably attributed to Reaganomics. Whether Reagan's affable sincerity was genuine, we will never know. But he was a model of successful self-invention who projected authenticity and a lack of pretense that made him one of the most popular presidents in recent history.

The senior George Bush was an American Brahmin on a more modest scale than FDR or JFK. With Reagan, he was the last of our presidents to have been forged in the crucible of World War II, in which he served as a very young and much decorated pilot. Bush received some of the highest acceptance ratings in polling history during his campaign against Iraq's Saddam Hussein, Desert Storm. And it was on Bush's watch that the Soviet Union—the "Evil Empire," as Reagan called it—dissolved in 1991. But Bush was ultimately undone by his inability to distance himself from his aristocratic roots. Constantly reminded by the brilliant, relentless coalition that put Clinton in the White House in 1992, the American public never forgot the image of Bush staring in wonder at an electronic supermarket scanner. The voting public may forgive you for going to Choate, but it will never forgive you for not knowing how the other half shops.

An orphan raised by an alcoholic step-father, President Clinton was brilliantly self-made, a man who was swept into office in 1992 by making voters believe in a place called Hope, the stranger-than-fiction name of his Arkansas birthplace. Clinton had the intelligence, the charm, the ability to find common ground—everything he needed to be one of the greatest presidents in history. Everything, that is, except the strong moral compass that all great leaders have. Clinton's case is tragic in the classical sense, that of a hero brought down by his own fatal flaw. Hounded throughout his two terms by Conservative opponents with Javert-like tenacity, Clinton still managed to preside over a period of prosperity, fueled by the soaring New Economy, unmatched in modern American history. He was ultimately impeached on, and acquitted of, charges that included perjuring himself about a dalliance with White House intern Monica Lewinsky.

Clinton's ability to recover from setbacks during his years in Arkansas politics won him the nickname "The Come-Back Kid." Time will tell if Clinton is able to re-invent himself out of office, as Carter did. Certainly Clinton has the talent and the drive to do so. Whether he has the requisite integrity—a quality that transcends traditional notions of propriety—remains to be seen.

It is still early in the process of determining what went wrong with the two-term presidency of George W. Bush. The psychoanalytically inclined tend to look for answers in the younger Bush's ambivalent feelings toward his powerful father. But no amount of armchair psychiatry can account for the speed with which Bush 43 managed to create an American presidency of unprecedented opacity and disdain for some of the nation's most cherished principles. When W. first took office, there was hope that he would undergo a Shakespearean transformation and grow into the presidency—that he would evolve from a fun-loving, Texas-style Prince Hal into an American Henry V. It was not to be, and the nation suffered mightily for it.

Like Clinton, W. represented a new generation of leaders whose crucible was not World War II but the more ambiguous proving-ground of the 1960s and early '70s, with their sex, drugs, rock 'n' roll, and mistrust of authority. The history-making election of Barack Obama marks another profound generational change. Conservative commentator David Brooks points out that Obama "is a child of a child of the 1960s." Brooks calls Obama's post-baby-boomer cohort the "temperate generation." It is also the first generation to grow up wired. Time will tell if Obama is a truly transformational figure. But in his sober, stirring victory speech, he made it clear that he will be president of all Americans as well as a citizen of the world. He promised a collaborative administration that would include Republicans. And he spoke of the need for sacrifice as the country faces its many challenges. A steady, deliberative leader whose mantra was "yes we can," Obama galvanized young voters as no president had since JFK, and it is likely that Obama's example will inspire many to enter public life. As Missouri senator Claire McCaskill observed, while the votes were still being counted: "Another generation of leaders was born in this election."

The Greeks believed that excellence was based on a perfect balance of eros and logos, or feeling and thought, which together allow us to understand the world on all levels, from "the concrete contemplation of the complete facts." True understanding derives from engagement and from the full deployment of ourselves. As John Gardner once said, talent is one thing, while its triumphant expression is another. Only when we are fully deployed are we capable of that triumphant expression. Full deployment, engagement, hone and sharpen all of one's gifts, and ensure that one will be an original, not a copy.

LEADERS, NOT MANAGERS

I tend to think of the differences between leaders and managers as the differences between those who master the context and those who surrender to it. There are other differences, as well, and they are enormous and crucial:

41

- The manager administers; the leader innovates.
- The manager is a copy; the leader is an original.
- The manager maintains; the leader develops.
- The manager focuses on systems and structure; the leader focuses on people.
- The manager relies on control; the leader inspires trust.
- The manager has a short-range view; the leader has a long-range perspective.
- The manager asks how and when; the leader asks what and why.
- The manager has his or her eye always on the bottom line; the leader's eye is on the horizon.
- The manager imitates; the leader originates.
- The manager accepts the status quo; the leader challenges it.
- The manager is the classic good soldier; the leader is his or her own person.
- The manager does things right; the leader does the right thing.

To reprise Wallace Stevens, managers wear square hats and learn through training. Leaders wear sombreros and opt for education. Consider the differences between training and education:

Education	Training
inductive	deductive
tentative	firm
dynamic	static
understanding	memorizing
ideas	facts

broad	narrow
deep	surface
experiential	rote
active	passive
questions	answers
process	content
strategy	tactics
alternatives	goal
exploration	prediction
discovery	dogma
active	reactive
initiative	direction
whole brain	left brain
life	job
long-term	short-term
change	stability
content	form
flexible	rigid
risk	rules
synthesis	thesis
open	closed
imagination	common sense

The Sum:	**Leader**	**Manager**

If the list on the left seems strange to you, it's because that isn't the way we are usually taught. Our educational system is really better at training than educating. And that's unfortunate.

Training is good for dogs, because we require obedience from them. In people, all it does is orient them toward the bottom line.

The list on the left is of all the qualities that business schools don't encourage enough, as they too often opt for the short-run, profit-maximizing, microeconomic bottom line. Bottom lines have nothing to do with problem-finding. And we need people who know how to find problems, because the ones we face today aren't always clearly defined, and they aren't linear. Frank Gehry and other great architects have moved away from the old divinity of right angles to rhomboids, rounded spaces, and parabolas. They are designing sombreros. Aspiring leaders must also think non-traditionally.

Leaders have nothing but themselves to work with. It is one of the paradoxes of life that good leaders rise to the top in spite of their weakness, while bad leaders rise because of their weakness. Abraham Lincoln was subject to fits of serious depression, yet he was perhaps this country's best president, guiding this country through its most severe crisis. On the other hand, Hitler imposed his psychosis on the German people, leading them through delusions of grandeur into the vilest madness and most horrific slaughter the world has ever known.

What is true for leaders is, for better or for worse, true for each of us: we are our own raw material. Only when we know what we're made of and what we want to make of it can we begin our lives—and we must do it despite an unwitting conspiracy of people and events against us. It's that tension in the national character again. As Norman Lear put it, "On the one hand, we're a society that seems to be proud of individuality. On the other hand, we don't really tolerate real individuality. We want to homogenize it."

For Oscar-winning movie director Sydney Pollack, the search for self-knowledge was a continuing process. "There's a sort of monologue or dialogue going on in my head all the time," he said. "Some of it's part of a fantasy life, some is exploratory. Sometimes I can trick myself into problem-solving by imagining myself talking about problem-solving. If I don't know the answer to something, I imagine being asked the question in my head. Faulkner said, 'I don't know what I think until I read what I said.' That's not just a joke. You learn what you think by codifying your thinking in some way."

That's absolutely true. Codifying one's thinking is an important step in inventing oneself. The most difficult way to do it is by thinking about thinking—it helps to speak or write your thoughts. Writing is the most profound way of codifying your thoughts, the best way of learning from yourself who you are and what you believe.

Newspaper executive Gloria Anderson added, "It's vital for people to develop their own sense of themselves and their role in the world, and it's equally vital for them to try new things, to test themselves and their beliefs and principles. I think we long for people who will stand up for what they believe, even if we don't agree with them, because we have confidence in such people."

Scientist Mathilde Krim agreed. "One must be a good explorer and a good listener, too, to take in as much as possible but not swallow anything uncritically. One must finally trust his own gut reactions," she said. "A value system, beliefs, are important so you know where you stand, but they must be your own values, not someone else's."

If knowing yourself and being yourself were as easy to do as to talk about, there wouldn't be nearly so many people walking around in borrowed postures, spouting secondhand ideas, trying desperately to fit in rather than to stand out. Former Lucky Stores CEO Don Ritchey said, on the need for being oneself, "I believe people spot phonies in very short order, whether that be on an individual basis or a company basis. As Emerson says, 'What you are speaks so loudly I cannot hear what you say.'"

ONCE BORN, TWICE BORN

Harvard professor emeritus Abraham Zaleznik posits that there are two kinds of leaders: once-borns and twice-borns. The once-born's transition from home and family to independence is relatively easy. Twice-borns generally suffer as they grow up, feel different, even isolated, and so develop an elaborate inner life. As they grow older, they become truly independent, relying wholly on their own beliefs and ideas. Leaders who are twice born are inner-directed, self-assured, and, as a result, truly charismatic, according to Zaleznik.

Once-borns, then, have been invented by their circumstances, as in the case of Johnson and Nixon, while twice-borns have invented themselves, as in the case of Roosevelt and Truman.

A couple of studies underscore the benefits, even the necessity, of self-invention. First, middle-aged men tend to change careers after having heart attacks. Faced with their own mortality, these men realize that what they've been doing, what they've invested their lives in, is not an accurate reflection of their real needs and desires.

Another study indicates that what determines the level of satisfaction in post-middle-aged men is the degree to which they acted upon their youthful dreams. It's not so much whether they were successful in achieving their dreams as the honest pursuit of them that counts. The spiritual dimension in creative effort comes from that honest pursuit.

There is, of course, evidence that women, too, are happier when they've invented themselves instead of accepting without question the roles they were brought up to play. Psychologist and author Sonya Friedman said, "The truth of the matter is that the most emotionally disturbed women are those who are married and into traditional full-time, lifetime homemaker roles. Single women have always been happier than married women. Always. And there isn't a study that has disproved that."

Staying single has historically been the only way most women were free to invent themselves. Nineteenth-century poet Emily Dickinson, a reclusive woman who never married and who surely invented herself, is supposed to have said to one of the rare visitors to her room, "Here is freedom!"

Fortunately, the changing times have meant changes in relationships, too. Many of the women leaders I talked with have managed to invent themselves even though married—as has Friedman herself.

I cannot stress too much the need for self-invention. To be authentic is literally to be your own author (the words derive from the same Greek root), to discover your own native energies and desires, and then to find your own way of acting on them. When you've done that, you are not existing simply in order to live up to an image posited by the culture or by some other authority or by a family tradition. When you write your own life, then no matter what happens, you have played the game that was natural for you to play. If, as someone said, "it is the supervisor's role in a modern industrial society to limit the potential of the people who work for him," then it is your task to do whatever you must to break out of such limits and live up to your potential, to keep the covenant with your youthful dreams.

Norman Lear would add to this that the goal isn't worth arriving at unless you enjoy the journey. "You have to look at success incrementally," he said. "It takes too long to get to any major success. . . . If one can look at life as being success-ful on a moment-by-moment basis, one might find that most of it is successful. And take the bow inside for it. When we wait for the big bow, it's a lousy bargain. They don't come but once in too long a time."

Applauding yourself for the small successes, and taking the small bow, are good ways of learning to experience life each moment that you live it. And that's part of inventing yourself, of creating your own destiny.

To become a leader, then, you must become yourself, be-come the maker of your own life. While there are no rules for doing this, there are some lessons I can offer from my decades of observation and study. And we'll turn to those lessons now.

3
Knowing Yourself

I have often thought that the best way to define a man's character would be to seek out the particular mental or moral attitude in which, when it came upon him, he felt himself most deeply and intensively active and alive. At such moments, there is a voice inside which speaks and says, "This is the real me."

—WILLIAM JAMES
Letters of William James

By the time we reach puberty, the world has reached us and shaped us to a greater extent than we realize. Our family, friends, school, and society in general have told us—by word and example—how to be. But people begin to become leaders at that moment when they decide for themselves how to be.

For some leaders, this happens early. Former Secretary of Education Shirley Hufstedler has spent her life in the legal profession, but she was something of an outlaw as a young girl. She told me, "When I was very young, the things I wanted to do were not permitted by social dictates. I wanted to do a lot of things that girls weren't supposed to do. So I had to figure out ways to do what I wanted to do and still show up in a pinafore for a piano recital, so as not to blow my cover. You could call it manipulation, but I see it as observation and picking one's way around obstacles. If you think of what you want and examine the possibilities, you can usually figure out a way to accomplish it."

Brooke Knapp, a trail-blazing pilot and businesswoman, also fought her way out of the mold. She said, "I was raised in the South, and I was raised to be a wife. When I went to college, the definition of success was to get married to a gentleman and help him succeed and have children . . . [but] I was a little savage, in the best sense of the word, because I was stronger than my mother, and there was no way to control me."

As Knapp learned, however, breaking out, being yourself, is sometimes anything but easy. She said, "In high school, I realized that I was going to be voted the most athletic, but I didn't want the 'lady jock' label, so I decided to become the most popular. I learned the name of every single person casting a ballot and called them all by name and won." Her popularity took a nosedive when "the mothers of the girls in my class started taking potshots at me. I concluded that success means that people don't like you and you become a bad person, so I shut down for a lot of years. It wasn't till after I got married that I began to experience my need to achieve again."

Know thyself, then, means separating who you are and who you want to be from what the world thinks you are and wants you to be. Author/psychiatrist Roger Gould also declared his independence very early. He said, "I remember, during arguments with my father, there seemed to be arbitrary rules, which I never understood. I used to ask 'why' all the time. One time, I must have been six, I was lying in bed and looking up at the stars and thinking, 'There're other planets out there, and maybe there's life on some of them, and the earth is enormous, with millions of people, and everyone can't be right all the time, so my father could be wrong, and I could be right.' It was my own theory of relativity. Then, in high school, I began reading the classics, and they were my transition in my own life, away from my parents. I had my own private life, which I could appreciate on its terms, and never talk to anyone else about it until I had digested it for myself."

Hufstedler, Knapp, and Gould clearly invented themselves, just as the other leaders I talked with did. They overcame a variety of obstacles in a variety of ways, but all stressed the importance of self-knowledge.

Some start the process early, and some don't do it until later. It doesn't matter. Self-knowledge, self-invention are lifetime processes. Those people who struggled to know themselves and become themselves as children or teenagers continue today to explore their own depths, reflect on their experiences, and test themselves. Others—like Roosevelt and Truman—undertake their own remaking in midlife. Sometimes we simply don't like who we are or what we're doing, and so we seek change. Sometimes events, as in Truman's case, require more of us than we think we have. But all of us can find tangible and intangible rewards in self-knowledge and self-control, because if you go on doing what you've always done, you'll go on getting what you've always got—which may be less than you want or deserve.

All of the leaders I talked with agreed that no one can teach you how to become yourself, to take charge, to express yourself, except you. But there are some things that others have done that are useful to think about in the process. I've organized them as the four lessons of self-knowledge. They are

- One: You are your own best teacher.
- Two: Accept responsibility. Blame no one.
- Three: You can learn anything you want to learn.
- Four: True understanding comes from reflecting on your experience.

Lesson One: You Are Your Own Best Teacher

Gib Akin, professor at the McIntire School of Commerce, University of Virginia, studied the learning experiences of sixty managers. In his classic study, published in *Organizational Dynamics*, Akin found that the managers' descriptions were "surprisingly congruous. . . . Learning is experienced as a personal transformation. A person does not gather learnings as possessions but rather becomes a new person. . . . To learn is not to have, it is to be."

Akin's roster of modes of learning includes

- Emulation, in which one emulates either someone one knows or a historical or public figure.
- Role taking, in which one has a conception of what one should be and does it.
- Practical accomplishment, in which one sees a problem as an opportunity and learns through the experience of dealing with it.
- Validation, in which one tests concepts by applying them and learns after the fact.
- Anticipation, in which one develops a concept and then applies it, learning before acting.

- Personal growth, in which one is less concerned with specific skills than with self-understanding and the "transformation of values and attitudes."
- Scientific learning, in which one observes, conceptualizes on the basis of one's observations, and then experiments to gather new data, with a primary focus on truth.

The managers Akin interviewed cited two basic motivations for learning. The first was a need to know, which they described, he said, "as rather like a thirst or hunger gnawing at them, sometimes dominating their attention until satisfied." The second was "a sense of role," which stems from "a person's perception of the gap between what he or she is, and what he or she should be."

In other words, the managers knew that they were not fulfilling their own potential, not expressing themselves fully. And they knew that learning was a way out of the trap, a major step toward self-expression. And they saw learning as something intimately connected with self. No one could have taught them that in school. They had to teach themselves. Somehow they had reached a point in life where they knew they had to learn new things—it was either that or admit that they had settled for less than they were capable of. If you can accept all that, as the managers did, the next step is to assume responsibility for your education as well as yourself. Major stumbling blocks on the path to self-knowledge are denial and blame.

Lesson Two: Accept Responsibility. Blame No One

The wisdom of this seems intuitively obvious to me. So I'll let you listen to Marty Kaplan, who is the best example of accepting responsibility for oneself that I know of.

Today, Kaplan is a research professor at the University of Southern California's Annenberg School for Communication who holds the Norman Lear Chair in Entertainment, Media, and Society. He is an accomplished screenwriter and producer as well as a regular contributor to the Huffington Post. But he was only in his 30s when, in the mid–1980s, he embarked on his third career—as Disney Productions' Vice President. He went to Disney with a wide-ranging background—from biology to the *Harvard Lampoon*, from broadcast and print journalism to high-level politics. He knew a lot about a lot of things, but very little about the movie business. His description of his self-designed university illustrates how he accepted the responsibility for creating his own success:

"Before starting this job, I put myself through a crash course, watching five or six movies every single day for six weeks, trying to see every successful picture of the last several years. Then I read as many of the scripts as I could get my hands on, to see what made these particular movies great. I kind of invented my own university, so that I could get some sense of both the business and the art. . . . I've always been in worlds where knowing the community has been important. In graduate school, when I was studying literature, to know the writers and critics was to know a universe. In Washington, I had to learn the political players, and here I had to learn the players. It became clear to me that there were about one hundred core writers, and I systematically set out to read a screenplay or two by each of them. When I got here, I was told it would take me three years to get grounded, but after nine months, the head of the studio told me I'd graduated and promoted me. Within a year I found—with some stumbles here and there—that I could perform the way my peers, who had spent their entire careers here, did. I attribute that partly to discipline, partly to desire, and partly to the old transferability of skills. You use many of the same muscles in molecular biology, politics, and the movies. It's all about making connections.

"One thing I did when I first got here was to sit in the office of the studio head all day, day after day, and watch and listen to everything he said or did. So when writers would come, when producers would come, I would just be there. When he was making phone calls, I would sit and listen to him, and I would hear him contend with what a person in his position contends with. How does he say no to someone, how does he say yes, how does he duck, how does he wheedle and coax? I would have a yellow pad with me, and all through my first many months, any phrase I didn't understand, any piece of industry jargon, any name, any maneuver I didn't follow, any of the deal-making business financial stuff I didn't understand, I'd write it down, and periodically I would go trotting around to find anyone I could get to answer.

"There was no situation that I could fail to learn from, because everything was new to me, and therefore no matter what it was, however obtuse the person I was meeting with, however stupid the idea, however low-powered the agent pitching me something, it was a useful encounter, because I would be for the first time in that position. Every single thing was new, and so I had a complete tolerance for every conceivable experience, and as I learned from what other people would regard as real tedium, and stupid and avoidable experiences, I would then begin to filter those out of my input until I was ultimately only doing what I thought was useful and important for me, or things from which I could learn, or had to do."

Lesson Three:
You Can Learn Anything You Want to Learn

If one of the basic ingredients of leadership is a passion for the promises of life, the key to realizing the promise is the full deployment of yourself, as Kaplan did when he arrived at Disney. Full deployment is simply another way of defining learning.

Learning, the kind Kaplan did, the kind I'm talking about here, is much more than the absorption of a body of knowledge or mastery of a discipline. It's seeing the world simultaneously as it is and as it can be, understanding what you see, and acting on your understanding. Kaplan didn't just study the movie business, he embraced it and absorbed it, and thereby understood it.

In our discussion, I suggested that this kind of learning has to do with reflecting on experience. Kaplan said, "I would add a component to that, which is the appetite to have experience, because people can be experience averse and therefore not learn. Unless you have the appetite to absorb new and potentially unsettling things, you don't learn. . . . Part of it is temperament. It's a kind of fearlessness and optimism and confidence, and you're not afraid of failure."

"You're not afraid of failure." Keep that in mind, because we'll get back to it later.

Lesson Four: True Understanding
Comes from Reflecting on Your Experience

Kaplan didn't simply watch all those movies and read all those scripts and spend all those hours in the studio head's office. He did all that, and then he reflected on what he'd seen and read and heard, and he came to a new understanding.

Reflecting on experience is a means of having a Socratic dialogue with yourself, asking the right questions at the right time, in order to discover the truth of yourself and your life. What really happened? Why did it happen? What did it do to me? What did it mean to me? In this way, one locates and appropriates the knowledge one needs or, more precisely, recovers what one knew but had forgotten, and becomes, in Goethe's phrase, the hammer rather than the anvil.

Kaplan stated it forcefully: "The habit of reflection may be a consequence of facing mortality. . . . To begin to understand any great literature is to understand that it's a race against death, and it's the redeeming power of love or God or art or whatever the artist is proposing that's the thing that makes the race against death worth racing. . . . In a way, reflection is asking the questions that provoke self-awareness."

Nothing is truly yours until you understand it—not even yourself. Our feelings are raw, unadulterated truth, but until we understand why we are happy or angry or anxious, the truth is useless to us. For example, every one of us has been yelled at by a superior and bitten our tongues, afraid to yell back. Later, we yell at a friend who has done nothing. Such displaced emotions punctuate our lives, and diminish them. This is not to suggest that yelling back at a superior is a useful response. Understanding is the answer. When you understand, then you know what to do.

The importance of reflecting on experience, the idea that reflecting leads to understanding, came up again and again in my conversations with leaders. Now executive director of the National School Boards Association, Anne Bryant was executive director of the American Association of University Women when she told me she has made reflection a part of her daily routine: "Every morning after the alarm goes off, I lie in bed for about fifteen minutes, going over what I want to get out of each event of my day, and what I want to get done by the end of the week. I've been doing it for two or three years, and if I don't do it, I feel I've wasted the day."

To look forward with acuity you must first look back with honesty. After spending four days a week at her Washington, D.C., office, Bryant spent the balance of the week at her home in Chicago, where she read, reflected on the week just past, and planned for the days ahead.

Those, then, are the four lessons of self-knowledge. But in order to put these lessons into practice, you need to understand the effect that childhood experiences, family, and peers have had on the person you've become.

All too often, we are strangers to ourselves. In his classic *The Lonely Crowd*, David Riesman wrote, "The source of direction for the individual is 'inner' in the sense that it is implanted early in life by the elders and directed toward generalized, but nonetheless inescapably destined roles," while "what is common to all the other-directed people is that their contemporaries are the source of direction for the individual—either those known to him or those with whom he is indirectly acquainted through friends and through the mass media. This source is internalized in the sense that dependence on it for guidance in life is implanted early. The goals toward which the other-directed person strives shift with that guidance: It is only the process of striving itself and the process of paying close attention to the signals from others that remain unaltered throughout life."

In other words, most of us are made by our elders or by our peers. But leaders are self-directed. Let's stop and think about that for a moment. Leaders are self-directed, but learning and understanding are the keys to self-direction, and it is in our relationships with others that we learn about ourselves. As Boris Pasternak wrote in *Doctor Zhivago,*

> Well, what are you? What is it about you that you have always known as yourself? What are you conscious of in yourself: your kidneys, your liver, your blood vessels? No. However far back you go in your memory it is always some external mani- festation of yourself where you come across your identity: in the work of your hands, in your family, in other people. And now, listen carefully. You in others—this is what you are, this is what your consciousness has breathed, and lived on, and en- joyed throughout your life, your soul, your immortality—your life in others.

How, then, do we resolve the paradox? This way: leaders learn from others, but they are not made by others. This is the distinguishing mark of leaders. The paradox becomes a dialec- tic. The self and the other synthesize through self-invention.

What that means is that here and now, true learning must often be preceded by unlearning, because we are taught by our parents and teachers and friends how to go along, to measure up to their standards, rather than allowed to be ourselves.

Alfred Gottschalk, chancellor emeritus of Hebrew Union College, told me, "The hardest thing I've had to do is convey to children, my own and others, the necessity of coming to terms with themselves. Their interests aren't deep. They don't think about things. They accept what they're told and what they read or see on TV. They're conformists. They accept the dictates of fashion."

Asked to define his philosophy, Gottschalk said, "I value the need for the individual to feel unique and for the collective to remain hospitable to diversity. I believe in unity without uniformity and in man's capacity to redeem himself."

Given the pressures from our parents and the pressures from our peers, how does any one of us manage to emerge as a sane—much less productive—adult?

William James wrote, in 1890 in *The Principles of Psychology*,

> A man's Self is the sum total of all that he can call his, not only his body and his psychic powers, but his clothes and his house, his wife and children, his ancestors and friends, his reputation and works, his lands and horses, and yacht and bank account. All these things give him the same emotions. If they wax and prosper, he feels triumphant; if they dwindle and die away, he feels cast down.

It's hard to conceive of a more apt description of the conspicuous consumer of any era. But as James concludes, ". . . our self-feeling in this world depends entirely on what we back ourselves to be and do."

Leaders begin, then, by backing themselves, inspiring themselves, trusting themselves, and ultimately inspire others by being trustworthy.

Famed psychoanalyst Erik Erikson has divided life into eight stages that are useful to look at during our examination of self-invention:

1. Infancy: Basic Trust vs. Basic Mistrust
2. Early childhood: Autonomy vs. Shame, Doubt
3. Play age: Initiative vs. Guilt
4. School age: Industry vs. Inferiority
5. Adolescence: Identity vs. Identity Confusion

6. Young adulthood: Intimacy vs. Isolation
7. Adulthood: Generativity vs. Stagnation
8. Old age: Integrity vs. Despair

Erikson believes that we do not proceed to the next stage until each stage's crisis has been satisfactorily resolved. Too many of us, for example, never overcome the inner struggle between initiative and guilt, and so we lack real purpose. A woman caught between motherhood and an urge for a career was thought only a generation ago to be at best selfish, at worst unnatural. Giving up motherhood was deemed unthinkable; trying to juggle her children and her career was a frustrating and usually unsupported choice. Whichever course she took, initiative and guilt struggled, unresolved. And, of course, these inner conflicts were made outwardly manifest, inflicted on the people in her life, as well as on herself. No one, including the hermit, suffers alone.

Traditionally, it has been easier for men to make their way through these stages and their attendant crises, but all too often, prodded by well-meaning parents and teachers, men, too, do what they're supposed to do in life, not what they want to do. In this way, the man who dreams of being a poet becomes an accountant and the would-be cowboy becomes an executive, and both suffer the torments of the unfulfilled. And who knows what they might have done if they had chosen to follow their dreams? Former Beatle John Lennon, possibly the most influential songwriter of his generation, gave the aunt who raised him a gold plaque engraved with her oft-repeated dictum, "You'll never make a living playing that guitar."

In the world according to Erikson, how we resolve the eight crises determines who we will be:

1. Trust vs. Mistrust = hope or withdrawal
2. Autonomy vs. Shame, Doubt = will or compulsion
3. Initiative vs. Guilt = purpose or inhibition
4. Industry vs. Inferiority = competence or inertia
5. Identity vs. Identity Confusion = fidelity or repudiation
6. Intimacy vs. Isolation = love or exclusivity
7. Generativity vs. Stagnation = care or rejectivity
8. Integrity vs. Despair = wisdom or disdain

With all the power that the world has over us as we proceed through the early years of our lives, it is a wonder that any of us manages to resolve any of these crises in a positive way. Or as a woman once said to me, the phrase "dysfunctional family" is redundant: "If there's a functional family anywhere, I certainly haven't seen it." What she meant by that is that the Cleavers, Waltons, Huxtables, and other fictional happy families are far from the reality most of us experience. TV sitcom children are a good deal more likely to enjoy wise, nurturing parents and happy childhoods than the population at large.

Analyst Gould told me he wanted to write a book on recovering from childhood that would focus on "overcoming the adaptational warp that takes place early in life. If you let it happen, you undergo an automatic recovery process in the course of facing and dealing with new realities. In order to respond to the challenges of each cycle of your life appropriately, you have to continually re-examine your defenses and assumptions, and in the course of that re-examination, you iron out the way. . . . Feelings are memories of past behavior. When you sort them out and see what's current and what's left over, you can literally begin to use your thinking process to change your behavior."

There is ample evidence that ego development does not stop with physical maturity, and so while we cannot change our height or bone structure, we can change our minds. Many people insist that "it's never too late to have a happy childhood." I wouldn't quite go that far. We cannot change the circumstances of our childhoods, much less improve them at this late date, but we can recall them honestly, reflect on them, understand them, and thereby overcome their influence on us. Withdrawal can be turned to hope, compulsion to will, inhibition to purpose, and inertia to competence through the exercise of memory and understanding.

There are people who would argue with this, who claim that our destiny resides wholly in our genes, that each of us is a mere product of heredity. Others argue fervently that each of us is an offspring of his or her environment and that our fate is determined by our circumstances. Studies of identical twins who have been raised separately indicate that there is more truth to the first perspective. But the real answer to how we become who we are is more complex.

Genetic research affirms that there is a strong hereditary component to disease. Equally compelling research suggests that stress and other environmental factors also affect our health. Similarly, some scientists see the brain and heart as mere organs, capable of nothing more than chemical reactions, while others see the brain and heart as the locus of reason and emotion, sophistication and poetry, all the qualities and capabilities that separate us from the apes. And while there is neurobiological evidence that part of the brain is hardwired prior to birth, it is increasingly clear that the brain is also plastic in nature, able to absorb and collate experiences that cause the brain itself to change.

There is growing evidence that even personality traits—introversion, humor, and so on—are genetic in origin. In the great debate between hereditary determinism and environmental determinism, there is not much room left for self-determination. In a sense, both schools justify removing responsibility for behavior from the individual, a new variation on the ancient Flip Wilson routine, "The devil made me do it!"

The truth is, we're products of everything—genes, environment, family, friends, trade winds, earthquakes, sunspots, schools, accidents, serendipity, anything you can think of, and more. The endless nature-nurture debate is interesting, even occasionally revelatory, but inconclusive. Like everyone else, leaders are products of this great stew of chemistry and circumstance. What distinguishes the leader from everyone else is that he or she takes all of that and creates a new, unique self.

Novelist William Faulkner told us that the past isn't dead. It isn't even past yet. Each of us contains his or her entire life. Everything we did or saw, everyone we ever encountered, is in our heads. But all that psychic baggage can be turned into comprehensible and useful experience by reflecting on it. Socrates said, "The unexamined life is not worth living." I'd go a step further: The unexamined life is impossible to live successfully. Like oarsmen, we generally move forward while looking backward, but not until we truly see the past—and understand it—can we successfully navigate the future.

Until you make your life your own, you're walking around in borrowed clothes. Leaders, whatever their field, are made up as much of their experiences as their skills, like everyone else. Unlike everyone else, they use their experience rather than being used by it.

William James again: "Genius . . . means little more than the faculty of perceiving in an unhabitual way." By the time we reach adulthood, we are driven as much by habit as by anything else, and there is an infinity of habits in us. From the woman who twirls a strand of hair when she's nervous or bored to the man who expresses his insecurity by never saying "thank you," we are all victims of habits. They do not merely rule us, they inhibit us and make fools of us.

To free ourselves from habit, to resolve the paradoxes, to transcend conflicts, to become the masters rather than the slaves of our own lives, we must first see and remember, and then forget. That is why true learning begins with unlearning— and why unlearning is one of the recurring themes of our story.

Every great inventor or scientist has had to unlearn conventional wisdom in order to proceed with his or her work. For example, conventional wisdom said, "If God had meant man to fly, He would have given him wings." But the Wright brothers disagreed and built an airplane.

No one—not your parents nor your teachers nor your peers—can teach you how to be yourself. Indeed, however well intentioned, they all work to teach you how not to be yourself. As the eminent child psychologist Jean Piaget said, "Every time we teach a child something, we keep him from inventing it himself." I would go a step further. Every time we teach children something, rather than helping them learn, we keep them from inventing themselves. By its very nature, teaching homogenizes, both its subjects and its objects. Learning, on the other hand, liberates. The more we know about ourselves and our world, the freer we are to achieve everything we are capable of achieving.

Many leaders have had problems with school, particularly their early school experiences. Albert Einstein wrote, "It is nothing short of a miracle that the modern methods of instruction have not yet entirely strangled the holy curiosity of inquiry. . . . It is a grave mistake to think that the enjoyment of seeing and searching can be promoted by means of coercion and a sense of duty."

Among the leaders I spoke with, scientist and philanthropist Mathilde Krim said, "To the extent that school is regimented, I don't like it." And Edward C. Johnson III, chairman of the board and CEO of Fidelity Investments, said, "Sitting in a classroom was never one of my strengths, but I've always been curious about ideas and objects." Johnson instinctively knew the difference between teaching and learning, between training and education.

Obviously, we cannot do away with—or do without—families or schools or any of the instruments of homogeneity. But we can see them for what they are, which is part of the equation, not the equation itself.

The prevailing equation is:

family + school + friends = you

But the only workable equation for anyone aspiring to selfhood is:

$$\frac{\text{family} + \text{school} + \text{friends}}{\text{you}} = \text{true you}$$

In this way, rather than being designed by your experience, you become your own designer. You become cause *and* effect rather than mere effect.

Self-awareness = self-knowledge = self-possession = self-control = self-expression.

You make your life your own by understanding it.

4
Knowing the World

I took a good deal o' pains with his education, sir; let
him run the streets when he was very young, and shift
for his-self. It's the only way to make a boy sharp, sir.

—CHARLES DICKENS
Pickwick Papers

One of the problems with standard leadership courses is that
they focus exclusively on skills and produce managers rather
than leaders, when they produce anything at all. Managerial
skills can, of course, be taught. And they are useful skills for
leaders to have. The ingredients of leadership cannot be
taught, however. They must be learned. As then CalFed CEO
Robert Dockson put it, "The things that matter can't be taught
in a formal classroom setting. Walter Wriston at Citicorp and
A. P. Giannini at the Bank of America weren't technicians.
They were men of vision. They knew what they wanted to do
and where they wanted to take their companies." Since by definition leaders are unique, what they learn and how they use it
to shape the future is unique, too.

As I noted in the last chapter, leaders are made at least as much by their experiences and their understanding and application of their experiences as by any skills. Norman Lear told me of an experience he had when he was in the Air Force, stationed in Italy: "I remember decking one guy—I hit one guy in my life before anybody hit me, in a bar in Foggia, Italy. He was a GI making an anti-Semitic joke. And I wrote an episode of 'All in the Family' about it. Mike hit somebody who was violating somebody else on the subway and scared himself with his own violence. And I had scared myself that way. I guess I see leadership in that, but I don't know where that comes from except that early feeling of how do I overcome this problem of being so much a minority and so unwanted."

Clearly, to become a true leader, one must know the world as well as one knows one's self. A variety of studies, as well as the lives of the leaders I talked with, demonstrates that certain kinds of experiences are especially significant for learning. These experiences include broad and continuing education, idiosyncratic families, extensive travel and/or exile, a rich private life, and key associations with mentors and groups.

I want to discuss the benefits of those experiences, but first I want to get into some ideas about learning itself.

In 1972, the Club of Rome began a groundbreaking study of learning, opening with a delineation of outer limits, which, in its words, "narrow our possibilities of material growth on a finite planet," and closing with a defense of "the inner free margins . . . which exist in ourselves and are pregnant with the potency of unparalleled developments."

Still relevant today, the Club's report was published in 1979 as *No Limits to Learning: Bridging the Human Gap*, by James W.

Botkin, Mahdi Elmandjra, and Mircea Malitza. Aurelio Peccei states in his foreword, "All we need at this point in human evolution is to learn what it takes to learn what we should learn—and learn it." The authors go on to define "the human gap" as "the distance between growing complexity and our capacity to cope with it. . . . We call it a human gap because it is a dichotomy between a growing complexity of our own making and a lagging development of our own capacities."

The authors describe the two principal modes of conventional learning:

- Maintenance learning, the most prevalent, is "the acquisition of fixed outlooks, methods and rules for dealing with known and recurring situations. . . . It is the type of learning designed to maintain an existing system or established way of life."
- Shock learning, almost as prevalent now, occurs when events overwhelm people. As the authors put it, "Even up to the present moment, humanity continues to wait for events and crises that . . . catalyze or impose this primitive learning by shock. . . . Shock learning can be seen as a product of elitism, technocracy and authoritarianism. Learning by shock often follows a period of overconfidence in solutions created solely with expert knowledge or technical competence and perpetuated beyond the conditions for which they were appropriate."

In other words, both maintenance learning and shock learning are less learning than they are accepting conventional wisdom. Society or one's family or school says this is the way things are and these are the things you need to know, and you accept what you're told as gospel. You forget that there is a self that must be listened to.

America's automotive industry prospered on maintenance learning, until it suddenly found itself up against the wall, outdone and outsold by the Japanese automotive wizards, and learned by shock that it was in crisis. Detroit was bankrupt creatively and facing financial ruin, but instead of trying to think its way out of the dilemma, it ran on shock for years, closing down plants, throwing thousands of employees out of work, buying any solution that looked good. It wasn't until recently that Detroit truly began to examine and recover from its self-inflicted wounds, evidence of what the Club of Rome calls "innovative learning that may come too late."

The authors write, "The conventional pattern of maintenance/shock learning is inadequate to cope with global complexity and is likely, if unchecked, to lead to . . . loss of control over events and crises. . . ."

What applies on a global basis applies on the personal level, too. Anyone who relies on maintenance and shock learning is bound to be more reactor than actor in his or her own life. For example, most families simply maintain. When someone in the family dies suddenly, the shock is so profound that the family frequently falls apart, at least temporarily. We all know husbands and wives who were so devastated by the death of a child that they wound up divorced. In the same way, people in business who simply accept conventional wisdom may reach the top of a bureaucratic organization, but they will never use their particular talents to their fullest. And if they ever confront their own lives, they will suffer the shock of failed aspirations—at the very least.

So innovative learning must replace maintenance/shock learning. The principal components of innovative learning are

- Anticipation: being active and imaginative rather than passive and habitual.
- Learning by listening to others.
- Participation: shaping events, rather than being shaped by them.

Obviously, then, innovative learning requires that you trust yourself, that you be self-directed rather than other-directed in both your life and your work. If you learn to anticipate the future and shape events rather than being shaped by them you will benefit in significant ways.

In making what the authors of the Club of Rome report call "the shift from . . . unconscious adaptation to conscious participation," we make or recognize new connections, generating useful syntheses, and our understanding deepens.

Movie director Pollack discussed the forces that work against innovative learning. "Everybody has the ability to free associate, but society tends to frown on active fantasies. Beyond a certain age, we stop playing games, 'let's pretend,' 'what if,' and all that. It goes on in your head anyway, but at some point you start to feel guilty. You know, you listen to a symphony and imagine that you're the conductor, and there you are, conducting like crazy, but then you get to be a grown man, and you say, 'Gee, I'd hate for anybody to know that I'm pretending I'm conducting the symphony.' But that kind of fantasy life is the real key to problem solving at every level. It's certainly the primary tool for problem solving in art, whether it's painting or dancing or choreography or directing films or writing scripts or writing novels or whatever." Creative problem solving is a form of innovative learning.

In innovative learning, one must not only recognize existing contexts, but be capable of imagining future contexts. American foreign policy was skewed for generations because our policy makers operated on the false assumption that communism was monolithic. It was a textbook example of maintenance learning. In fact, even during the Soviet era, there were many varieties of communism. Maintenance learning sees communism as purely political, rather than social, economic, and political. Innovative learning sees through the political similarities to the social and economic differences that make the few remaining communist societies distinct.

Innovative learning is a way of realizing vision. Attorney Shirley Hufstedler spoke about looking ahead. "You have to be able to envision in fairly concrete terms what ought to be done or what you want to do or where you want to go. . . . A certain amount of conceptualization is required. It's not unlike planning a trip. First you have to figure out where you want to go. Then you have to devise a mode of transportation. If no one's done it before, you may have to make it up. You have to maintain a certain amount of flexibility in organizing people to go with you. You have to know from the beginning how much baggage you have to haul, or how light you can travel. It requires a combination of historical perspective, vision, and institutional appreciation—what its texture is, what its possibilities are."

Maintenance learning, which most organizations and educational institutions practice, seeks to preserve the status quo and make good soldiers of us all. It's a monologue based in authority— hierarchical, exclusive, and isolating. Being limited and finite, it is a static body of knowledge. It requires us to adjust to things as they are.

Shock learning keeps us in line and obedient, by confirming our inability to control events or prepare for the future as individuals, and by affirming the need for authority and hierarchical organizations to protect us.

Innovative learning is the primary means of exercising our autonomy, a means of understanding and working within the prevailing context in a positive way. It is a dialogue that begins with curiosity and is fueled by knowledge, leading to understanding. It is inclusive, unlimited, and unending, knowing and dynamic. It allows us to change the way things are.

In sum, we have the means within us to free ourselves from the constraints of the past, which lock us into imposed roles and attitudes. By examining and understanding the past, we can move into the future unencumbered by it. *We become free to express ourselves, rather than endlessly trying to prove ourselves.*

In the same way, through the exercise of innovative learning, we no longer follow along, but rather lead our own lives. We do not accept things as they are, but rather anticipate things as they can be. We participate in making things happen.

We shape life, rather than being shaped by it. This dictum is borne out again and again.

In the early 1960s, Victor and Mildred Goertzel set out to discover what several hundred successful men and women had in common, and published their findings in *Cradles of Eminence*. Their subjects ranged from writers and actors to politicians and businessmen.

Their findings are instructive. Most of their subjects came from small towns or villages. In almost every household, there was a love of learning, "often accompanied by a physical exuberance and a persistent drive toward goals." Half of the parents were opinionated about controversial subjects. Nearly half the fathers "were subject to traumatic vicissitudes in their business or professional careers," while one-fourth of the mothers were "described as dominating."

Wealth was much more frequent than abject poverty. One-fourth of the subjects were physically handicapped. The homes of the subjects "were exceptionally free of mental illnesses requiring hospitalization." As children, the subjects enjoyed being tutored, "most frequently disliked secondary school," and most frequently liked "the prestige college." A full three-fourths "expressed dissatisfaction with schools and school teachers, although four-fifths showed exceptional talent." Finally, three-fourths of the subjects were troubled as children—by poverty, a broken home, difficult parents, financial ups and downs, physical handicaps, or parental dissatisfaction over their children's school failures or vocational choices.

The Goertzels include a statement from T. H. Huxley that sums up the need to examine and overcome one's past that I outlined earlier. Huxley said, "Sit down before fact as a little child, be prepared to give up every preconceived notion, follow humbly wherever and to whatever abyss nature leads, or you shall learn nothing."

There is nothing you can do about your early life now, except to understand it. You can, however, do everything about the rest of your life. As John Gardner once said, "The maturing of any complex talent requires a happy combination of motivation, character, and opportunity. Most talent remains undeveloped."

Universities, unfortunately, are not always the best place to learn. Too many of them are less places of higher learning than they are high-class vocational schools. Too many produce narrow-minded specialists who may be wizards at making money, but who are unfinished as people. These specialists have been taught how to do, but they have not learned how to be. Instead of studying philosophy, history, and literature—which are the experiences of all humankind—they study specific technologies. In the long run narrow specialties may be more prone to obsolescence and may fail to deliver big salaries, let alone the incalculable rewards of a more broadly examined life.

Educator and former Disney executive Marty Kaplan said, "You spend your early years asking your parents all the big questions—where am I from, why did Grandpa die and where did he go, and who is God? Kids are sponges for that stuff. What do undergraduates talk about in the middle of the night but that stuff? What am I doing with my life, who am I, all those questions that we encourage in a liberal arts confrontation with the abyss. I think that's at the core of our notion of what Western values are, the confrontation with the abyss, and some people will call the abyss death in a sort of casual biological sense, while some people have a much more metaphysical conception of nothingness, but I think it starts in the child, and we either let it flourish or repress it, but it's always there, and it's always going to be there."

Poet Richard Wilbur wrote, "But ceremony never did conceal,/Save to the silly eye, which all allows,/How much we are the woods we wander in." We need to wander through all the woods at our disposal, and out of all that to begin to understand ourselves and the world.

In the mid–1980s, the issue of our cultural illiteracy reached the best-seller lists, with Allan Bloom's *The Closing of the American Mind* and E. D. Hirsch, Jr.'s *Cultural Literacy: What Every American Needs to Know*. A nationwide test of history and literature given to 7,800 high school juniors proved Bloom and Hirsch's thesis. The average score, as reported in *What Do Our 17-Year-Olds Know?* by Diane Ravitch and Chester E. Finn, Jr., was in the 50s—an F.

The authors wrote,

Perhaps the most obvious indicator of how process-driven our schools have become is the dominant role played by the Scholastic Aptitude Test. Looming over our educational land-scape is an examination that, in its verbal component, carefully avoids assessing substantive knowledge. . . . Whether test-takers have studied the Civil War, learned about the Magna Carta or read Macbeth are matters to which the SAT is studiously indifferent.

Whatever our schools are teaching—or at least testing—has increasingly less to do with what we have historically considered education, and more to do with the ubiquitous bottom line. A study by the Carnegie Foundation shows that an increasing number of young people choose fields that promise to be instantly profitable, such as business, engineering, computer science, and health programs.

Yet Lynne Cheney, former chairman of the National Endowment for the Humanities and wife of former Vice President Dick Cheney, wrote in *Newsweek* that many of the country's most successful people had a liberal arts background, including President Reagan and a majority of his cabinet, 38 percent of all CEOs, and nine of the top thirteen executives at IBM. According to Cheney, an AT&T study showed that social science and humanities graduates moved faster into middle management than engineers and were "doing at least as well as their business and engineering counterparts in reaching top management levels." She concludes, "Students who follow their hearts in choosing majors will most likely end up laboring at what they love. They're the ones who will put in the long hours and intense effort that achievement requires. And they're the ones who will find the sense of purpose that underlies most human happiness."

Roger Smith, former chairman and CEO of General Motors, agrees. Smith wrote in the book *Educating Managers,*

> The art of management begins with vision, a quality that has never been so crucial as it is today. . . . Competitiveness—and, for some companies, survival itself—depends on the manager's ability to envision new things (as well as new ways of doing old things), to extrapolate on the basis of what worked in the past, to organize and reorganize operations . . . and to imagine how, and by what kind of intervention, the course of events might be changed. . . . When students are trained to recognize recurring elements and common themes in art, literature, physics and history, they are . . . learning about the kind of creativity that leads to visionary solutions to business problems. . . . People trained in the liberal arts would be able to understand, function in and contribute to the loose-tight, entrepreneurial organization that so many other businesses are striving to become. . . . They learn to tolerate ambiguity and to bring order out of apparent confusion. Intellectual integrity is paramount, and reasoning processes are just as important as the conclusions to which they lead. . . . [They have] the kind of sideways thinking and cross-classifying habit of mind that comes from learning, among other things, the many different ways of looking at literary works, social systems, chemical processes, or languages. . . . [T]he attributes of excellence . . . all depend on communication skills and sensitivity to people. . . . Everything we do depends on the successful transfer of meaning from one group to another.

CBS, Inc. also agrees. In 1984, the Corporate Council on the Liberal Arts, representing twelve major companies, was established with a $750,000 grant from CBS in association with the American Academy of Arts and Sciences. The council's purpose, according to its then chairman, Frank Stanton, a former CBS president, is to "heighten awareness of a liberal arts education—insight, perception, critical inquiry and imagination—and to understand the relationship between liberal arts learning and leadership in the corporate world."

That relationship is very real and very strong. This is not to suggest, however, that if you majored in business or computer science, you've fouled up. One of the marvelous things about life is that any gaps in your education can be filled, whatever your age or situation, by reading, and thinking about what you read.

FILLING IN THE GAPS

Author Ray Bradbury, giving advice to managers on how to feed creativity, started his recipe with this:

Well now, when was the last time you ran to a library and took home more books than you could read, like stacked loaves of bread, warm in your arms, waiting to be chewed? When, for that matter, was the last time you opened a book, placed it to your nose, and gave a great sniff? Heaven! The smell of bread, baking. When was the last time that you found a really great old book store and wandered through it hour after hour, alone, finding yourself on the shelves. With no list, no intellectual priorities, just wandering, snuffing the dust, plucking the pigeon books off the shelves to read their entrails and, not in love, putting them back, or in love, toting them home? To be lost in time is to find your roots.

If you want a more formal approach, many colleges, universities, and community colleges offer classes in literature, philosophy, and history. Just to let you know that I sometimes practice what I preach: I once went to Cambridge with two of my children so that we could all take classes together. My choice was Charles Dickens and Victorian England. My daughter Kate studied Shakespearean comedies, and my son Will took Darwin and modern science. We stayed on one floor of Trinity Hall at Trinity College and spent a marvelous three weeks immersed in our books, excitedly swapping the best of what we were learning.

Now a professor of constitutional law at American University, Jamie Raskin was an assistant attorney general in Boston when he warned against letting your ambition get in the way of your intellectual growth: "'Ambition is the death of thought,' as Wittgenstein said. A number of my friends are as ambitious as I am, but they suppress any thoughts that might be subversive or dangerous to their ambitions. Your intellectual life is really the ability to see how things can be different, and big institutions in society, whether public or private, often ask people to toe the line in any number of ways—personal, political, ideological. And clearly one can get ahead by doing that. I guess the only way to prevent ambition from killing your intellectual life is not to be afraid of losing, or to say something people might think is wrong, or crazy, something the institution isn't ready to hear yet. . . . If you want a concrete tip, learn how to speed read. People say they don't have time to read. My feeling is, 'When in doubt, read it.' I can read a book in a couple of hours."

Then CBS executive Barbara Corday said, regarding education, "If I were talking to young executives, I'd advise them to forget their MBAs. A lot of young leaders are very taken with their own credentials, and they forget that most American leaders of the past 150 years didn't have MBAs, didn't have Ph.D.s. I barely graduated from high school and have never had another day of formal education. I'm not saying that because I'm particularly proud of it, but I'm also not embarrassed about it. In my business, very few people have an academic background that matches in any way what they're doing now. A liberal arts education is probably the best thing for my business, and I feel I have that, even though I don't have a degree to show. . . . A lot of the young people I've dealt with in the last five years have all sorts of degrees, but they lack some of the personality traits, the showmanship and enthusiasm and childlike qualities, that the entertainment business requires, and it makes me sad to see that. . . . People who go to plays, read books, know the classics, who have an open mind and enjoy experiences, are more apt to be successful in my business than someone with an MBA in finance."

Charles Handy, one of Great Britain's thought leaders, would agree with her. He told me that the primary lesson he learned at the Sloan School of Management was that he didn't need to go to school.

James E. Burke, former CEO of Johnson & Johnson, learned a lot while getting an MBA, however: "I went to that school [Harvard Business School] with a set of values that I had gotten, as people suggest you should, from family and church and so forth. I was young, and I wasn't sure that I could succeed in business with my value system. I was really torn. . . . I had somehow picked up, as many people do in this country—I don't know where—that there was something, not immoral, about business, but a sense that you had to play the edges in order to be successful. I think a lot of people feel that way. The business school was a tremendous release, because everything I was taught at the business school said that's not true. The way to be successful is to be straight."

The education of former Xerox executive Renn Zaphiropoulos, who founded Versatec, a major producer of electrostatic printers, began at home: "I was brought up in Egypt by Greek parents. My father was a sea captain, a pilot in the Suez Canal. He didn't have any collegiate degrees, but he'd been everywhere and was a heavy reader. He used to say, 'Your house is your university.' He was a poet. Instead of going to church, we all listened to classical music on Sundays. His advice to me was never to do anything because other people did it, but because it made good sense to me. I was a good student, not straight A's, but good. Straight-A students never seem to get over it. I had a lot of other interests. I studied painting, composed music, did some woodworking, wrote poems. . . . It's easy enough to learn marketing, selling, engineering, whatever. It's harder to learn how to optimize your own performance and that of your subordinates. It's vital to possess an adequate understanding of the first principles of human behavior in order to perform as optimum supervisors and directors of people."

John Sculley, like Jim Burke, believes in formal education and took an MBA. Sculley's curriculum vitae is well known. He left Pepsico after a very successful run when Apple co-founder Steve Jobs challenged him by asking whether he really wanted to spend the rest of his life selling sugar water or he wanted a chance to change the world. Sculley was CEO of Apple when he told me he saw genuine and valuable links between education and business. "The people I gravitate to are dreamers. I wouldn't live anywhere except near a great university, because I like access to the libraries, to academics. Most new industries tend to grow up around major university communities, which means that potential leaders are developing in a very different context [from] the traditional narrow one. This isn't a high-tech phenomenon. The question isn't how many computer scientists use our computers, but how many artists use them."

Don Ritchey summed it up thusly: "Education helps produce conceptual skills. The majority of people don't learn those skills without the help of some education. I don't know that the humanities are better than a business education, but I think a university helps you learn how to think and to analyze problems, to see things as a whole and see how you can put them together. It seems to me that the people with an educational match to the practical experience turn out to be the best combination."

At Hebrew school, a teacher told Roger Gould, "They can take our jewels and cars and furs and houses, but they can never rob us of our education." Gould himself said, "The capacity to learn is always present. The inherent opposition to learning is variable. Everyone has certain built-in defenses. Their rigidity and influence is central." Gould himself has no such defenses. He says, "When I read something, I absorb it, pulverize it, cut it up, use it here and there, so by the time I'm finished using it, it no longer exists in its original form."

This is how learning is meant to be—active, passionate, and personal. What you read should be grist for your own mill; you should make it yours. One last word from Frances Hesselbein: "If there's anything I really believe in, it's the joy of learning and learning every day."

THE BROADENING EXPERIENCE

Travel is another kind of learning. All the clichés about it are true. It does broaden. It is revelatory. It changes your perspective immediately, because it requires new and different responses from you. Things are done differently in other countries. People are more relaxed, or less so, more reserved, or more volatile. Their rituals vary. In Paris, many shops close down entirely in August. In Spain, an afternoon siesta follows a long lunch, and dinner is very late. Language is suddenly a barrier. The simplest transaction can turn complex all of a sudden. A friend of mine once went from London to Paris, and she was so preoccupied with re-gearing her brain to figure in francs rather than pounds that she said, "For twenty-four hours I couldn't speak English or French. I went into a tobacco shop and asked for *quatorze* packets of Kents. The shopkeeper looked at me as if I were quite mad. People buy one or two or even ten packages of cigarettes, but they don't buy fourteen. I'd meant to say four packs, of course."

The extent to which travel broadens depends at least partly on how much you give yourself to the experience. Those who immerse themselves in a different culture are likely to learn more than those who head for the Paris McDonald's. At the same time, there's a difference between immersing oneself in a new culture and "going native." Sitting in Les Deux Magots wearing a beret is not necessarily being a critical learner. If you lose perspective on yourself and your own roots, you have merely put on the garb of another culture. You need to keep the sense of difference.

Henry Thoreau wrote that one sees the world more clearly if one looks at it from an angle. In a foreign land, one sees everything from an angle. Thorsten Veblen theorized that many Jews developed acute intelligence because they were perpetual exiles. The stranger in a strange land sees more and sees fresh. Being on the road not only requires the full deployment of one's self, it redeploys one, tests one's strengths and weaknesses, and exposes new strengths and weaknesses. Our two most sophisticated Founding Fathers, Thomas Jefferson and Benjamin Franklin, were inveterate travelers, and both spent much time in Europe. Those who travel farther from home learn even more.

Alfred Gottschalk learned the outsider's lesson at an early age: "I came to America as a refugee. I had no identity, or only a negative identity. I was Jewish. I was German. I dressed funny. I couldn't speak the language, and I was poor—financially. But I graduated from Brooklyn Boys High with a 92 average, and I played football. I became independent very early."

As leaders have traditionally been travelers, they've also traditionally had rich private lives. They've been Sunday painters, poets, even chefs, and they've always made time to reflect. Joseph Campbell, the world's foremost authority on mythology, told Bill Moyers in an interview shortly before his death, "You must have a room, or a certain hour or so a day, when you don't know what was in the newspapers that morning, you don't know who your friends are, you don't know what you owe anybody, you don't know what anybody owes to you. This is a place where you can simply experience and bring forth what you are and what you might be. This is the place of creative incubation. At first, you may find that nothing happens there. But if you have [such] a sacred place and use it, something eventually will happen."

Whether one chooses a daily retreat or a formal sabbatical, one has access to one's soul, to one's imagination, and one can truly reflect on one's experience, and learn from it, and emerge renewed and refreshed.

FRIENDS AND MENTORS

As much as we each need such regular respite, we need true engagement too; we need mentors and friends and groups of allied souls. I know of no leader in any era who hasn't had at least one mentor: teachers who found things in them they didn't know were there, parents or older siblings, senior associates who showed them the way to be, or in some cases, not to be, or demanded more from them than they knew they had to give.

When asked who had inspired him, Jamie Raskin said, "The people I've admired most are the people I know or know of historically who've been able to see seemingly unrelated things coming together. One of my favorite people was Martin Luther King. Something I read by him when I was a kid had such an effect on me. He said that all life was interrelated, all humanity part of one process, and to the degree that I harm my brother, to that extent I am harming myself. A lot of leadership is based on the ability to see how all humanity is related, how all parts of society are related, and how things move in the same direction. My father has this quality, too. He's able to make those kinds of connections and see the humanity in everyone. . . . My dad taught me how to think and my mom taught me how to write."

Aviator Brooke Knapp said, "I learned my sense of quality and performance from my grandmother, the matriarch of the family. It was she who demanded that I finish college."

Former college president Alfred Gottschalk learned from many sources. "I learned how to cook and sew and clean from my mother, and I worked during the summers as a waiter in the Catskills. My father died when I was 16, so I was required to learn courage early. . . . My mentors would include my father, my mother, my rabbi, and my football coach. The football team was made up of Irish and blacks and Italians and Poles, and they were my family. That's where, in a sense, I became an American, and where I learned that you must never quit."

Roger Gould's mentors came from the university. He said, "I had forty cousins, and I was the only one of us who went to college. They were affluent, but they put absolutely no premium on education. They valued wiles, street smarts, never education. So I faced a blank screen . . . no preconceptions, restrictions, or restraints. I was very inspired by the classics. They were my transition into another life, my own private underground, which I could appreciate by myself and never talk to anyone about. In my first semester in college, it was as if someone had opened a great big candy store of ideas, and it was all up for grabs. A professor of philosophy immediately became my intellectual father. I decided I wanted to be a philosopher, and therefore I had to know everything."

Former CalFed CEO Robert Dockson found his principal mentors and models entirely in books. "My mentors were people I read about, such as Richard Byrd, the explorer, rather than people I knew. I was just terribly inspired by Byrd. I don't envy any man and I haven't tried to emulate anyone—except on the golf course."

Friends offer inspiration and encouragement, and more. Then AAUW head Anne Bryant told me, "Friends are vital. You learn from them, because they tell you the truth."

Barbara Corday's writing partner was also her best friend. She said, "Barbara Avedon and I had a great partnership. My daughter used to say that what we did for a living was laugh, because every time she called the office we were laughing. For eight or nine years we were not only collaborators and partners, we were best friends. We raised our children together, and went on vacations together, and our families were very close. It happened coincidentally to be in the early days of the women's movement, and I think that was an interesting time to go through together. We each went through a divorce and a remarriage with the other, we each went through the child rearing with the other. We really had a very special time. And I loved it."

Given this, it seems fitting that the Corday-Avedon relationship produced "Cagney and Lacey," the long-running and highly acclaimed TV series about a pair of policewomen who were close friends as well as partners. The series was not only the first hit show to feature female buddies, but the first cop show to focus as much on the personal lives of its protagonists as on their work.

During John Sculley's tenure at Apple, he found both inspiration and friendship in his own field from Alan Kay, one of the polymath gurus of the computer age. "Alan Kay is sort of my spiritual leader," Sculley said. "He doesn't look like a leader or dress like a leader, but if you believe in the power of ideas, he's a fountainhead, a wonderfully inventive person who's able to skip across an intellectual landscape comprising many disciplines." Computer whiz Kay played a kind of Merlin to Sculley's Arthur.

Groups, gatherings of friends or associates, sometimes simply sustain and encourage their members, as with old school friends, army buddies, business pals. But sometimes they make history, as with FDR's brain trust, Eisenhower's general staff, John Kennedy's Irish Mafia, the Bloomsbury writers, and the Bauhaus designers.

J. Robert Oppenheimer, Jr., directed what has been called the most exclusive club in the world at Los Alamos, New Mexico, in the early years of World War II. Oppenheimer said of the scientists who gathered to develop the atomic bomb, "It was a remarkable community inspired by a high sense of mission, of duty and of destiny . . . coherent . . . dedicated . . . and remarkably unselfish . . . devoted to a common purpose."

Former Johnson & Johnson CEO Jim Burke told me of a very different but equally remarkable group of friends, all of whom achieved extraordinary success in business: "My six closest friends in the world all became close friends at Harvard Business School. I think I have more close friends than most people, and I made most of them there. A lot of it came out of the bonding of our values. We also were alike in wanting to work very hard, and we were all excited about the opportunities to do something with our lives . . . . Our lives are all wound up with each other. There is in fact a value system that runs through us all, and we view the world in identical terms. On top of that, we have a helluva lot of fun."

LEARNING FROM ADVERSITY

Study, travel, people, work, play, reflection, all are sources of knowledge and understanding, but so, curiously, are mistakes. John Cleese, who, in addition to his memorable comic turns in movies and with Monty Python, writes and produces equally memorable business training films, said, "It's self-evident that if we can't take the risk of saying or doing something wrong, our creativity goes right out the window. . . . The essence of creativity is not the possession of some special talent, it is much more the ability to play."

He continued, "In organizations where mistakes are not allowed, you get two types of counterproductive behavior. First, since mistakes are 'bad,' if they're committed by the people at the top, the feedback arising from those mistakes has to be ignored or selectively reinterpreted, in order that those top people can pretend that no mistake has been made. So it doesn't get fixed. Second, if they're committed by people lower down in the organization, mistakes get concealed."

The leaders I talked with are far from believing that mistakes are "bad." They not only believe in the necessity of mistakes, they see them as virtually synonymous with growth and progress.

Former Lucky Stores executive Don Ritchey said, "Even if you're pretty analytical by nature, you have to be willing to make a decision somewhere short of certainty. You just haven't got the time or the resources, even if it was possible to actually get that last finite piece of information that lets you deal with certainty. You have to get 80 or 85 percent of it and then take your best shot and go on to something else. That means you'll blow it now and then, but you also develop a momentum and a pace that gets to be exciting."

Like Barbara Corday, leaders don't always see "failures" as mistakes. "My favorite project," she said, "a TV series called 'American Dream,' had a lot of things to say, was executed brilliantly, written and acted well, and produced beautifully. It was a critical success, but for whatever reason, the public chose not to watch it, and it lasted only five or six episodes. It was a flop, but I don't see it as a failure. So it also wasn't a mistake. Mistakes aren't failures either, and I don't take them seriously. It's okay to make mistakes, as long as you make them in good conscience and you're doing the best you can at that moment. . . . I'm not afraid to make a mistake, and I'm not afraid to say afterward, 'Boy, that was a mistake. Let's try something else.' I think that wins people over. Now, I don't make mistakes purposely to win people over, but when I make one, I admit it. I can also say, 'You have a better idea than I have. Let's do your idea.' I don't second-guess people. If I hire you to do something, I let you do it."

Jim Burke actually encouraged mistakes at Johnson & Johnson, saying, "I decided that what we needed more than anything else was a climate that would encourage people to take risks. . . . I started with the premise that we could accomplish anything we wanted to accomplish, if the people around me were permitted to do what they wanted to do. From the benefit of hindsight, it was somewhat naive on my part, assuming that anybody can do anything. On the other hand, I think many of my successes are wrapped up in the same thing. If you believe that growth comes from risk taking, that you can't grow without it, then it's essential in leading people toward growth to get them to make decisions, and to make mistakes."

Burke went on to tell of his own experience with a mistake: "I once developed a new product that failed badly, and General Johnson called me in, and I was sure he was going to fire me. I had just come in late when his secretary called, and he was always in early. I can remember walking over to his office. . . . Johnson said to me, 'I understand you lost over a million dollars.' I can't remember the exact amount. It seemed like a lot then. And I said, 'Yes sir. That's correct.' So he stood up and held out his hand. He said, 'I just want to congratulate you. All business is making decisions, and if you don't make decisions, you won't have any failures. The hardest job I have is getting people to make decisions. If you make that same decision wrong again, I'll fire you. But I hope you'll make a lot of others, and that you'll understand there are going to be more failures than successes.'"

Sydney Pollack said, "When I work with inexperienced actors, I try to convince them that it's not possible to make a mistake. I say the only way they can make a mistake is by trying not to make a mistake, because that'll create tension and tension will tie them up every time. . . . There is an enormous timidity about trusting the impulse. One spends an awful lot of time in life trying to get insurance beforehand that whatever bit of behavior is going to happen is at best impressive, but at the very least, acceptable and not foolish. A really good actor has got to be capable of making an enormous fool out of himself. Otherwise, no original work gets done."

Trusting the impulse always leads to growth, although sometimes through mistakes. Sometimes trusting the impulse leads directly to brilliance. That kind of impulse—the blessed impulse—we'll return to in the next chapter.

Horace B. Deets, executive director of AARP until he retired in 2002, was equally emphatic about the need to establish a tolerant culture. Now a senior advisor to the organization, Deets said, "I try to encourage as much openness and contrary views as possible. It's important to encourage dissent and embrace error."

Shirley Hufstedler summed it up, saying, "If you haven't failed, you haven't tried very hard."

There are lessons in everything, and if you are fully deployed, you will learn most of them. Experiences aren't truly yours until you think about them, analyze them, examine them, question them, reflect on them, and finally understand them. The point, once again, is to use your experiences rather than being used by them, to be the designer, not the design, so that experiences empower rather than imprison.

Entrepreneur Larry Wilson, a founder of innovative learning centers who once described himself as a "game changer," had a crucial experience as a boy. "I learned about risk when I was seven years old. I had just moved from Minneapolis to Little Rock, and I was the littlest one in the class—boys and girls. Even the desks were bigger. Worse, I was a slow runner and had a Northern accent. These factors combined to put me in jeopardy every noon hour. Every day the Civil War got replayed in the school yard, and I kept losing. I was in a lot of pain.

"One day the priest came to do catechism, and I suddenly found myself jumping up in front of the class like Lawrence Welk, trying to lead them in a chorus of 'Sister Loves Father.' You have to be Catholic to understand the magnitude of my sin. In a matter of seconds, I went from being the class doormat to class hero . . . . They just sat there with their mouths open. I got into big trouble with the teacher [the nun], but the benefit was incredible. I learned then that the risk is easily worth taking, for the incredible benefit."

Thus was an entrepreneur born from a painful experience in a Little Rock parochial school classroom that might have branded a less determined human being, might have caused him to retire from the spotlight forever if he had assimilated it differently. Wilson went on, "For most entrepreneurs, certainly for me, the primary pull is the vision. You are simply passionately compelled to make it come about. I think that a compelling vision combined with a unique ability to manage risk is the magic behind successful entrepreneurs. It's as if you already handled the risk ahead of time in your mind, so you can go where angels fear to tread, because you've already skipped ahead to the gain."

Leaders, then, learn from their experiences. Learning from experience means

- Looking back at your childhood and adolescence and using what happened to you then to enable you to make things happen now, so that you become the master of your own life rather than its servant.
- Consciously seeking the kinds of experiences in the present that will improve and enlarge you.
- Taking risks as a matter of course, with the knowledge that failure is as vital as it is inevitable.
- Seeing the future—yours and the world's—as an opportunity to do all those things you have not done and those things that need to be done, rather than as a trial or a test.

How do you seize the opportunity? First you must use your instincts to sense it, and then follow the "blessed impulse" that arises. "Operating on Instinct" is where our story takes us next.

5
Operating on Instinct

Two things seemed pretty apparent to me. One was, that in order
to be a [Mississippi River] pilot a man had got to learn more than
any one man ought to be allowed to know; and the other was, that
he must learn it all over again in a different way every 24 hours.

—MARK TWAIN
Life on the Mississippi

Life has never been simple and is growing more complex all
the time, yet we persist in attempting to reduce it to bumper-
sticker dimensions. The advocates of simplicity see reality as
mechanical, static, segmented, and rational, when it is, in fact,
organic, dynamic, whole, and ambiguous. They see relationships as linear, sequential and serial, discrete, singular and independent, when they are, in fact, parallel and simultaneous,
connected, murky, multiple and interdependent. They are de-
terminists, believers in cause-and-effect, when, in fact, proba-
bility is the rule and the inevitable hardly ever happens. They
wear square hats, when they should try sombreros.

Lest anyone feel overwhelmed by complexity, however, I'd like to offer this thought from Carl Sagan's *The Dragons of Eden*:

> We can imagine a universe in which the laws of nature are immensely more complex. But we do not live in such a universe. Why not? I think it may be because all those organisms who perceived their universe as very complex are dead. Those of our arboreal ancestors who had difficulty computing their trajectories as they brachiated from tree to tree did not leave many offspring.

The universe may not be very complex, but it is, nevertheless, complex. And as I mentioned earlier, the social laws are more complex and less certain than the natural ones. But despite the complexity, we cannot stand still. We must continue to swing from tree to tree, although the trees may be ideas, and we may be using axons instead of arms to make the connections. We might want to take Alfred North Whitehead's advice here: "Seek simplicity, then distrust it."

It was the mechanistic view that produced the organization man, and it was the organization man, as I have noted, who ironically enough has caused many of the problems in our organizations. It is the individual, operating at the peak of his or her creative and moral powers, who will revive our organizations, by reinventing both self and them.

Recent research has made it clear that the geography of the brain is not as strictly delineated as we once thought. But it is still useful to think of American organizational life as a left-brain culture, meaning logical, analytical, technical, controlled, conservative, and administrative. We, to the extent we are its products, are dominated and shaped by those same characteristics. Our culture needs more right-brain qualities, needs to be more intuitive, conceptual, synthesizing, and artistic. And so, of course, do we. As I talked with the people I interviewed for this book, I was struck again and again by the fact that, whatever their occupations, they relied as much on their intuitive and conceptual skills as on their logical and analytical talents. These are whole-brained people, capable of using both sides of their brain.

In any corporation, managers serve as the left brain and the research and development staff serves as the right brain, but the CEO must combine both, must have both administrative and imaginative gifts. One of the reasons that so few corporate executives have successfully made the leap from capable manager to successful leader is that the corporate culture, along with society as a whole, recognizes and rewards left-brain accomplishments and tends to discount right-brain achievements. Bottom-line thinking is a manifestation of left-brain dominance. Habits are born in the left brain and unmade in the right.

When Anne Bryant was executive director of the AAUW, she used something she calls "the hot air balloon exercise" to encourage her staff to think imaginatively. "You take people up in an imaginary balloon and from up there you can see the entire entity. Then you examine what you see, who you see, what they're doing, and what other things they might be doing. You imagine, for instance, what might happen if you put $500,000 toward child development research or what might be done about teen pregnancy."

Acknowledging the constant dilemma of organizations, and the pull between left-brain habits and right-brain visions, Richard Schubert, then CEO of the American Red Cross, told me, "I'm constantly torn between the obvious need to support the existing structure and the equally obvious need to change it."

As executive director of the Girl Scouts of the USA, Frances Hesselbein saw social changes, including the increase in minorities, and envisioned how her organization could prepare for them: "So girls' needs are changing, and we're exploring different ways to meet those needs and deliver our services. I'm establishing a center for innovation. It isn't a place. It's people and a concept. The team . . . will work directly with Girl Scout Councils in developing models through which we can reach highly diverse communities and locate and train indigenous leadership, which will be increasingly important."

Bryant, Schubert, and Hesselbein each took a whole-brain approach in leading their nonprofit organizations out of traditional patterns and into innovative modes. Not coincidentally, all three of them had been previously successful in the private sector and made major career changes in midlife. And all three said they'd never done anything that they enjoyed as much as their nonprofit assignments. Schubert said succinctly, "This is the most exciting, challenging thing I've ever done."

Scientist Mathilde Krim, who also moved from the private to the public sector, said, "Growth requires curiosity to experience both the difference and the synchrony, to explore and immerse yourself in new surroundings, to be able to contemplate your experiences and get something out of them."

A part of whole-brain thinking includes learning to trust what Emerson called the "blessed impulse," the hunch, the vision that shows you in a flash the absolutely right thing to do. Everyone has these visions; leaders learn to trust them.

I want to remind you here of something Norman Lear said regarding the profound influence that Emerson's "Self Reliance" had on his growth as a leader: "Emerson talks about listening to that inner voice and going with it, all voices to the contrary. I don't know when I started to understand that there was something divine about that inner voice—I certainly didn't in high school, college, or even in young manhood—but somewhere along the line, I appreciated that, too. How is it possible that as a writer I can go to bed a thousand times with a second act problem and wake up with the answer? Some inner voice. To go with that—which I confess I don't do all of the time—is the purest, truest thing we have. And when we forgo our own thoughts and opinions, they end up coming back to us from the mouths of others. They come back with an alien majesty. . . . So the lesson is, you believe it. *When I've been most effective, I've followed that inner voice.*"

Following the "blessed impulse" is, I think, basic to leadership. This is how guiding visions are made real. But the need for other right-brain qualities came up again and again in my conversations.

Author and feminist leader Gloria Steinem said of being an entrepreneur, "It helps if you're a nonlinear thinker. And it takes a certain amount of persuasion, which means empathy. . . . Entrepreneurs always seemed to me like the artists of the business world, because we put together things that haven't gone together in the past." She used similar words when she talked about success: "To me, the model of progress is not linear. Success is completing the full circle of yourself."

Herb Alpert described how he works this way: "I'm a right-brain animal. I'm not a businessman in the traditional sense. And I do a lot of buckshotting and I rely on my gut reaction. When my shoulders feel tight, I know something's off. I use my body as a barometer. . . . I try to listen like a piece of Silly Putty when someone plays me a song. I try to let my biases just blow in the breeze. For the most part, I'm listening for the feeling."

That reliance on instinct has made Alpert a successful recording star and an equally successful businessman. His longtime partner in A&M Records Gil Friesen said of Alpert, "Instinctively he knows what's right and what should be done. And he has the ability to detach himself from time to time and look and see and ask questions. He's running his own career within the framework of the company, which is an ideal scenario. As he makes decisions, he reinvents his career."

Alpert believes that you need a vision of the future at the same time that you're dealing with the present. And Alpert believes in trust. In speaking of Friesen and A&M founding partner, Jerry Moss, Alpert said, "The real motor of this company is the basic trust that Jerry, Gil, and I have for each other, and the trust that artists have for us. They say they're more comfortable and more inspired because our people care about what they're doing. Also, we're a privately owned and independent label, so we're able to move quickly."

Friesen continued, "I can't tell you how important that word independent is, how important it is to our staff and to the artists. It has a kind of magic about it." Then he added with a smile, "And we never refer to our recordings or our artists as 'product,' because we think it's demeaning."

As Apple CEO John Sculley encouraged diversity of opinion around him, and went with vision over market research. "One of the biggest mistakes a person can make is to put together a team that reflects only him. I find it's better to put teams together of people who have different skills and then make all those disparate skills function together. The real role of the leader is to figure out how you make diverse people and elements work together.

"Often people don't know what they want and can't describe it until they see it. If we'd done market research on the Macintosh prior to its introduction, and asked people to describe the ideal personal computer, they would have come up with something entirely different. But when we show people the Macintosh and say, 'Is this what you want?' they say, 'Yes.' You have to be able to make the abstract recognizable, because only then can people accept or reject it."

As an academic administrator, Alfred Gottschalk looked for right-brain characteristics when he hired. "I first look for character, whether the individual can inspire trust. Then I look for imagination and perseverance, steadfastness of purpose. If, for example, I am engaging somebody who is going to be the chief controller of the institution, and I see that as an undergraduate he had difficulty with intermediate algebra or calculus, and he nevertheless manages to go into accounting, I wonder what kind of a financial imagination he has. I try to find out as much as I can about the individual, and then a largely intuitive decision is made. I have to feel right about the person."

Right-brain characteristics come in handy even when you're dealing with things, not people. Mathilde Krim talked about the importance of instinct in her early work: "I always had a good instinct for biological problems. I don't remember ever having worked at something that fizzled into nothing. . . . I could recognize a chromosome. One time a colleague said that he had isolated a new cell line from a dog. And I looked at it and saw immediately that it wasn't a dog cell. I could tell that it was a rat cell just by looking at the chromosomes, and I was right, because we did cellulogical tests afterwards. In the case of prenatal diagnosis, it was obvious to me from the beginning, the first time I looked at the lymphatic cells, that there was a difference between male and female cells, so then we studied it systematically. At the time it made quite a splash in the press, but it was a very simple kind of work to do."

For Krim, who had the vision and trusted her instincts, it was a very simple kind of work to do. But it had never been done before.

The leaders I spoke with believed also in the importance of luck, but they put a particular spin on it, one reminiscent of Vince Lombardi's dictum that luck is a combination of preparation and opportunity. Former Johnson & Johnson CEO Jim Burke is best known for how ably he dealt with the discovery that bottles of Tylenol had been tampered with. Burke, who described himself as an "intuitive, instinctive person" with an overlay of logic, said of leadership positions, "A lot of luck occurs to get people to these places. A lot of what happened in my life was an accident. You wouldn't be here talking to me if it hadn't been for Tylenol. I happened to be exquisitely prepared for that problem—by accident, though."

Then Boston prosecutor Jamie Raskin also spoke of luck and preparation. "The general advice I would have for people about leadership is to find out what's truest in yourself and stick to it. But I really believe in the role of luck in human affairs. Machiavelli said that fortune favors the bold. I think the prepared mind is basically the same thing as the bold, but fortune is in there. Napoleon said that of all the qualities his lieutenants had, the one he most favored was luck. Luck continues to intervene at every point in your life."

Sydney Pollack described right-brain leadership best, when he said that it comes out of "a certain kind of controlled free association. All art comes out of that. We say daydreams, we say inspiration, but scientifically what it is, is free association. It's the ability to be in touch with that. That's where you get the ideas. And then it's the ability to trust the ideas once you have them, even though they may break certain rules. And then it's the confidence and courage to carry out the ideas once you've found them and once you've trusted them. Then you can't be afraid to fail. Otherwise it's just imitative. Otherwise you go to leadership school, and try to pitch your voice the same way that the boss did there, and have your office decorated the same way his is, and that's not real leadership. Real leadership probably has more to do with recognizing your own uniqueness than it does with identifying your similarities."

Pollack told me a story that illustrates marvelously the "blessed impulse" of leadership. "Years ago, I did a film with Barbra Streisand and Robert Redford called *The Way We Were*. Streisand played a character who wanted desperately to be a writer, who worked very, very hard at it, but nothing came easily to her. Redford played a character where everything came easy. He was a kind of a prince. He had no particular aspirations to be a writer, but he happened to be good and talented. She had worked and struggled and worked and struggled in her writing class to do a very serious paper, a little short story. And the professor chose that day to read Redford's story. It just devastated her. She ran out of the classroom, and the scene called for her to run to a trash basket, rip up her story, throw it in the trash basket, and just sob.

"I had set up the shot so that the camera was at the trash basket pointing toward a tree behind which she was standing, so that when I would call, 'Action,' she would emerge running from behind this tree, run toward the camera, straight at us, throw the story in the trash basket, and I would move into her face when she leaned against the trash basket and cried. The first assistant director on the picture, Howard Koch, Jr., had been the first A.D. on her previous picture, *Up the Sandbox*. Howard came to me while we were working on the scene and said, 'You know, she's very nervous.' I asked why. He said, 'She's very uptight because she thinks she can't cry. She had some terrible problems crying in *Up the Sandbox*, and in her head she equates that with being a bad actress, so she's very nervous.'

"We have a device in the picture business, little ammonia crystals that go into a little test tube with holes in the bottom like a salt shaker and gauze over the front end. The makeup man blows in it, and the ammonia aroma comes out and gets in your eyes and makes tears. It makes your eyes bloody and it stinks, but it works for film. Barbra had the makeup man behind the tree. I said to Howard, 'I don't believe she can't cry. Anybody who sings the way she sings can cry. You stay here. I will go behind the tree. When I wave my hands, you roll the camera.'

"I went back to the tree, and I found Barbra pacing. The makeup man was there with his test tube, and I sent him away. She got alarmed and said, 'Where are you going? Wait, wait, what are you doing?' I said, 'Just relax. Just relax.' I went over and I put my arms around her, and the minute I put my arms around her, she just started to sob. And I waved my hand, and he rolled the camera, and around the tree she went.

"Now, I didn't say anything to her. I didn't think up some wonderful piece of direction to give her. But I knew that there was juice going on in her, and she was just too tense to let it come out. She had built it all up in her mind, and something touched her when I put my arms around her. Something just made her let loose. And she cried all the way through the picture. You can say, 'How did you think of it? What made you know what would work?' To tell you the truth, I didn't have the faintest idea what I was going to do when I sent away the makeup man. I just was so convinced that she could cry, because I had seen so much emotion in her work, and I knew her to be a very emotional woman, and I had no idea what to do—and then the impulse. I don't know where the impulse to hug her came from.

"Now where did the impulse happen? Did it happen on the walk to the tree? I don't think so. I don't think the impulse happened until I saw her. What does it represent in terms of problem solving? It represented a very efficient and quick solution at the time, probably better than a lot of talk, or a lot of saying, 'Well, think about the time something bad happened to you.' If I had come near her and said, 'Look, I know you can do this, I believe in you,' she would have said, 'Get out of here!' That would have just put more pressure on her. I think what happened was—and I'm guessing—that she felt a sense of real support, and that touched her. I think that moment was a simple, emotional thing, that somebody was really on her side, and it touched her, and that's all."

These leaders have proved not only the necessity but the efficacy of self-confidence, vision, virtue, plain guts, and reliance on the blessed impulse. They have learned from everything, but they have learned more from experience, and even more from adversity and mistakes. And they have learned to lead by leading.

Grace under pressure might be this group's motto. None began life with an edge. Some began with genuine handicaps. All have risen to the top because leaders are made, and made by themselves. To quote Wallace Stevens, they have lived "in the world, but outside of existing conceptions of it." And they have made new worlds, because they themselves are, each and every one, originals. They have worn sombreros.

They would say themselves that they can teach you nothing, but they have shown you the ways to learn everything you need to know.

No leader sets out to be a leader. People set out to live their lives, expressing themselves fully. When that expression is of value, they become leaders.

So the point is not to become a leader. The point is to become yourself, to use yourself completely—all your skills, gifts, and energies—in order to make your vision manifest. You must withhold nothing. You must, in sum, become the person you started out to be, and to enjoy the process of becoming.

Henry James, midway through a life filled with writing marvelous novels, wrote in his *Notebooks*,

I have only to let myself go! So I have said to myself all my life— so I said to myself in the far-off days of my fermenting and passionate youth. Yet I have never fully done it. The sense of it—of the need of it—rolls over me at times with commanding force: it seems the formula of my salvation, of what remains to me of a future. I am in full possession of accumulated resources—I have only to use them, to insist, to persist, to do something more—to do much more than I have done. The way to do it—to affirm one's self *sur la fin*—is to strike as many notes, deep, full and rapid, as one can. All life is—at my age, with all one's artistic soul the record of it—in one's pocket, as it were. Go on, my boy, and strike hard. . . . Try everything, do everything, render everything—be an artist, be distinguished to the last.

James's major novels were written after this self-exhortation. So strike hard, try everything, do everything, render everything, and become the person you are capable of being.

6
Deploying Yourself:
Strike Hard, Try
Everything

There is a self, and what I have sometimes referred to as
"listening to the impulse voices" means letting the self emerge.
Most of us, most of the time (and especially does this apply to
children, young people), listen not to ourselves but to Mommy's
introjected voice or Daddy's voice or to the voice of the
Establishment, of the Elders, of authority, or of tradition.

—ABRAHAM MASLOW
Farther Reaches of Human Nature

"Letting the self emerge" is the essential task for leaders. It is
how one takes the step from being to doing in the spirit of expressing, rather than proving. The means of expression discussed in this chapter unfold from one another as the opening
petals of a flower.

Suppose you were required, as a child, to recite a poem in
front of your class. You forgot the second verse, were scolded
by your teacher, and laughed at by your classmates, and ever
since you've broken into a cold sweat at the thought of speaking in public.

Now you've been offered a job that requires making regular speeches to large groups. You want the job very much, but your fear of public speaking prevents you from accepting it immediately. In other words, your feeling of fear overpowers your confidence in your ability to do the job and prevents you from acting. You have three choices:

- You can surrender to your fears and pass on the job.
- You can attempt to analyze your fear objectively (but as analyst Roger Gould points out, that will probably not result in any significant change).
- You can reflect on your original experience in a concrete way. You were, after all, a child. And you probably didn't like the poem very much, so it was hard to memorize. But most important, although you got scolded and laughed at, your life was not changed in any significant way by the lapse. Neither your grades nor your standing with your classmates suffered. Indeed, everyone forgot your lapse immediately—except you. You have clung to that feeling all these years, without ever thinking about it. Now is the time to think about it.

REFLECTION AND RESOLUTION

Reflection is a major way in which leaders learn from the past. Jim Burke told me, "At Holy Cross, studying with the Jesuits, I had to take twenty-eight hours of scholastic philosophy, which forces you through a logical, disciplined way of thinking. I've often felt this was very important to my business success, because I was naturally intuitive and instinctive, so this overlay of logic was useful. It helped me get through Harvard Business School, which reinforced it. Most of what I've done in business is to look at something and say, 'That's the way to go.' Then I pull myself back and subject it to a very rigorous logic. I'm much more inclined to emotionally arrive at a decision than I am to use logical resources, and the blend has caused me to be reflective. Also, I've always felt that society lacks philosophers. We ought to have people who dedicate their lives just to thinking. We have plenty of economists, and we have all the sciences covered, but only a handful of thinkers. So maybe that makes me reflective. But I think of myself as an activist."

In fact, what we do is a direct result of not only what and how we think, but what and how we feel as well. Roger Gould agreed: "It's how you feel about things that dictates how you behave. Most people don't process their feelings, because thinking is hard work. And abstract thinking doesn't usually lead to a change in behavior. It leads to conflict about change. I use two analytic skills in everything. One is perspective—I always like multiple frames of reference. And I always look for the heart of the issue, the core."

Reflection may be the pivotal way we learn. Consider some of the ways of reflecting: looking back, thinking back, dreaming, journaling, talking it out, watching last week's game, asking for critiques, going on retreats—even telling jokes. Jokes are a way of making whatever-it-was understandable and acceptable.

Freud said that the goal of analysis is to make the unconscious conscious. He talks about the importance of anniversaries, for example—the number of men who die on the same day their fathers died. The anniversary had remained trapped in the unconscious, never reflected on. The wound experienced on the day had never been given air and allowed to heal. Reflection is a way of making learning conscious. Reflection gets to the heart of the matter, the truth of things. After appropriate reflection, the meaning of the past is known, and the resolution of the experience—the course of action you must take as a result—becomes clear. I like the word *resolution*, by the way, and tend to use it in two of its several meanings: a course of action decided upon, and an explanation or solution. And *resolution* has a musical overtone that I like as well: the progression of a dissonant chord to a consonant one.

On the subject of reflection, Barbara Corday said, "Unfortunately, too often it's people's failures that get them to reflect on their experiences. When you're going along and everything is working well, you don't sit down and reflect. Which is exactly the moment when you should do it. If you wait for a giant mistake before you reflect, two things happen. One, since you're down, you don't get the most out of it, and two, you tend only to see the mistake, instead of all the moments in which you've also been correct."

It's true. Most of us are shaped more by negative experiences than by positive ones. A thousand things happen in a week to each of us, but most of us remember the few lapses rather than our triumphs, because we don't reflect. We merely react. Playwright Athol Fugard said that he worked his way out of a depression by starting every day thinking of ten things that gave him pleasure. I've found thinking of the things in my life that bring me pleasure a peaceful and positive way to start the morning, and I've started doing it regularly. Thinking of the small pleasures around one—the glow of the morning light on the ocean, the fresh-cut roses next to the word processor, the tall café latte waiting at the end of a morning walk, even the dog that wants to be fed—is a much better way to deal with a perceived failure than to ruminate on it. When you're down, think of the things you have to look forward to. When you are no longer in the grip of the mishap, *then* you are ready to reflect on it.

In fact, mistakes contain potent lessons—but only if we think them through calmly, see where we went wrong, mentally revise what we're doing, and then act on the revisions. When a great batter strikes out, he doesn't linger for a moment over the goof, but instead sets about to improve his stance or his swing. And great batters do strike out—Babe Ruth not only set a home run record, he set a strikeout record as well. Think what a great batting average is: .400—which means a great batter fails to get a hit more than half the time. Most of the rest of us are paralyzed by our failures, large and small. We're so haunted by them, so afraid that we're going to goof again, that we become fearful of doing anything. When jockeys are thrown, they get back on the horse, because they know if they don't, their fear may immobilize them. When an F–14 pilot has to eject, he or she goes up the next day in another plane. Most of us have lesser fears to face—but most of us have to cope with them through thought, before we act again. Reflection comes first, and then strategic action. As Roger Gould phrased it, reflection permits us to process our feelings, understand them, resolve our questions, and get on with our work. Wordsworth defined poetry as strong emotion recollected in tranquillity. That's the time to reflect, in tranquillity—and then to resolve.

The point is not to be the victims of our feelings, jerked this way and that by unresolved emotions, not to be used by our experiences, but to use them and to use them creatively. Just as writers turn experiences from their lives into novels and plays, we can each transform our experiences into grist for our mill. Isak Dinesen said, "Any sorrow can be borne if we can put it in a story."

Your accumulated experience is the basis for the rest of your life, and that base is solid and sound to the degree that you have reflected on it, understood it, and arrived at a workable resolution.

Gloria Steinem, like many pioneers, has made a vocation of venturing into uncharted, untested waters. Her approach is direct: "I'm not very reflective. I work out whatever it is by acting or doing or saying it. It's the Midwest in me. In the Midwest, introspection is practically forbidden. As a result, I'm future oriented, which isn't great, because you can only live in the present, not the future. . . . There are learning moments. I think things happen over and over again, and we learn in a spiral, not a straight line . . . and then one day we get it. So I don't have the sensation of reflecting or examining. I have the sensation of, 'Oh, that's why.' If you've experienced the dynamic before, you sort of understand when it's happening again. There's a plateau for a long time, and then a sudden leap forward, and then another plateau. I think of those leaps as learning moments. But I think you often know things intellectually before you understand them emotionally. I wrote a piece about my mother that I can't read, because now I understand it, and it makes me too sad."

As both Steinem and Gould have said, too much intellectualizing tends to paralyze us. But true reflection inspires, informs, and ultimately demands resolution. Steinem leaps first and looks or reflects later. There is something to be said for that headlong approach, but only if you are able to see mistakes, failures, as a basic and vital part of life. Most of us, unfortunately, aren't that wise or that cool-headed. It is the pioneers like Steinem, the ones who head straight for the unmapped territory marked only by the legend "Here there be tygers," who believe so much in what they're doing that they accept the risks inherent in such undertakings as part of the job.

To do anything well requires knowing what it is that you're doing, and you can only know what you're really doing by making the process conscious—reflecting on yourself, reflecting on the task, and coming to a resolution.

As I mentioned in an earlier chapter, Erik Erikson sees our development as a series of resolved conflicts, one for each stage of life. He further postulates that until each conflict is resolved positively, we cannot move to the next stage or conflict.

These conflicts are so basic, and resolving them is so vital, that I've come to see them in much broader terms and a more general frame than Erikson's. We are subject to these conflicts all of our lives, and the way we resolve them determines how we will live. Here is how I would reframe them:

Conflicts	Resolutions
Blind trust vs. Suspicion	Hope
Independence vs. Dependence	Autonomy
Initiative vs. Imitation	Purpose
Industry vs. Inferiority	Competence
Identity vs. Confusion	Integrity
Intimacy vs. Isolation	Empathy
Generosity vs. Selfishness	Maturity
Illusion vs. Delusion	Wisdom

Physicist Neils Bohr said, "There are two kinds of truth, small truth and great truth. You can recognize a small truth because its opposite is a falsehood. The opposite of a great truth is another truth."

Our lives are made less of small truths and falsehoods than of great truths and the truths that are their opposites, which is

113

why the resolution of these basic conflicts is so difficult sometimes. It's almost never a choice between a right and a wrong. For example, hope lies somewhere between blind trust and suspicion, but so does its opposite, despair. And wisdom usually follows illusion, delusion, and disillusion.

Once you have learned to reflect on your experiences until the resolution of your conflicts arises from within you, then you begin to develop your own perspective.

PERSPECTIVE

John Sculley touched on the need for perspective: "It's important to change your perspective, maybe by living or traveling extensively abroad. Shifting your stance changes you. You take the same set of facts and shift the vantage point and everything looks different. One of the things leaders have to be good at is perspective. Leaders don't necessarily have to invent ideas, but they have to be able to put them in context and add perspective. . . . What I look for in people is the ability to transform their experience into ideas and to put those ideas in context."

What is your perspective? The following questions should give you some idea.

1. When you consider a new project, do you think first of its cost or its benefits?
2. Do you rank profit or progress first?
3. Would you rather be rich or famous?
4. If offered a promotion that required you to move to another city, would you discuss it with your family before accepting it?

5. Would you rather be a small fish in a big pond, or a big fish in a small pond?

Your answers will reveal something important about your perspective. If you think first of the cost of a project or rank profit higher than progress, then your perspective is short-term. A person who would rather be famous than rich is the more ambitious because—unless you're in show biz—fame requires more talent and originality than the making of a fortune. If you would discuss a promotion with your family before accepting it, you're more humane than ambitious. And if you'd rather be a big fish in a small pond, you may lack drive (or you may simply agree with Julius Caesar, who is reputed to have said, "I would rather be first in a small Iberian village than second in Rome").

Perspective is no more and no less than how you see things, your particular frame of reference. Without it, you're flying blind. But it's also your point of view, and as Marvin Minsky, a pioneer in artificial intelligence, said, point of view is worth 80 I.Q. points. Marty Kaplan told me, "I think one of the reasons for the fame or notoriety of this studio [Disney] is that the people who run it have a very strong point of view, which I guess I would add to leadership. . . . To the outside world we couch a rejection in subjective terms. 'Gosh, we just didn't like it.' But inside the company, a decision is not viewed as a kind of soft, mushy, relativistic thing. We have a viewpoint, and a project either works with our viewpoint or doesn't work with our viewpoint."

If you know what you think and what you want, you have a very real advantage. In this era of experts, when we have nutritionists to fine-tune our diets, turn family dogs over to professional trainers and even pet psychologists, and bring in consultants on any major decision, a point of view is not only rare, but valuable. Establishing a pattern that would survive his own demise, the late Morton Downey, Jr., became rich and famous almost overnight by becoming the Archie Bunker of late–twentieth-century talk show hosts. It's not so much that people liked his biased, rude, macho act (although some obviously did), it's that they responded to the fact that he had a point of view and that he expressed it without apology. Like the steady stream of bigoted but confident radio and TV pundits that followed him, Downey was admired not so much for what he said, but that he said anything at all.

I am not for a moment suggesting that you emulate television and talk radio's narrow-minded big mouths. In fact, I'd rather you didn't—we have more than enough already. I am suggesting that anyone who wants to express him- or herself fully and truly must have a point of view. Leadership without perspective and point of view isn't leadership—and of course it must be your own perspective, your own point of view. You cannot borrow a point of view any more than you can borrow someone else's eyes. It must be authentic, and if it is, it will be original, because you are an original.

Once you master the arts of reflection, understanding, and resolution, perspective and point of view will follow. Your next task is to figure out what to do with all that.

TESTS AND MEASURES

Some people are born knowing what they want to do, and even how to do it. The rest of us aren't so lucky. We have to spend some time figuring out what to do with our lives. Vague goals, such as "I just want to be happy" or "I want to live well" or "I want to make the world a better place" or even "I want to be very, very rich," are nearly useless. But so are overly specific goals, such as "I want to be chairman of the XYZ Corporation" or "I want to be a nuclear physicist" or "I want to discover a cure for the common cold," because they leave out all the other values in life.

Jamie Raskin told me, "One of my heroes is a professor at Harvard Law School named Derek Bell. He told me that it's important not to have any specific ambitions or desires. It's more important to have ambitions in terms of the way you want to live your life, and then the other things will flow out of that."

What do you want? The majority of us go through life, often very successfully, without ever asking, much less answering, this most basic question.

The most basic answer, of course, is that you want to express yourself fully, for that is the most basic human drive. As one friend put it, "We all want to learn how to use our own voices," and it has led some of us to the peaks and some of us to the depths.

How can *you* best express *you*?

The first test is knowing what you want, knowing your abilities and capacities, and recognizing the difference between the two.

Gloria Anderson said, "I always felt it wasn't right to be like everyone else. I thought I had to meet different standards and do different things." Journalism was an obvious choice of expression for her, because journalists, by definition, stand apart from other people. As reporters, they cover the action, rather than taking part in it, and as editors, they have the opportunity to speak out on issues they believe in.

Anne Bryant was first chosen by others. "In elementary school," she said, "I got awards for leadership activities, which always surprised me. In high school, I was asked to be a leader. Of course, I was taller than everyone else, so I sort of loomed over everyone, which may have helped. But I never ran for things. I do like taking charge of things. I always have." Since she likes "taking charge of things," it's not surprising that Bryant became an executive and led an organization, the American Association of University Women, with 150,000 members and assets of over $47 million, whose goals include promoting equity for women, self-development, and positive social change.

Betty Friedan was always an organizer. "In fifth grade, we had a substitute teacher who didn't like children, so I organized a club, the Baddy-Baddy Club, and at a signal from me, everybody dropped their books on the floor and did other things that would irritate the teacher. The principal called me to his office and said, 'You have a great talent for leadership. You must use it for good, not evil.' . . . In my adult professional life, I'm theoretically a writer, but I spend much time on my political activity. I organized three of the key organizations of the women's movement and then bowed out of active leadership."

The second test is knowing what drives you, knowing what gives you satisfaction, and knowing the difference between the two.

Roger Gould said, "I remember dreaming every night about how I was going to save everyone, not just me, but everyone. I must have been 12 or 13 at the time." So Gould grew up to become a psychoanalyst, a kind of secular savior.

Mathilde Krim needed to be useful: "I spent three summers working on an isolated farm. It was horrible, but it gave me a fantastic feeling of self-confidence. I thought if I could do that, I could do anything. I did it because it was the right thing to do' at the time, and I tried to do a good job of it, to be really useful, but it was very hard." This was a good start for someone who went on to become a scientist and was a pioneer in the fight to defeat AIDS. "I spend all my time on the AIDS issue now," she told me. "I'm incapable of doing anything else."

John Sculley's route was slightly more circuitous, although no less logical: "I've always had a sort of insatiable curiosity about things, everything, electronics for a while, then art, then art history and architecture, all sorts of stuff. When I get interested in something, I become totally absorbed by it, and I always run out of physical energy before my curiosity is satisfied. I never intended to become a businessman. That was the furthest thing from my mind. I thought I'd be an inventor or architect or designer. I was interested in visual things, and I was always interested in ideas and comfortable with them—in everything from calculus to architecture." It's hard to imagine a better background for heading an innovative, design-savvy technology firm such as Apple.

The point of the first two tests is that once you recognize, or admit, that your primary goal is to fully express yourself, you will find the means to achieve the rest of your goals—given your abilities and capacities, along with your interests and biases. On the other hand, if your primary aim is to prove yourself, you'll run into trouble sooner or later, as Ed, the lead character in the cautionary tale in chapter one, did. The man who follows his father into law or medicine in order to prove himself, or the woman who decides to be a stockbroker to show that she can make a lot of money, is playing the fool's game and will almost inevitably fail and/or be unhappy.

The third test is knowing what your values and priorities are, knowing what the values and priorities of your organization are, and measuring the difference between the two.

If you've found a way to express yourself fully and well, and are reasonably satisfied with your pace and performance, but you don't feel you'll get very far in your present position, it may be that you're in sync with yourself, but you're out of sync with your environment—your partner, company, or organization.

Herb Alpert said, "I used to record for a major company. And I didn't like the way I was being treated. I was sort of being fed through their computer. And it just seemed like they were on the wrong track. . . . I had this spark of an idea for Tijuana Brass, which involved overdubbing the trumpet, which I was experimenting with in my own little garage studio at home. They said it was impossible, that it violated union regulations, because I'd be putting some musician out of work. Well, they missed the point altogether. So I just decided that when I had my own company, the artist would be the heartbeat of the company and his needs would come first."

Alpert and Jerry Moss went on to found A&M Records, which is legendary for its fine treatment of artists, although their then partner Gil Friesen said, "A&M has a certain reputation for being artist oriented and having a sort of family atmosphere, but it's nothing we consciously do. It isn't calculated. . . . Actually, I think you do it by not doing it, by not managing very much."

Alpert's decision to start his own company in order to create the kind of environment he wanted to work in was as ultimately sensible as it was seemingly radical: he and A&M became major industry powers.

In the same spirit, Gloria Anderson founded her own newspaper. She said, "*Miami Today* was my first opportunity to do things my way, and I'm very proud of it. But when I realized that my partner didn't share my vision and never would, I decided to move on and do something on my own."

Anne Bryant, on the other hand, recommends walking more carefully. "Too often you come into a new job on a wave of fresh energy and, not by design, you tend to debunk what's been previously done. That's very hard on the people who've been with the organization for a while. It's better to try to put yourself in their shoes and acknowledge the good things that have been done and reinforce those things, before going forward with your own plans. If the existing personnel feel supported and are made to feel a part of the new plans, they're thrilled."

Being in sync with your organization is almost as important as being in sync with yourself, in other words. Some leaders are inevitably drawn to form their own organizations, while others, like Bryant, prefer the path of accommodation.

The fourth test is—having measured the differences between what you want and what you're able to do, and between what drives you and what satisfies you, and between what your values are and what the organization's values are—are you able and willing to overcome those differences?

In the first instance, the issues are fairly basic. Almost every one of us has, at one point in our lives, wanted to be an NFL quarterback or a movie star or a jazz singer, but we simply didn't have the requisite equipment. And although I've said— and believe—that you can learn anything you want to learn, certain occupations require gifts beyond learning. I know a highly successful radiologist who has always dreamed of being a singer, but he has no voice. Instead of abandoning his dream, he writes songs. A would-be quarterback who's fast and smart, but who weighs only 140 pounds, might well become a coach or manager. Or he might organize a Saturday afternoon touch-football league among his friends and co-workers.

Whatever it is you want to do, you shouldn't let fear get in your way. Fear, for most leaders, is less a crippler than a motivator. As Brooke Knapp said, "I started flying because I was afraid of it. If you give not 90 percent or 95 percent but 100 percent, you can make anything happen. The greatest opportunity for growth lies in overcoming things you're afraid of." She went on to become one of America's leading flyers.

In the second instance, the issue is more complex. We all know people who are driven to succeed, never mind at what or how, who are never satisfied, and who are often unhappy. It is entirely possible to succeed and satisfy yourself simultaneously, but only if you are wise enough and honest enough to admit what you want and recognize what you need.

For the third instance I'll refer again to that feckless fellow Ed. If he had thought more about what he wanted and what his company needed, he wouldn't have driven himself off the track. But he spent his energies doing and proving, not being. Some corporate cultures are so rigid that they require absolute obedience to the corporate line. Others are flexible, adjustable, and adaptable. By knowing the flex in yourself and the flex in the organization, you'll know whether you're a fit or not.

DESIRE

Brooke Knapp said, "Some people are lucky enough to be born with desire and the ability to make things happen. I've always had a desire to achieve. It's not calculated. It's as natural as eating to me."

Former CalFed CEO Robert Dockson was lucky, too. "I don't think you can be taught dedication, purpose, and a sense of vision," he said. "I don't know where that comes from."

If Knapp is right, and desire is as natural as eating, then it exists in all of us. And while Dockson may be right that it can't be taught, it can be activated. Virtually every one of us was born with a hunger for life itself, with what I call a passion for the promises of life, and that passion can take one to the heights. Unfortunately, in too many of us, it devolves into drive. Entrepreneur Larry Wilson defined *the difference between desire and drive as the difference between expressing yourself and proving yourself*. In a perfect world, everyone would be encouraged to express, but not required to prove him- or herself. But neither the world nor we are perfect. In order to avoid booby-trapping ourselves, then, we must understand that drive is healthy only when married to desire.

Drive divorced from desire is often hazardous, sometimes lethal, while drive in the service of desire is often both productive and rewarding. Knapp, like the other leaders I spoke with, has that passion for the promises of life, and the drive to realize her passion. "I was raised with eight boys on my block," she said, "and I was stronger than all of them. I was the one with the energy and enthusiasm and drive and determination, so I became the leader."

Although she went through a docile period, her desire emerged intact some years later. "I'm an entrepreneur in spirit," she told me. "I see a window of opportunity and take advantage of it. Jet Airways [a company she founded that flies executives around the country] happened almost by accident. Deregulation had killed off a lot of small airlines, so corporations were having a tough time getting their people into small towns, and I wanted to buy a Lear Jet." Her desire to have her own plane and the need for cost-effective executive transportation were happily combined. Knapp remains restless and inventive. After founding Jet Airways, she managed a securities portfolio and became involved in the Florida citrus industry and with high-end real estate in southern California.

Barbara Corday credits her success partly to enthusiasm. "A corporation, or a show, is only as strong as the caring and enthusiasm that the people who are involved in it on a daily basis put into it. And I don't think you can expect caring and enthusiasm from people you, the leader, don't care about and are not conscious of. . . . I think my enthusiasm is catching. I think when I get on a project, if I love it, I can make you love it."

Jamie Raskin agreed that passion is infectious: "If you hold your ground and make your conviction known, people will come around. I'm committed to radical principles. As Oscar Wilde said, 'I'm on the left, which is the side of the heart, as opposed to the right, which is the side of the liver.'"

Gloria Anderson summed it up. "You can't make being a leader your principal goal, any more than you can make being happy your goal. In both cases, it has to be the result, not the cause."

MASTERY

When I asked Marty Kaplan to describe the qualities of leadership, he said, "Competence, first. A true sense of mastery of the task at hand. Another is the ability to articulate, because if someone is a complete master of what they need to know, but is unable to explain why I should care about it, or want to help, then they can't get me to support them. And something I prefer to see in a leader, but isn't essential, is a level of human sensitivity, tact, compassion, and diplomacy. I've known leaders who have had none of it and nevertheless were lead-

ers, but those who have had that quality have moved and inspired me more."

He's right. "A true sense of mastery of the task at hand." Leaders haven't simply practiced their vocation or profession. They've
mastered it. They've learned everything there is to know about it,
and then surrendered to it. For example, the late Fred Astaire
mastered the choreography, and then surrendered to it. He became one with it, so it was impossible to say where he stopped
and the routine began. He was the routine. Franklin Roosevelt
mastered the presidency; Jimmy Carter was mastered by it.

Such mastery requires absolute concentration, the full deployment of oneself. Astaire had it. That's what got our attention before he did anything. Martin Luther King, Jr.,
galvanized America with a few words. He didn't simply have a
dream, he was the dream, just as Magic Johnson was the Lakers
and Bill Gates is Microsoft.

The Chinese practice something called *wushu*, which Mark
Salzman, an American writer who has lived in China, describes
as a means of achieving "perfect form and concentration.
[One's] movements become instinctive and express a harmony
of mind and body that the Chinese believe is crucial to spiritual as well as physical health. In classical *wushu* . . . the *wushu-
jia* devotes most of his training time to the practice of *taolu*, or
routines . . . choreographed sequences of movements, one to
twenty minutes in length, that must be carried out according
to strict esthetic, technical and conceptual guidelines. . . . An
unbroken thread of intent must exist between the movements
of a *taolu*, like the invisible line that passes through and con-
nects the separate pieces of Chinese calligraphy."

Salzman quotes his instructor, Pan Qingfui, a master whose
nickname is Iron Fist, as saying, "The eyes are the most

important, because in them you can see a person's *yi* [will or intent]." Salzman goes on to say, "Chinese boxing depends on *yi* for its strength, so you have to train your eyes.... You must practice the *taolu* as if you had complete confidence in your strength, as if a single blow of your hand could destroy your opponent.... You must hit him with your eyes, your heart. Your hands will follow."

Author George Leonard writes of mastery, "Experienced pilots can tell a lot about how good another pilot is by the way he or she gets into the pilot's seat and straps on his or her safety harness. There are some people who are so obviously on that they give us a lift just by walking into the room. [Some people] can demonstrate mastery simply by the way [they] stand."

Leonard describes some other elements of mastery, too: "The path of mastery is built on unrelenting practice, but it's also a place of adventure.... Whether it's a sport or an art or some other work, those we call masters are shamelessly enthusiastic about their calling.... Those on the path of mastery are willing to take chances, play the fool.... The most powerful learning is that which is most like play.... The word *generous* comes from the same root as *genial*, *generative*, and *genius*.... [The genius] has the ability to give everything and hold nothing back. Perhaps, in fact, genius can be defined in terms of this givingness."

Barbara Corday said of a kind of self-mastery, "In my business, if you love something and want to make it happen, you can convince other people to go along with you. Personal style, personal belief, a tremendous desire to make something happen, tenacity, the ability to never give up, no matter how many people say no, are vital. I am in a business that is built on rejection, daily rejection. You have to be able to go beyond that, to simply turn a deaf ear to rejection, to keep moving forward, to build into your own psyche the ability to stay true to yourself and what you believe in. If you had a good idea yesterday, it's going to be a good idea tomorrow, and just because you haven't convinced anyone to go with it today doesn't mean you won't convince someone to go with it tomorrow."

Mastery, absolute competence, is mandatory for a leader. But it's also more fun than anything else you'll ever do. Jim Burke said, "It should be fun, the process ought to be exciting and fun. The person who's not having any fun is doing something wrong. Either his environment is stultifying or he's off base himself."

Roger Gould simply loves what he does. "I'd never known a psychiatrist and didn't really know what they did, but it seemed right for me. I like people and love talking to them on a deep level. I love being an analyst. I have a great feeling for people and like helping them. But at the core of it all is a profound curiosity about the thinking process. That's what drives me."

STRATEGIC THINKING

There's an old saying: "Unless you're the lead dog, the scenery never changes." To extend that thought, for the leader the scenery is always changing. Everything is new. Because, by definition, each leader is unique, his or her circumstances are also unique.

Sydney Pollack, when asked if leadership could be taught, responded, "It's hard to teach anything that can't be broken down into repeatable and unchanging elements. Driving a car, flying an airplane—you can reduce those things to a series of maneuvers that are always executed in the same way. But with something like leadership, just as with art, you reinvent the wheel every single time you apply the principle."

Robert Dockson agreed: "Leaders aren't technicians."

Creativity is required, then, for the banker as well as the motion picture director. The creative process that underlies strategic thinking is infinitely complex, and as unexplainable finally as its inner mechanism, but there are basic steps in the process that can be identified. When you reduce something to its most elemental state, its nuclear core, you can generalize from there.

First, whether you're planning a novel or a corporate reorganization, you have to know where you're going to end up. Mountain climbers don't start climbing from the bottom of the mountain. They look at where they want to go, and work backward to where they're starting from. Like a mountain climber, once you have the summit in view, you figure out all the ways you might get there. Then you play with those—altering, connecting, comparing, reversing, and imagining—finally choosing one or two routes.

Second, you flesh out those routes, elaborate them, revise them, make a kind of map of them, complete with possible pitfalls and traps as well as rewards.

Third, you examine this map objectively, as if you were not its maker, locate all its soft spots, and eliminate them or change them.

Finally, when you have finished all that, you set out to climb your mountain.

Frances Hesselbein and her husband and their families were part of Johnstown, Pennsylvania, for four generations. They had a communications business, and she worked as a Girl Scout volunteer there, but she also did management training for Girl

Scout Councils around the country. Asked to take over the CEO slot of the local council temporarily, she agreed. Six years later, although she hadn't applied for the job, she was made executive director of the Girl Scouts of the USA. She and her husband moved to New York City and set about reorganizing the Scouts, to reflect everything she had learned on her way up the ladder.

"The first thing we did," Hesselbein said, "was to develop a corporate planning system in which planning and management were synonymous. It was a common planning system for 335 local councils and the national organization. We developed a corporate planning monograph to mobilize the energy of 600,000 adult volunteers in order to carry out our mission to help young girls grow up and reach their highest potential as women. Today, our people feel we've achieved more unity and cohesion than anyone can remember.

"I just felt there was a compelling need to have a clear planning system that defined roles, differentiating between the volunteers, the operational staff, and the policy planners, one that permitted whatever was going on in the smallest troop—needs, trends, whatever—to flow through to the policy makers, so they had a clear idea of what was going on and what needed to go on. We have three million members, and we really listen to the girls and their parents, and we've devised ways to reach out to the girls wherever they are. We say, 'We have something of value to offer you, but you in return have something to offer us. We respect your values and culture, and if you open our handbooks, even if you're a minority, a Navajo, you're there.'

"I think we have the best staff anywhere. They're wonderful, and my job is to keep opening up the system and increase their freedom and scope. I can't stand to box people in. Everyone's in a circle. It's rather organic. If I'm in the center, then there are seven bubbles around me, and the next circle would be group directors, and then team directors, and so on. Nothing moves up or down, but rather laterally, across. It's so fluid and flexible that people who're used to a hierarchy have a bit of trouble adjusting, but it works. We sell it to outside groups.

"But the best thing about it is that every girl in America can look at the program and see herself."

There are risks to assume in making the results of your strategic thinking real. But as Carlos Casteneda said, "The basic difference between an ordinary man and a warrior is that a warrior takes everything as a challenge, while an ordinary man takes everything as a blessing or a curse."

Unless you are willing to take risks, you will suffer paralyzing inhibitions, and you will never do what you are capable of doing. Mistakes—missteps—are necessary for actualizing your vision, and necessary steps toward success.

SYNTHESIS

Finally, the leader combines all the means of expression, in order to act effectively.

Little children are naturally creative, and so are the elderly. Novelist Carlos Fuentes said, "I really think youth is something you win from age. You are rather old and stupid when you are young. The youngest men I ever met in my life were Luis Buñuel, who made his greatest films between the ages of 60 and 80, and Arthur Rubinstein, a man who became a genius at 80, being able to strike a note by raising his hand to heaven and making it fall exactly as Beethoven and Chopin demanded. Pablo Picasso painted his most erotic and passionate works when in his 80s. These are men who earned their youth. It took them 80 years to become young."

I think what Fuentes was getting at was that, subject to all the usual peer, familial, and social pressures, we lose track of ourselves when we are adolescents. We become lost in the crowd, more connected and responsive to it than to ourselves, and so we lose our ability to create, because creation is the province of the individual, not the committee.

But leaders, having achieved self-possession, have long since recovered their creative powers, too, and have continued to grow. We tend to think of growth in quantitative terms: heights and weights. When our bodies stop growing, our minds stop growing, or so we think. But, as the leaders I talked with have shown in their own lives, our intellectual and emotional growth doesn't have to stall, nor should it. Leaders differ from others in their constant appetite for knowledge and experience, and as their worlds widen and become more complex, so too do their means of understanding.

Dialectical thinking, a variation on the Socratic dialogue, is one such means. It presumes that reality is dynamic rather than static, and therefore seeks relationships between ideas, to aim at synthesis. You might find it useful to think of reflection and perspective as two horns, with synthesis balanced between them.

Frances Hesselbein demonstrates synthesis as she describes her approach to her work with the Girl Scouts: "First, you have to figure out how to organize your job, the management of time, what your responsibilities are. Second, you have to learn to lead, not contain. Third, you have to have a clear sense of who you are and a sense of mission, a clear understanding of it, and you must be sure that your principles are congruent with the organization's principles. Fourth, you have to demonstrate

131

through your behavior all the things you believe a leader and a follower should do. Fifth, you need a great sense of freedom and scope so that you can free the people who work with you to live up to their potential. If you believe in the team approach, you must believe in people and their potential. And you must demand a great deal of them, but be consistent."

John Sculley saw synthesis as the difference between management and leadership. "Leadership is often confused with other things, specifically management. But management requires an entirely different set of skills. As I see it, leadership revolves around vision, ideas, direction, and has more to do with inspiring people as to direction and goals than with day-to-day implementation. . . . One can't lead unless he can leverage more than his own capabilities. . . . You have to be capable of inspiring other people to do things without actually sitting on top of them with a checklist—which is management, not leadership."

Robert Terry, formerly an executive at the Hubert H. Humphrey Institute of Public Affairs, defines leadership as "a fundamental and profound engagement with the world and the human condition."

Roger Gould demonstrated that engagement when he said, "Once you have a vision that you've tested over and over again, you've got the tiger by the tail. You almost can't stop leading, because that would mean being unfaithful to your vision of reality."

Betty Friedan concurred, saying, "When I see a need, I get people together to do something about it. My version of religion is 'You are responsible.'"

For all their particular talents, these leaders see themselves less as soloists than as collaborators. Leaders and followers are engaged in the same dance.

Robert Dockson said, "The leader guides people, he doesn't force them, and he always treats them fairly. . . . Too many people claim that our only responsibility is to our shareholders. I believe we're responsible to them, but we're also responsible to our employees, our customers, and the community at large. There's something wrong with the private enterprise system if it doesn't recognize its responsibility to the community."

Former Red Cross director Richard Schubert, too, believes in relating well to others: "How you attract and motivate people determines how successful you'll be as a leader. Above all, the Golden Rule applies. Whether it's an employee or a customer or a senior vice president, the leader treats people the way he would like to be treated. Ninety-six percent of our people at disaster sites are volunteers. If we don't attract the right people and motivate them positively, we aren't going to make it." This concept is so important that I'll elaborate on it in chapter eight, "Getting People on Your Side."

Leaders who trust their co-workers are, in turn, trusted by them. Trust, of course, cannot be acquired, but can only be given. Leadership without mutual trust is a contradiction in terms. Trust resides squarely between faith and doubt. Leaders always have faith in themselves, their abilities, their co-workers, and their mutual possibilities. But leaders also have sufficient doubt to question, challenge, probe, and thereby progress. In the same way, his or her co-workers must believe in the leader, themselves, and their combined strength, but they must feel sufficiently confident to question, challenge, probe, and test, too. Maintaining that vital balance between faith and doubt, preserving that mutual trust, is a primary task for any leader.

Vision, inspiration, empathy, trustworthiness are manifestations of a leader's judgment and character. Former university president Alfred Gottschalk said, "Character is vital in a leader, the basis for everything else. Other qualities would include the ability to inspire trust, some entrepreneurial talent, imagination, perseverance, steadfastness of purpose. . . . Character, perseverance, and imagination are the sine qua non of leadership."

An Irish proverb is pertinent: "You've got to do your own growing, no matter how tall your grandfather is."

All of these leaders have consciously constructed their own lives and the contexts in which they live and work. Each is not just actor, but playwright, hammer and anvil, and each, in his or her own way, is altering the larger context.

The means of expression are the steps to leadership:

1. Reflection leading to resolution.
2. Resolution leading to perspective.
3. Perspective leading to point of view.
4. Point of view leading to tests and measures.
5. Tests and measures leading to desire.
6. Desire leading to mastery.
7. Mastery leading to strategic thinking.
8. Strategic thinking leading to full self-expression.
9. The synthesis of full self-expression = leadership.

Leadership is first being, then doing. Everything the leader does reflects what he or she is. So that is the next turn in our tale—to follow the leader, "Moving Through Chaos."

7
Moving Through Chaos

> If you want to truly understand something, try to change it.
>
> —KURT LEWIN

Leaders are, by definition, innovators. They do things other people have not done or dare not do. They do things in advance of other people. They make new things. They make old things new. Having learned from the past, they live in the present, with one eye on the future. And each leader puts it all together in a different way. To do that, as I noted earlier, leaders must be right-brain, as well as left-brain, thinkers. They must be intuitive, conceptual, synthesizing, and artistic. They must—like Wallace Stevens—wear sombreros.

Robert Abboud was once fired from the top slot in a Chicago bank. He went to work for Armand Hammer and was fired again. Then he moved to Texas and became CEO of the First National Bankcorp. When asked how he could account for his success, after all that failure, he cited an exchange on "The Andy Griffith Show" that summed it up: Barney, Andy's deputy, asked Andy how one acquired good judgment. Andy said he guessed it came from experience. Barney asked how you got experience. Andy said, "You get kicked around a little bit." Abboud shrugged and said, "I got kicked around a little bit."

Abboud learned from his experience, rather than being defeated by it, because he didn't simply accept it. He reflected on it, understood it, and used it. Leaders learn by doing—they learn where there are challenges, where the task is unprogrammed, where the job is being done for the first time. How do you rescue a bank? You learn by doing it. You learn through all the things that happen on the job. Much of this chapter appears to revolve around learning from adversity. But I don't think of it that way. I think of it as learning from surprise.

Sydney Pollack told me how he learned from experience. "The first time I ever directed anything," he said, "I acted like a director. That's the only thing I knew how to do, because I didn't know anything about directing. I had images of directors from working with them, and I even tried to dress like a director—clothes that were kind of outdoorsy. I didn't put on puttees, or anything like that. But if there had been a megaphone around, I would have grabbed it."

Pollack created entire worlds every time he made a movie— both the world on-screen and the world behind the camera. "On a motion picture I have a team of anywhere from one hundred to two hundred people. Some are technicians, some are artists, some are craftsmen, and some are just laborers. Part of the trick is not creating situations where you're inviting contests of egos. And oddly enough, the more willing you seem to be to let people participate, the less need they have to force participation. It's the threat of being left out that exacerbates their ego problems and creates clashes."

Here is one of the important things Pollack learned about leadership: "The things people always talk about in any interview about leadership aren't the things that are the most difficult or the most interesting about leadership. They're the more tangible things. We know that you have to delegate responsibility, you have to encourage people to have initiative, and you have to encourage people to take chances. The artistic part of leadership is in a way, I think, not different from art, in that in a sense it's all innovation, and like all creative acts comes out of a certain kind of controlled free association."

Learning to lead is, on one level, learning to manage change. As we've seen, a leader imposes (in the most positive sense of the word) his or her philosophy on the organization, creating or re-creating its culture. The organization then acts on that philosophy, carries out the mission, and the culture takes on a life of its own, becoming more cause than effect. But unless the leader continues to evolve, to adapt and adjust to external change, the organization will sooner or later stall.

In other words, one of a leader's principal gifts is the ability to use his or her experiences to grow in office. Teddy Roosevelt was described as "a clown" before he became president. His cousin, Franklin D. Roosevelt, was dismissed by Walter Lippman as "a pleasant country squire who wants to be president." The Roosevelts are now regarded as two of this country's best presidents. For leaders, the test and the proof are always in the doing.

Jacob Bronowski wrote, in *The Ascent of Man*, "We have to understand that the world can only be grasped by action, not by contemplation. . . . The most powerful drive in the ascent of man is his pleasure in his own skill. He loves to do what he does well and, having done it well, he loves to do it better."

The leader does it better and better and better, but is never satisfied. Aeschylus said that wisdom is gained through pain and reflection. The leader knows better than anyone that the fundamental problems of life are insoluble, but persists anyway, and continues to learn.

Leaders learn by leading, and they learn best by leading in the face of obstacles. As weather shapes mountains, so problems make leaders. Difficult bosses, lack of vision and virtue in the executive suite, circumstances beyond their control, and their own mistakes have been the leaders' basic curriculum.

Korn/Ferry International co-founder Richard Ferry belongs to what might be called the throw-them-into-the-water-and-they'll-learn-to-swim school: "You can't really create leaders. How do you teach people to make decisions, for example? All you can do is develop the talents people have. I'm a great believer in trial by fire, on-the-job experience. Put them out there in the plants, put them in the markets, send them to Japan and Europe. Train them on the job."

Jim Burke and Horace Deets were succinct. Burke said, "The more experience and the more tests you survive, the more apt you are to be a good leader." Deets, speaking of his job as executive director of the American Association of Retired Persons, said, "It's a tough job and, I would wager, can only be learned by experience. You can't learn it by reading up on it, you've got to do it. The only real laboratory is the laboratory of leadership itself."

When I talked with her, Barbara Corday was working her way through a difficult lesson: "When Tri-Star and Columbia merged, they woke up the next day with two presidents of their two television divisions, and so one of us had to go. It turned out to be me. It's been three months—the longest period of time I've gone without working for twenty-five years. It's been a real learning experience, a real time of change and reflection, and I think I'm just really getting ready to plunge back in again. . . . I think getting up in the morning is more exciting when you're nervous. If you're not nervous, you're dead. . . . It's time to change your life or your work the moment you stop having butterflies in your stomach."

College president emeritus Alfred Gottschalk is another advocate of learning from adversity. "I lost some jobs as a kid and did poorly in some courses, and I learned that the world didn't end. Adversity has a great deal to do with the development of leaders. Either it knocks you out or you become a bigger and better person."

On the risks of leadership, Gottschalk said, "Today there are risks in being at the head of the pack. You can get shot in the back. People try to trip you. People want you to fail. And at some point or another, every leader falls off his pedestal. They're either pulled down, shot down, or they do something dumb, or they just wear out."

According to a study by behavioral scientists Michael Lombardo and Morgan McCall at the Center for Creative Leadership, adversity is as random—and as prevalent—as good luck. After interviewing nearly 100 top executives, they found that serendipity was the rule, not the exception, and that the executives' ascensions were anything but orderly. Key events included radical job changes and serious problems, as well as lucky breaks. Problems cited included failure, demotions, missed promotions, assignments overseas, starting new businesses from scratch, corporate mergers, takeovers and shake-ups, and office politics.

Lombardo and McCall concluded that adversity instructs, that successful executives ask endless questions, that they surpass their less successful compatriots primarily because they learn more from all their experiences, and that they learn early in their careers to be comfortable with ambiguity.

In 1817, poet John Keats wrote in a letter to his brothers that the basis for real achievement was "negative capability . . . when a man is capable of being in uncertainties, mysteries, doubts, without any irritable reaching after fact and reason." There's probably no better definition of a contemporary leader than that.

John Gardner, the late founder of Common Cause and a former Health, Education, and Welfare secretary, listed creeping crises, the size and complexity of organizations and institutions, specialization, the current anti-leader climate, and the general and specific rigors of public life as the principal obstacles to leadership.

Norman Lear, too, sees obstacles as an integral part of leadership. "To be an effective leader, you not only have to get the group of followers on the right path, but you must be able to convince them that whatever obstacle stands in the way ahead, whether it's a tree or a building that blocks the view, you're going to get around it. You're not going to be put off by the apparent barriers to your goal. All journeys are filled with potholes and mines, but the only way we can move beyond them is to approach them, and recognize them for what they are. You have to see that it's only a tree, or whatever, and it's not insurmountable. Everywhere you trip is where the treasure lies."

Everywhere you trip is where the treasure lies. That's learning from surprise, as well as adversity. Virtually every leader I talked with would agree.

A number of them learned valuable lessons from difficult bosses—some even from bad bosses. The difference between the two is that bad bosses teach you what not to do. The difficult boss offers more complex lessons. A difficult boss can be challenging, picky, intimidating, arrogant, abrupt, and mercurial. But at the same time he can inspire, provide vision, and occasionally even care about you. A classic example of a difficult boss was media mogul Robert Maxwell. A true visionary who was discovered to be a crook after his mysterious death in 1991, Maxwell admitted to all of the flaws listed above during a "60 Minutes" interview. He once fired his son for forgetting to pick him up at the airport, and then rehired him six months later.

Anne Bryant told me of a difficult boss: "I worked for a woman whom I admired, thought was fabulous, but she always looked for the flaws in people, so she lost lots of good people. She is exciting, brilliant, a visionary, and she really moves and changes organization, but working for her is tough. I learned a lot from her—on both the positive and negative sides. If you're strong, you can learn from bad bosses, but if you're not strong, it's tough."

Barbara Corday described both a bad boss and a difficult one: "I think I learned some really important things from bad leaders. It's like having a parent where you say, 'I'll never treat my children that way.' . . . I worked years ago in New York for a man who was very abusive to people who worked for him—physically as well as mentally. He would take a guy and throw him up against a wall and yell at him. And then he would put an extra $50 in the pay envelope. I did not see any loyalty or good work coming out of that atmosphere. And I just went completely the other way. . . . My partner Barbara and I once worked for a man, a very famous, talented producer, who was unhappily married and had no particular interest in going home at night. Well, of course, what that translated to was that we wound up working terrible hours, well into the nights and weekends, because our boss didn't have a life that he cared about. The theory I got from that is that you can't force your lifestyle and your personal life on the people who work for you. . . . I think if I am known for anything in this industry, it is that anybody who has ever worked for me wants to work for me again."

Former Lucky Stores CEO Don Ritchey said that difficult bosses really "test your beliefs, and you learn all the things you don't want to do or stand for. I once was in a situation where I had to put up or shut up, and I quit, went back to school, to start a new career as a college administrator. Then a couple of years later, he was gone and I was rehired. Ultimately I became CEO." Ritchey worked for some very good bosses, but it was the difficult boss who had a crucial impact on his career.

With a weak boss, a leader in training may have to "manage upward."

Shirley Hufstedler said, "Some people, at bottom, really want the world to take care of them, rather than the other way around. Such people expect their followers to care for them. For such people, only a crisis—such as a serious illness, a life-threatening situation, a great personal or financial loss—can change them and/or their direction."

The ideal boss for a growing leader is probably a good boss with major flaws, so that one can learn all the complex lessons of what to do and what not to do simultaneously.

Ernest Hemingway said that the world breaks all of us, and we grow stronger in the broken places. That's certainly true of leaders. Their capability to rebound permits them to achieve, to realize their vision.

Robert Dockson told me of the time he was fired by the Bank of America: "It was one of the best things that ever happened to me, because if you can bounce back, you can learn a great deal."

Mathilde Krim overcame a deeper, more personal obstacle: "I always felt I was a little different," the distinguished scientist and activist told me.

This brings me to what I think of as the Wallenda Factor, a concept I described in detail in *Leaders* and so will recap only briefly here. Shortly after the great aerialist Karl Wallenda fell to his death in 1978 while doing his most dangerous walk, his wife, also an aerialist, said, "All Karl thought about for months before was falling. It was the first time he'd ever thought about that, and it seemed to me that he put all his energies into not falling rather than walking the tightrope." If we think more about failing at what we're doing than about doing it, we will not succeed.

Few other American leaders—none that I talked with—have experienced anything like the Tylenol crisis that Jim Burke had to deal with in the early 1980s. It was a calamity that could have destroyed Johnson & Johnson, but both the company and Burke emerged stronger and wiser than before. Burke talked at length about the crisis, and it was clear to me that at no moment did he think about not succeeding.

As you will recall, several people died from poison that had been inserted into Tylenol capsules. The story swept across the country like a fire storm, made more dramatic—and frightening—by the fact that no one knew who had poisoned the Tylenol or why or how many packages had been tainted. Burke took charge immediately. "I knew I had to and I knew I could," he said. "I had never been on television in my life, but I understood it, and I understood the public. I had three separate organizations doing research, one looking at it from an overall

Johnson & Johnson point of view, another looking at it from a product point of view, and then a group of our people out with TV cameras talking to consumers. I took tapes home every night and saw that everyone else who was making decisions saw them, so we could listen to the people, see them, and get some sense of their emotions, their reactions.

"I've been trained in market research and consumer marketing. I know the media. I was a news freak, and I'd dealt with the networks several times. I knew the heads of news, who to call, how to talk with them. I wasn't anxious to go to TV myself, but I was trying to get them to understand the problem and the need to handle it responsibly. I knew that the public, in the long run, was going to make the decision, not just for Tylenol and Johnson & Johnson, but how we marketed over-the-counter drugs in general. I was in this room twelve hours a day. I solicited advice from everyone, because no one had ever dealt with this kind of issue before. It was brand-new.

"My son said an interesting thing. He said that I had a philosophy of life which I felt strongly about, and all of a sudden, through an accident, that philosophy was tested, and all my experience was utilized in a unique way. Several very capable people told me they couldn't do what I was doing, and only one person here supported what I was doing. I knew we were not the bad guys, and I believed in the intrinsic fairness of the system, and I believed we'd be fairly treated. But when I decided to go on '60 Minutes,' the head of public relations told me it was the worst decision anyone in this corporation had ever made, and anyone who would risk this corporation that way was totally irresponsible, and he walked out and slammed the door.

"I had double-dated with Mike Wallace years before, and I met with him and his producer, who was the toughest monkey

I ever met. He'd been a prosecuting attorney, and he acted like one. What it came down to was that if we were absolutely straight with them, we'd do fine. And we did. After the show, we did some research, and the people who saw it were five times more apt to buy our products than those who didn't see it. I did 'Donahue,' too. He was very supportive, very helpful.

"I think it all worked because I was convinced that we had tremendous strengths as a company that we'd never used before. And there wasn't a doctor in the country we didn't call to ask about Tylenol. And we had everything we needed internally, including the moral strength. We put together the new packaging overnight practically, when it would have normally taken two years. But most important was the fact that we put the public first. We never hid anything from them and were as honest as we knew how to be. It just confirmed my belief that if you play it straight, it works.

"I lived on junk foods and about three or four hours' sleep a night, but it never seemed to bother me. I think it's true that the body creates the chemistries it needs to deal with emergencies. I also think I was sustained by the fact that I knew we were doing well. I was convinced we were going to save the brand, and we did."

Burke appeared on the cover of *Fortune* in June 1988, as part of a story on innovators—a highly deserved tribute.

Our leaders transform experience into wisdom and, in turn, transform the cultures of their organizations. In this way, society as a whole is transformed. It is neither a tidy nor necessarily logical process, but it's the only one we have.

Lynn Harrell, one of our great cellists and a former USC faculty member, once wrote in *Ovation* magazine: "It is, alas, almost impossible to teach magic. In my class at USC, twelve talented individuals and I search constantly for some way to define the undefinable. . . . But, in the end, they have to go out into the orchestra and do it for themselves. There is no substitute for the magic [of the orchestra]. It is why I snarl like a guard dog if I sense they are being walled off or screened from this experience. . . . I remember how it feels to be opened in this way when you are young, before the shell and the ordinariness sets in."

There is magic in experience, as well as wisdom. And more magic in stress, challenge, and adversity, and more wisdom. Crisis is so often the crucible in which leaders are formed. Look at the transformation of Rudolph Giuliani following 9/11.

Before the terrorist attacks on New York, Giuliani was a lame-duck mayor with a reputation for toughness rather than compassion, a reputation somewhat tarnished by his bitter breakup with wife Donna Hanover. But tragedy showed Giuliani to be a genuine leader, one who was able to communicate his vision of a brave, resilient New York in ways that comforted and inspired the devastated city. Following the collapse of the Twin Towers, he was a constant, tireless presence, skillfully handling such disparate details as keeping celebrities away from Ground Zero and walking brides down the aisles whose firefighter fathers or brothers had died in the attacks. Just as the chaos of the Blitz brought out the leader in Churchill, the chaos of 9/11 allowed Giuliani to become, in the words of the media, "Churchill in a baseball cap."

8
Getting People
on Your Side

Once more unto the breach, dear friends, once more . . .
Follow your spirit, and upon this charge
Cry "God for Harry, England, and Saint George!"

—WILLIAM SHAKESPEARE
The Life of King Henry V

What is it that makes us go riding unto the breach—following
even those leaders who don't have Will Shakespeare writing
their speeches? Some would argue that the answer is charisma,
and either you have it or you don't. I don't think it's that simple. In the course of my study, I met many leaders who couldn't
be described as charismatic by any sort of rhetorical stretch,
but they nevertheless managed to inspire an enviable trust and
loyalty in their co-workers. And through their abilities to get
people on their side, they were able to effect necessary changes
in the culture of their organizations and make real their guiding visions.

Ed, the fellow who surrendered to the context early in this
book, was not one of this group. When I first met him, the

147

complaint was only that he had no people skills. Ultimately, of course, Ed's problem was much deeper than that, but people skills deserve more attention than they often receive in discussions of leadership. Some of them can be taught; I'm not certain that all of them can. Empathy, for example—like charisma—may be something that people either have or don't have. Not all leaders have it, but many do—and as Marty Kaplan said, "I've known leaders who have had none of it and nevertheless were leaders, but those who have had that quality have moved and inspired me more." Gloria Steinem added, "There are a lot of excellent people who can't empathize very well."

As a CBS executive Barbara Corday worked through empathy, which she sees as particularly female: "I think women generally see power in a different way from men. I don't have any need for personal power, especially over people. I want to have the kind of power that is my company working well, my staff working well. . . . As moms and wives and daughters we've been caretakers, and a lot of the caretakers in our lives were women, and we continue in caretaking roles even as we get successful in business. And that feels natural to us. I have always been very pleased and happy and proud of the fact that I not only know all the people who work for me, but I know their husbands' and wives' names, and I know their children's names, and I know who's been sick, and I know what to ask. That's what's special to me in a work atmosphere. I think that's what people appreciate, and that's why they want to be there, and that's why they're loyal, and that's why they care about what they're doing. And I think that is peculiarly female."

The men I spoke with also talked of empathy, however. Herb Alpert said, "One of the keys to dealing with artists is to be sensitive to their feelings and their needs, to give them their day in court so they can air their grievances or their brilliant ideas."

Empathy isn't simply the province of artists. Former Lucky Stores CEO Don Ritchey said, "I think one of the biggest turn-ons is for people to know that their peers and particularly their bosses not only know they're there but know pretty intimately what they're doing and are involved with them on almost a daily basis, that it's a partnership, that you're really trying to run this thing well together, that if something goes wrong our goal is to fix it, not see who we can nail."

And, of course, empathy isn't the only factor in getting people on your side. Roger Gould explained how he took charge without taking control: "I've always been kind of a lone wolf, but when I was head of outpatient services at UCLA, I developed a kind of consensus leadership, based on getting the group to formulate the problems. If we had a problem or complaint, we dealt with it openly and immediately. The fact that I was the boss didn't mean that I would or could take sole responsibility. Everyone was living with the same complexity, so we had to deal with it as a group."

Sydney Pollack described the leader's need to have people on his side this way: "Up to a point, I think you can lead out of fear, intimidation, as awful as that sounds. You can make people follow you by scaring them, and you can make people follow by having them feel obligated. You can lead by creating guilt. There is a lot of leadership that comes out of fear, dependence, and guilt. The marine boot camp is famous for it. But the problem is that you're creating obedience with a residue of resentment. If you want to make a physics analogy, you'd be moving through the medium, but you'd be creating a lot of drag, a lot of backwash. There're two other qualities that I think are more positive reasons to follow someone. One is an honest belief in the person you're following. The other is selfish. The person following has to believe that following is the best thing to do at the time. I mean it has to be apparent to them that they are getting something better by following you than they ever would by not following you. You don't want people to follow you just because that's what they're paid for. Sometimes you can teach them something. 'You're going to learn more by doing this movie than you would by doing another movie,' let's say. You try to make everyone feel they have a stake in it."

Barbara Corday used some of the same words: "Getting people on your side has a lot to do with spirit, a lot to do with team atmosphere. I think it has a lot to do with not putting people in direct competition with each other, something that is not a universally held philosophy. I don't believe in personal competition in the workplace. I have always, in any place I've worked, worked very hard to rid the company or the show or the staff of internal politics. I've never worked well under the intimidation theory."

Former CEO Don Ritchey agreed. "A real essential for effective leadership is that you can't force people to do very much. They have to want to, and most times I think they want to if they respect the individual who is out front, if they have confidence that the person has some sort of vision for the company. . . . I don't have any flashes of brilliance of how you teach somebody to be a leader, but I know you can't lead unless somebody's willing to follow."

Gloria Steinem saw getting people on your side as the difference between "movement" leadership and "corporate" leadership—although she admitted that this might not be fair to the better kind of corporate leadership, such as Ritchey's surely was. "Movement leadership requires persuasion, not giving orders. There is no position to lead from. It doesn't exist. What makes you successful is that you can phrase things in a way that is inspirational, that makes coalitions possible. The movement has to be owned by a variety of people, not one group. For example, before we popularized the phrase 'reproductive freedom,' people talked about 'population control.' And that was divisive, because some poor people and some racial groups felt that this was directed at them. The problem was the phrase, which said that someone else was going to make the decision, not you. 'Reproductive freedom' tells you that the center of authority is in the individual. And that made coalitions possible. . . . There is no human being who's going to do what I say. None. Not even my assistant, who is too smart. The only power I have is the power of persuasion, or inspiration."

Betty Friedan also discussed the idea of leading through voice rather than position. "I have never fought for organizational power. I can have a great deal of influence just by my voice. I don't have to be president. I recently gave a speech at a university where only 2 percent of the faculty is women. I had a big crowd. I said, 'I must be in a place that is for some reason an anachronism.' I read the figures to them. I said, 'I'm surprised that you have not had a major class action suit.' You could see the tension in the room. I said, 'Of course, we have had eight years of Reagan, and the laws that affect discrimination haven't been enforced, but now we've got the Civil Rights Restoration Act. And you are really in a vulnerable position, since over 50 percent of your financing is federal funding. Just as a warning. Watch it.' Then I went on with the rest of my lecture. And something happened in that room. So the last ten years, I haven't been the head of any organization, but I don't need to be."

The underlying issue in leading from voice is trust—in fact, I believe that trust is the underlying issue in not only getting people on your side, but having them stay there. There are four ingredients leaders have that generate and sustain trust:

1. *Constancy*. Whatever surprises leaders themselves may face, they don't create any for the group. Leaders are all of a piece; they stay the course.
2. *Congruity*. Leaders walk their talk. In true leaders, there is no gap between the theories they espouse and the life they practice.
3. *Reliability*. Leaders are there when it counts; they are ready to support their co-workers in the moments that matter.
4. *Integrity*. Leaders honor their commitments and promises.

When these four factors are in place, people will be on your side. Again, these are the kinds of things that can't be taught. They can only be learned. Someone like Ed never understands their importance.

Frances Hesselbein said of her work with the Girl Scouts, "I think I've kept my promises. I've been able to communicate a vision, a future for the organization, and a respect for people. Personal and organizational integrity are key. But I have a passion for doing everything better and better, and a striving for excellence in everything we do. We're not managing for the sake of being great managers, we're managing for the mission. I don't believe in a star system. I believe in helping people identify what they can do well and releasing them to do it. Our whole focus is on membership, the delivery of services to the membership, and the opportunity that gives this organization and its six hundred thousand volunteers. It's a very exciting time. We're shifting the whole ecology of learning away from a specific class or place into problem areas and issues, so that the so-called problems become opportunities to serve in new ways."

As president of the Red Cross in the late 1980s, Richard Schubert used his voice to seek nothing less than a revolution in an old American institution. "It's harder to run the Red Cross than Bethlehem Steel because, first, you do everything in a fish-bowl here, and second, you're working for the most part with volunteers, and third, the nature of the organization demands full-time leadership. You can't ever just manage, you have to lead. I spend a lot of time in the trenches. It's important to me to understand the people we serve and their views of us. And I always keep in mind the global nature of the organization. There are really only two services that every chapter of the Red Cross must provide: disaster and support services to military families during crises. But we've created a new focus. We're not going to try to be all things to all people. We're going to be an emergency organization, and we basically let our chapters determine their community's needs in this area. Hence, anything you can think of in health and welfare is done by some Red Cross chapter."

Like Steinem and Friedan, Hesselbein and Schubert must lead with their voices. They understand the lesson of taking charge without taking control, that they must inspire their volunteers, not order them.

Leading from voice is a necessary condition for movement leadership, or for any situation in which the leader is dealing with volunteers. But the same ability to inspire and persuade through empathy and trust can be and should be present in all organizations. In his book *Leadership Is an Art*, Max De Pree,

CEO of Herman Miller, argues that's the best way to treat everyone: "The best people working for organizations are like volunteers. Since they could probably find good jobs in any number of groups, they choose to work somewhere for reasons less tangible than salary or position. Volunteers do not need contracts, they need covenants. . . . Covenantal relationships induce freedom, not paralysis. A covenantal relationship rests on shared commitment to ideas, to issues, to values, to goals, and to management process. Words such as love, warmth, personal chemistry, are certainly pertinent. Covenantal relationships . . . fill deep needs and they enable work to have meaning and to be fulfilling."

British philosopher Isaiah Berlin said, "The fox knows many things; the hedgehog knows but one." Leaders are both fox and hedgehog. They have mastered their vocation or profession, do whatever they do as well as it can be done, but they are also masters of the more fundamental, human skills. They're able to establish and maintain positive relationships with their subordinates inside the organization and their peers outside the organization. They have not only the ability to understand the organization's dimensions and purposes, but to articulate their understanding and make it manifest. They have the ability to inspire trust, but not abuse it. Don Ritchey said, "They [your co-workers] have to believe that you know what you're doing. You have to believe that they know what they're doing, too, and let them know that you trust them. I always took a little more time, told people more than they needed to know. . . . You have to be absolutely straight with people, not clever or cute, and you can't think that you can manipulate them. That doesn't mean you have to think they're all stars or that you have to agree with everything they do, but the relationship, I think, ought to be for real."

Ultimately, a leader's ability to galvanize his or her co-workers resides both in self understanding and in understanding the co-workers' needs and wants, along with understanding of what Hesselbein has called their mission. In such leaders, competence, vision, and virtue exist in nearly perfect balance. Competence, or knowledge, without vision and virtue, breeds technocrats. Virtue, without vision and knowledge, breeds ideologues. Vision, without virtue and knowledge, breeds demagogues.

As Peter Drucker has pointed out, the chief object of leadership is the creation of a human community held together by the work bond for a common purpose. Organizations and their leaders inevitably deal with human nature, which is why values, commitments, convictions, even passions are basic elements in any organization. Since leaders deal with people, not things, leadership without values, commitment, and conviction can only be inhumane and harmful.

Especially today, in the current volatile climate, it is vital that leaders steer a clear and consistent course. They must acknowledge uncertainties and deal effectively with the present, while simultaneously anticipating and responding to the future. This means endlessly expressing, explaining, extending, expanding, and when necessary revising the organization's mission. The goals are not ends, but ideal processes by which the future can be created.

INTEGRITY IS THE BASIS OF TRUST

A major challenge that all leaders are now facing is an epidemic of institutional malfeasance, as we read nearly every day in the news. And if there is anything that undermines trust, it is the feeling that the people at the top lack integrity, are without a solid sense of ethics. The characteristics of empathy and trust are reflected not just in codes of ethics, but in organizational cultures that support ethical conduct. Long before Enron became synonymous with corporate corruption, scholarly studies linked a lack of professional ethics to a business climate that not only condones greed, but rewards it. One classic study, done in the late 1980s by M. Cash Mathews at Washington State University, found that, ironically, corporations with codes of ethics are more frequently cited by federal agencies than those without such standards, because the codes usually emphasize improving company balance sheets. Further, Mathews noted that three-fourths of all such codes do not address such things as environmental and product safety. Mathews's conclusion is as valid as it ever was: "The codes are really dealing with infractions against the corporation, rather than illegalities on behalf of the corporation."

Frederick, who surveyed personal values in more than 200 Pittsburgh area managers, found that "people's personal values are getting blocked by the needs of the company." He mentioned an earlier study that included interviews with 6,000 executives and found that 70 percent of those surveyed felt pressure to conform to corporate standards and often compromised their own ethics on behalf of their employer. If executives didn't continue to feel pressure to conform to dubious corporate ethics, the subprime mortgage debacle would have never happened.

This corporate ethical decline is a direct result of the bottom-line mentality. Norman Lear condemns this kind of thinking: "I think that where the greatest impact on the culture might have been, in other times, the church, education, the family, the greatest impact now is business. Everywhere one looks, it seems to me that short-term thinking in business is the greatest impact on our culture. And that's leadership, because it's certainly educating kids to believe there's nothing between winning and losing. . . . Short-term thinking is the societal disease of our time."

Other leaders agreed with Lear, noting that if companies devoted as much time and attention to product quality as they do to trying to skirt laws and buy officials, their bottom lines would probably improve.

While studies of the relationship between corporate ethics and corporate bottom lines have been inconclusive (most show there is no relationship), Jim Burke pointed out that ethical corporations can be consistently profitable, as Johnson & Johnson was on his watch. He said, "It's possible to create a culture that attracts the qualities that you value in people. You can call that leadership, or you can call it creating a positive culture and articulating a vision."

Former Lucky Stores CEO Don Ritchey agreed. "I start out with the presumption that most people want to be ethical. It's sort of a Golden Rule philosophy. So if you set up a climate where you not only say it, but where people see that you mean it, and it works, then nobody has to make expedient choices because somebody was leaning on him, telling him on the one hand to be ethical and on the other hand to make the number even if he has to be cute about it. The fact that you are very hard-nosed about weeding out unethical behavior helps. If we caught somebody cheating on the gross profit, for instance, we'd tell him to get there the right way, or we'd rather he was short. And the next time it happens, he's out. . . . Ethics is not

Pollyanna stuff. It works better. . . . I was particularly fortunate, working for this company. I never had to choose in daily decisions between what was the right thing to do and what was good business."

But according to then Korn/Ferry International CEO Richard Ferry, Burke, Ritchey, and the others concerned with more than the short-term bottom line are still exceptions. He said, "There are some brilliant CEOs running American companies, executives who clearly understand what it'll take to be competitive in the future, but they're caught in a bind. The only way they can protect themselves against hostile takeovers is to get the stock price up. Anyone who's really thinking about the future is putting the company—and his or her career—at risk, because investing a fair amount of money in areas such as research and development and new products has no immediate payoff. . . . Companies may write a fancy job description. There'll be a lot of discussion about long-term strategy, but, in the end, they want an executive who is going to deliver earnings."

Burke, for one, was committed to fighting this social disease. And Norman Lear's description of how Burke raised the consciousness of his fellow CEOs is still relevant today. Lear said: "Jim Burke has put together some lunches where he has invited other CEOs, and at the beginning they are all interested in how the image of business can be improved. They aren't willing to admit readily the enormous contribution business is making to its own poor image. And as the time passes and people relax, you find them all aware that they need help. That business needs help. They're not villains—they didn't start the obsession with short-term thinking. They know it's wrong, but they're in traps that they can't find their way out of. They need somebody to put a spotlight on it, so that what's wrong will be seen by everybody. They can contribute quietly, but they can't say, 'I'm not going to be involved in short-term thinking.' Their obligation is to shareholders, and the shareholders are represented by Wall Street, and that's a vise they can't get out of. But if they can find a way to focus on it, the climate can change, and then they can change with it."

USING YOUR VOICE FOR CHANGE

Leading through voice, inspiring through trust and empathy, does more than get people on your side. It can change the climate enough to give people elbow room to do the right things. When they use their voices among their peers, leaders like Burke improve the general climate as well as reshape their own organizations to deal more effectively with the world.

The leader may discover that the culture of his or her own organization is an obstacle to positive change, because as currently constituted, it is more devoted to preserving itself than to meeting new challenges.

While at Apple, John Sculley talked about the need for organizations to change: "If you look at the post-World War II era, when we were at the center of the world's economy during the industrial age, the emphasis was on self-sufficiency in every sort of enterprise—in education, business, or government. Organizations were very hierarchical. That model is no longer appropriate. The new model is global in scale, an interdependent network. So the new leader faces new tests, such as how does he lead people who don't report to him—people in other companies, in Japan or Europe, even competitors. How do you lead in this idea-intensive, interpendent-network environment? It requires a wholly different set of skills, based on ideas, people skills, and values. The things I'm talking about aren't really new, but are now in a new context. What used to be peripheral is now mainstream. A shift in orientation has occurred in just the last ten years. Traditional leaders are having a hard time explaining what's going on in the world, because they're basing their explanations on their experience with the old paradigm, and if you place the same set of events or facts in a different paradigm, you may not be able to explain them."

Sculley continued: "My former boss at Pepsico and the current head of IBM were both World War II fighter pilots. The World War II fighter pilot is no longer going to be our principal paradigm for leaders. The new generation of leaders is going to be more intellectually aware. What does it mean to go from an industrial age to an information age? Beyond the ways we have to change as leaders and managers within the context of our enterprise, the world itself is changing, becoming more idea-intensive, more information-intensive, so the people who're going to surface, to rise to the top, are going to be people who are comfortable with and excited by ideas and information.

"I used to go on corporate boards so I could learn, but since coming to Apple, I've resigned from all of them."

Robert Dockson had to change a negative climate when he arrived at CalFed: "When I came here, no one ever tried to teach me the business. It was a divided company, and it had factions with walls around them. They refused to speak to each other. I wondered if I'd made a terrible mistake. There were eleven senior vice presidents, and they all wanted my job. I decided that I wasn't going to clean house, that I was going to win all of them over, make them work with me instead of against me, and that's what I did.

"I think the first thing one has to do [in setting out to change a culture] is get people on one's side and show them where you want to take the company. Trust is vital. People trust you when you don't play games with them, when you put everything on the table and speak honestly to them. Even if you aren't very articulate, your intellectual honesty comes through, and people recognize that and respond positively.

"I think you have trust in a man who has vision and can make you see that his vision is the right thing to do. I believe that this company can be one of the dominant financial institutions in the Pacific basin, and I want my successor, whoever he is, to have that vision. I don't want him to manage, I want him to lead."

Jim Burke found much that was good at Johnson & Johnson, but he found some gaps, too. "I had a real vision. I thought I saw what the future was going to be, and I understood what we needed in order to achieve that future. I began to see what was here in terms of a value system, and what wasn't here in terms of understanding sophisticated marketing principles. There was a kind of vacuum.

"The environment at Johnson & Johnson helps people learn to lead because we have a high degree of decentralization. General Johnson utilized a system of product managers because he saw that as institutions became larger and larger, it was more and more important to set up smaller entities within the whole in order to get things done. He wanted to find that unit within the whole that would liberate creative energy by permitting decision making.

"I've always operated on the assumption that creative confusion and conflict are healthy. Sometimes I take the opposite side simply to stir up controversy, because I think better that way, and the system works better that way.

"The freer the organization is, the more heterogeneity there is in the system, the more leaders will emerge. One of the problems with American business is its habit of marching to the style of one leader, and his style becomes enmeshed in the organization. This leads to vertical, hierarchical organizations, and I think that's the wrong way to get things done. Here we're decentralized and open, and people get things done in very different ways."

All of the leaders I talked with believe in change—in both people and organizations. They equate it with growth—tangible and intangible—and progress. Indeed, it might be said that their real life's work has been change. But change in the world at large can be an obstacle, too. "Circumstances beyond our control" is an organizational reality all too often.

Change, of course, isn't new. As Adam and Eve left Eden, Adam might have said, "We're now entering a period of transition." I've written more than thirty books, and in one sense or another, every single one of them has had to do with change, and coping with change. Still, the world has never been more volatile, more turbulent, and more spastic than it is now. Uncertainty is rampant. What's worse, in too many cases we can't even identify the causes or sources of this turbulence.

Leaders not only manage change, they must be comfortable with it in their own lives. Barbara Corday, as noted above, said, "I've had at least four completely different careers, and may very well have a fifth." Since then, she has done just that, becoming a professor of media and an administrator at the University of Southern California.

Marty Kaplan went from the Aspen Institute to Washington, D.C., to Walt Disney Pictures, and, most recently, to USC. When I interviewed him at Disney, he said, "One of the nice things about this industry is that you can be in it in a lot of quite different capacities. I'm not all that interested in slithering up a greasy pole, and I've pretty much decided that sometime within the next year I'll change my capacity in the business and go to a world in which it's time to start learning again. My guess is that I'll be a screenwriter and producer."

Alfred Gottschalk insisted that an escape clause be inserted in his contract with Hebrew Union: "I can stay basically until retirement. That's what they would like. I insisted they put it in, in case one or the other of us becomes disaffected, at which point we have to talk. I don't intend to stay one day longer than I'm happy with what I'm doing, and they don't have to keep me for one day longer than they're happy with what I'm doing, and for the last seventeen years it's worked. . . . They know what the core issues are for which I stand, and if it comes to a showdown on those, they know I have my resignation in my pocket."

Don Ritchey, too, said, "You should preserve the ability to say, 'Shove it,' and go your own way. That really frees you."

These leaders have dealt with and continue to deal with this mercurial world by anticipating, looking not just down the road, but around the corner; by seeing change as an opportunity, rather than an obstacle; and by accepting it, rather than resisting it. One of the hardest lessons any novice skier has to learn is to lean away from the hill and not into it. The natural inclination is to stay as close to the slope as possible, because it feels safer and more secure. But only when the skier leans out can he or she begin to move and gain control, rather than being controlled by

163

the slope. The organizational novice does the same thing: leans close to the company's slope, submerging his or her own identity in that of the corporation. The leader stands tall and leans out, taking charge of his or her own course, with a clear view of where the course is going—at least until the snow starts to fall.

Resisting change is as futile as resisting weather, and change—relentless change—is our weather now. It is that constant and that unpredictable. Leaders live in it, and so do organizations. And there is much organizations can do to make the process easier.

9
Organizations Can Help—or Hinder

I am tempted to believe that what we call necessary
institutions are no more than institutions to which we have
become accustomed. In matters of social constitution, the
field of possibilities is much more extensive than men
living in their various societies are ready to imagine.

—ALEXIS DE TOCQUEVILLE
Democracy in America

Buffeted by the tides of change, by forces that didn't even exist
a generation ago, under siege on all sides, too many organizations have simply hunkered down defensively. But like the old
joke, they prepare for nuclear attack by gathering the wagons
into a circle. They will not move and will not be moved. Meanwhile, outside the circle, everything is in motion.

Although more and more organizations claim to welcome
change, it is as unsettling as it ever was. In recent years, nonprofit organizations have seen their costs soar, their sources of
revenue dry up, their endowments shrink, and their missions
challenged. Corporate America has been roiled by scandal on a

scale not seen since widespread corruption kept muckrakers busy early in the twentieth century. Instant communication and globalization are our new realities, and, as a result, the markets dance to hitherto unheard-of rhythms. The character of work itself has changed, as more and more people have a string of careers instead of making a lifetime commitment to a single institution. J. Paul Getty once said that he had three secrets for success: one, get up early; two, work hard; three, find oil. Somehow nothing seems that simple anymore.

Change cannot be viewed as the enemy—instead, it is the source of both personal growth and organizational salvation. Only by changing themselves can organizations get back into the game and get to the heart of things.

There are three major forces working on the world today:

- *Technology*

    The most significant invention of the last fifty years is the integrated circuit. Forty workers can now produce what it once took 1,200 workers to produce. Someone said that factories of the future will be run by a man and a dog. The man's role will be to feed the dog. The dog's role will be to prevent the man from touching the machinery. Change *man* to *person*, and the observation continues to ring true.

    The computer and the creation of the World Wide Web have transformed the world. The web has sped the creation of virtual communities, groups of like-minded people who would never have found each other without it. The results have been positive and negative. Creative collaboration is now possible on an unprecedented scale, by people based all over the world. Today, backyard astronomers help discover heavenly bodies overlooked by the great academic astronomers of the past. On the downside, international terrorists are using the Internet to organize attacks on crowded buildings, night clubs, and other "soft targets" around the globe. Another technology-related fear is that the unwired minority may become even more of an underclass than it already is.

It is hard to overstate the extent to which digital technology is reshaping our lives. Virtually unheard of in the twentieth century, blogs have become a staple of everyday life throughout the increasingly wired world. There were some 15,000 blogs (short for "web logs") in 2002. By mid-2007 some 70 million filled the so-called blogosphere. Thanks to free, easy-to-use software, anyone can create a blog, and it often seems that everyone has. Genuine experts use their blogs to share what they know, companies use them to build brands and practice crisis control, people use them to promote themselves, crackpots fill them with their eccentric views. Blogs on all sides of the political spectrum were a major force in the 2008 American presidential election. For better or for worse, they have eroded the already waning power of mainstream media, allowing a vast corps of self-selected citizen journalists to emerge. When they function as digital whistleblowers, bloggers make corporate and political leaders more accountable. Bloggers in China, Iran, and other countries are forcing greater and greater transparency on authoritarian governments that try, with less and less success, to maintain control. Blogs are the midwives of countless new fads and a challenge to traditional notions of expertise. Social networks such as MySpace and Facebook have also changed how we relate to each other, organize behind causes or against them, and present ourselves to the world. On the downside, the Internet can ruin reputations as well as make them, as we are reminded by the occasional, tragic suicide of some teen who has been digitally assaulted.

On another front, imaging technology is unlocking the secrets of the brain, revealing the specific areas of the brain that engage in economic decision-making and other forms of human behavior. We now know that the brain is far more plastic than previously thought, capable of growth and repair well into adult life. Current reproductive technology allows children to come into the world in ways that were once confined to science fiction. The genetic code has been cracked, and an animal cloned. And as remarkable as all these breakthroughs are, they will undoubtedly pale next to some dazzling discovery not quite ready yet to emerge from an obscure bioengineering lab.

- *Global interdependence*

Twenty years ago, Japan was quickly becoming the major player in the world economy, and an American business day often began with a check of the yen-dollar ratio. Fifty percent of downtown Los Angeles was owned by the Japanese, and foreign investment throughout the country—in real estate, finance, and business—was widespread enough to be a matter of national concern.

Today, global interconnectivity means every economy and every nation is vulnerable to a misstep or malfeasance in any single country. Lead-tainted toys made in China threaten children and hurt Christmas sales in the United

States. The subprime mortgage crisis born in the U.S. rattles economies around the world. Economic rewards are also more broadly shared. Silicon Valley has clones throughout the United States, in Austin, Texas, for example, and there are thriving high-tech centers in Ireland, India, China, and many other countries as well. When the Irish economy began to slump recently, once-strife-ridden Northern Ireland began attracting high-tech jobs. Who could have imagined twenty years ago that many of the former Soviet socialist republics would be absorbed into a single Europe, with a common currency and passport? Today the twenty-seven nations that make up the EU (Croatia, Macedonia, and Turkey remain candidates for inclusion) have a population of almost 500 million and generate some 30 percent of the world's Gross National Product—$16.8 trillion in 2007. China's economic clout is enormous and continues to grow as that nation unleashes the frustrated entrepreneurial energy of 1.3 billion people. McKinsey researchers predict that, over the next decade, the global marketplace will swell by almost a billion new consumers as people in emerging nations begin to earn annual salaries of $5,000 or more, the minimum required for discretionary spending.

- *Demographics and values*

    The American population is aging. Is it ever. According to the 2000 census, 77 million Americans are 50 or older. That's an increase of 21 percent in a decade. Those over 50 are the nation's fastest growing age group, and they require a whole constellation of new goods and services. In 2008 38.7 million Americans were 65 or older—12.7 percent of the population. That number is expected to grow to 88.5 million by 2050, when one in five will be 65 or older. One consequence of the graying of America is a growing fear on the part of younger Americans that they will have to bear the financial burden for their retired elders. In large part because older Americans are healthier than ever, they are redefining age, increasingly bringing the activism they exercised in the 1960s and '70s to bear on age-related causes. At the same time, America continues to be obsessed with youth. And Baby Boomers and other older Americans worry about such catastrophic ailments as Alzheimer's disease—a fear that has created its own lingo, with the term "senior moment" used almost as a magic charm every time an older person forgets a name or phone number.

The demographics of the workplace have also changed. At the beginning of the twenty-first century, only 15 percent of those entering the work force were white males, with 25 percent white females, and the balance Latino, black, and Asian. Latinos are the fastest growing minority in America. Their numbers increased more than 50 percent between 1990 and 2000, to 35.3 million. In 2008, the country's Latinos numbered 46.7 million—15 percent of the population. Since 2000, the Latino community has grown larger than the African American community, which numbered 41.1 million, or 13.5 percent, in 2008. That disparity is expected to grow wider by 2050, when the Latino population is projected to reach 132.8 million, the African American population, 65.7 million. (In 2008 the Asian and Pacific Islander population was 5 percent.) The Latinization of America is changing everything from national politics to the way consumer goods are marketed. At the same time, more and more Americans identify themselves as of more than one race or ethnicity—a trend that many hail as a welcome antidote to tribalism and separation. The new president, whose father was a black Kenyan and whose mother a white Kansan, may have accelerated the trend when he playfully referred to himself as a "mutt" at his first post-election press conference.

The American consumer is increasingly sophisticated, demanding more emphasis on quality and safety in products, more and better service, and more products that save time as well as energy. As evidenced by the brisk sales of hybrid cars and the cachet of bamboo flooring and other green products, more and more Americans are concerned about the environment and the health of the planet. And as more and more mothers as well as fathers work, Americans long for better balance in their lives and seek ways—from aromatherapy to yoga—to reduce stress and simplify their hectic lives.

Each of these alterations is enormous in its impact and implications separately, but taken together, along with all their multiple interactions, they constitute a revolution. And a revolution in progress always triggers additional shifts and slides as it moves through the territory.

Once upon a time, a company introduced a new product, marketed it, and sold it. There was competition, of course, but there was plenty of room in the consumer arena for everyone. Now it's very different. Tom Peters sketched a typical scenario for doing business in the 1980s. As a company prepared to go to market with a product, it found the following entities there:

- A new competitor from Korea.
- An established Japanese company that had slashed costs and improved quality.
- A new American company—or several—starting up.
- An old-line American company with a new approach.
- A longtime competitor who's sold off a company with a great distribution setup.
- A company that now has an electronically based distribution system enabling it to slash delivery time by 75 percent.

And it found that it must accomplish new tasks:

- Target the market in segments.
- Respond to new consumer demands and tastes, which change rapidly.
- Deal with gyrating currencies.
- Suffer disruptions in service from offshore suppliers, as when their mother countries default on debt payments.

Today, the market is even more complex—although the company bringing its new product to market need only worry about the gyrating euro in selling to much of Europe. Niche marketing is more and more important than Tom imagined—it has transformed the magazine business, for example, and special-interest magazines now seem to be the only ones that thrive, including a raft of magazines such as *Real Simple* that offer tips on how to slow down and mellow out. Guerrilla marketing is the norm today, facilitated by the Internet. New competitors can now appear almost overnight and wrest market share away from corporate giants that can't move with the speed of light.

Along with Peters's list, consider some other phenomena of the age:

- The Internet and the World Wide Web.
- Cable TV and satellite transmissions.
- Single-parent families, working mothers, one-person households, and non-traditional families.
- Exploding housing costs such that only one in five families can afford to buy a house, in many parts of the country.
- HMOs, rising patient dissatisfaction, and exploding health and medical costs.
- E-commerce.
- The litigious, adversarial character of society.
- Fractured and fragmented constituencies.
- Rising non–English-speaking and illiterate population.
- Persistent poverty, drug abuse, and homelessness.
- International terrorism.

Since the organization is now the primary social, economic, and political form, and since business is a dominant cultural force in America, organizations in general and business in particular must deal with these sweeping and profound alterations in American society. Many new organizations and businesses have been, to lesser and greater degrees, designed to function effectively in this volatile climate. But the last great overall transformation in American business took place between 1890 and 1910, when the modern corporation was forged. It had two primary characteristics: multiple operating units and managerial hierarchies. Clearly, it is time for another transformation, and the key to such a transformation is the organization's attitude toward its workers.

Because the organization is the primary form of the era, it is also the primary shaper. The organization is, or should be, a social architect—but this means that its executives must be social architects, too. First of all, they must guarantee that their organizations are honest, ethical institutions. Then, they must redesign their organizations in order to redesign society along more humane and functional lines. They need, in a word, to be leaders, rather than managers.

The great American corporations reflected and were extensions of their founders. The Ford Motor Company was Henry Ford. General Motors was Alfred Sloan. RCA was Robert Sarnoff. Today's corporations, too, are reflections of their chiefs, but things aren't as simple now, and the reflections are often fractured. Further, the great old corporations were agents of change—Henry Ford paid assembly line workers an unheard-of wage: $5 per day!—while today's large corporations are, too often, its victims.

In this service-intensive, information-intensive age, every organization's primary resource is its people. Until the dot-com debacle of the 1990s, more and more organizations had come to appreciate that ideas and the people who have them are their treasure. Good people were wooed, facilitated, and rewarded. But as soon as the economy began to cool in 2000, too many organizations once again began to see workers, not as unique assets, but as interchangeable liabilities. This archaic attitude allows the organization to dismiss the potential contributions of *all* its members and prevents it from fully using its major resource in its effort to remake itself. Like the individual, the organization must learn from its experience and fully deploy itself and all of its assets; and like the individual, it must lead, not merely manage, if it is to fulfill its promise.

Despite his anti-Semitism and other character flaws, Henry Ford was a leader with an extraordinary vision. That vision was made manifest in the Ford Motor Company. But vision, like the world itself, is dynamic, not static, and must be renewed, adapted, adjusted. And when it becomes too dim, it must be abandoned and replaced.

The Ford Motor Company ran on its founder's vision until it ran down. Today, Ford, like the rest of America's auto industry, is fighting for survival. After bleeding billions of dollars for years, the industry is trying to reinvent itself in a twenty-first-century context. In late 2008, Ford and the other car companies hoped for a government rescue package that would buy them time to reinvent themselves, likely by building more hybrids and other green cars and marketing to consumers who care more about endangered species than trunk capacity. If the Ford Motor Company ultimately succeeds, it will be a collaborative effort, including corporate leaders, innovative designers, factory workers, unions, and public officials who believe the auto industry is worth saving. In musical terms, the rescue of Ford and its competitors will depend on the coordinated efforts of a full orchestra of contributors working in harmony. It won't be the one-man-band that made Henry Ford rich and famous in a simpler time.

Only the most innovative organizations have begun truly to tap into their primary resource, their people, much less given them the means to do what they are capable of doing. Indeed, many have taken the opposite tack, eschewing loyalty to workers, pruning rather than nurturing, and focusing almost exclusively on the bottom line. In the 1980s, the *New York Times* described the corporate scene as characterized by "a generation of ruthless management." Starting in 1993, "re-engineering the corporation" was the rage (the term was the title of a best-seller by Michael Hammer and James Champy), which often meant slashing staff, not rethinking every operation as the authors intended. Ruthless management may succeed in holding change at bay for a while, but only visionary leadership will succeed over time. Proof of that was the wild success, for a time, of the dot-coms, where talent was king. When visionary leadership is combined with sound business practices, the result can be success that lasts.

In *Thriving on Chaos,* Tom Peters says that organizations that succeed over time will have certain characteristics in common:

- A flatter, less hierarchical structure.
- More autonomous units.
- An orientation toward high-value-added goods and service.
- Quality controls.
- Service controls.
- Responsiveness.
- Innovative speed.
- Flexibility.
- Highly trained and skilled workers who use their minds as well as their hands.
- Leaders at all levels, rather than managers.

These leaders will take on new tasks within their organizations, tasks unimagined a generation ago, but vital now. They include

- Defining the organization's mission, so as to frame its activities and inform its work force.
- Creating a flexible environment in which people are not only valued, but encouraged to develop to their full potential, and treated as equals rather than subordinates.

176

- Reshaping the corporate culture so that creativity, autonomy, and continuous learning replace conformity, obedience, and rote; and long-term growth, not short-term profit, is the goal.
- Transforming the organization from a rigid pyramid to a fluid circle, or an ever-evolving network of autonomous units.
- Encouraging innovation, experimentation, and risk taking.
- Anticipating the future by reading the present.
- Making new connections within the organizations, and new relationships within the work force.
- Making new alliances outside the organization.
- Constantly studying the organization from the outside as well as the inside.
- Identifying weak links in the chain and repairing them.
- Thinking globally, rather than nationally or locally.
- Identifying and responding to new and unprecedented needs in the work force.
- Being proactive rather than reactive, comfortable with ambiguity and uncertainty.

In sum, Peters describes a world of people who are leading—not merely managing.

To succeed in this volatile environment, leaders must be creative and concerned, yet neither creativity nor concern is high on the agenda of many corporations, or not as high as, say, cost-consciousness would be. True leaders must be global strategists, innovators, masters of technology—all of which require new knowledge and understanding, which far too few companies supply, or even encourage. Albert Einstein said, "The world that we have made, as a result of the level of thinking we have done thus far, creates problems that we cannot solve at the same level at which we created them." Or, as a friend of mine put it, "Sometimes the only way to make the Coke machine work is to give it a good kick."

We've talked about people who followed failures with success because they got kicked around a little. Being kicked around can be a real eye opener. When I was a graduate student at MIT, I was required for a course in clinical psychology to go to a Boston psychiatric hospital and find a patient whom I would see once a week, under supervision. The first time I went there, I extended my hand, and the patient proceeded to kick me in the shins. As a result, I had to examine everything I had assumed about social etiquette from a new and different level. In the same way, organizations now need a good kick to get them started again, to upend their assumptions.

Gandhi said, "We must be the change we wish to see in the world." As organizations transform themselves, they will transform the world. To date, organizations have done far more to stifle leadership than to encourage it.

I think we've covered all the modes of discouragement, along with their effects. So how do organizations encourage leadership? As we have seen, the basis for leadership is learning, and principally learning from experience. In their book *Lessons of Experience*, Morgan W. McCall, Jr., Michael M. Lombardo, and Ann M. Morrison report that when they asked top executives what advice they would give to younger executives, there were three basic themes:

1. Take advantage of every opportunity.
2. Aggressively search for meaning.
3. Know yourself.

These are, of course, the same themes expressed by leaders with whom I spoke. Therefore, the organization must offer its employees the kinds of experiences that will enable them to learn and, finally, to lead.

Leaders are not made by corporate courses, any more than they are made by their college courses, but by experience. Therefore, it is not devices, such as "career path planning," or training courses, that are needed, but an organization's commitment to providing its potential leaders with opportunities to learn through experience in an environment that permits growth and change. Organizations tend to pay lip service to leadership development, but a study done by Lyman Porter and Lawrence McKibbon showed that only 10 percent of the companies surveyed devoted any time to it. A few companies have found creative ways to ensure future leaders. One of the best is General Electric's "People Factory"—a veritable leadership university that then CEO Jack Welch established at Crotonville, New York. Intel is another pioneer in leadership development, investing more than $5,000 a year for each employee. But these organizations are the exception, and that must change. Here, then, are the ways in which organizations can encourage and stimulate learning.

OPPORTUNITY = EMPOWERMENT

Leadership opportunities should be offered to all would-be leaders early in their careers, because they build drive, trigger a can-do spirit, and inspire self-confidence. Such opportunities include line-to-staff transfers to utilize, test, and develop strategic and conceptual skills in addition to tactical skills, task force assignments to review and revise old policy or make new policy, troubleshooting, and overseas posts.

Special projects are also an excellent proving ground. For example, in the 1980s, PacBell sent teams to set up temporary communications systems at both the Democratic National Convention and the 1984 Olympics in Los Angeles. In each case, the teams had to invent, improvise, and devise ways to make these temporary systems work efficiently, and they had to do it under severe time constraints. Above all, they had to do it so that PacBell made a profit.

It was a revelatory experience for everyone involved. In effect, what the teams were asked to do was to design, build, and operate a highly sophisticated phone system, sufficient to serve a small town, starting from scratch, in a very short time. They then had to dismantle it with equal speed and efficiency. Having done it successfully, the teams were changed in some basic way. They had been given an extraordinary test, and they had passed with flying colors. According to PacBell, team members were transformed by this experience into potential leaders.

Other corporations have devised ingenious ways to test and season aspiring leaders, according to McCall et al. Among them are

1. Establishing venture capital pools to enable potential leaders to start new entities.
2. Turning small low-margin businesses over to young managers.
3. Hanging on to troubled businesses and giving would-be leaders a shot at turning them around.

180

More often than not, new blood brings with it a fresh approach and new ideas, and so fix-its, slack areas, resistant personnel, may all be galvanized by the deployment of a young executive with the authority to lead, not merely manage.

In the same way, if there's a new venture in the works—whether it's an entire new division, a new product, a new service, or a new marketing campaign—aspiring leaders should at the very least be included on the team, and at best put in charge. The venture will benefit from their fresh perspective and they will learn from the experience of creating something from the ground up.

Robert Townsend, the iconoclastic leader who turned Avis around in the 1960s, was a great believer in executives knowing the business from the ground up, and from the customers' point of view. Every Avis executive was required to don the Avis red jacket and work at the company checkout stations regularly. Similarly, the great German composer-conductor Gustav Mahler required every member of his symphony orchestra to sit out in the audience at regular intervals to see how it sounded and looked from the audience's point of view. Clifton Wharton, former Chairman and CEO of TIAA-CREF, the world's largest pension plan, said, "You can spot people with potential as they're coming up the ranks. It's important to nurture that potential and help bring it along. There's no obvious consistency in personality types or models. But there are underlying similarities, one of which is having almost a sixth sense about how to make things work. Some people just seem to know, to have a grasp, and the ability to provide vision. They have the commitment and enthusiasm necessary to bring things about."

Job rotation is another means of affording would-be leaders an opportunity to learn more about the organization as well as to see it from another perspective. It is common practice now for marketing people to sit in on product planning, but it should be equally common practice for product designers and planners to go out into the marketplace. Other areas into which aspiring leaders should rotate are long-term planning, client negotiations, sales, and—again—overseas slots.

The higher the stakes, the more opportunities there are for learning—and, of course, the more opportunities there are for failures and mistakes. But as we have seen, failures and mistakes are major sources of vital experience. As virtually every leader I talked with said, there can be no growth without risks and no progress without mistakes. Indeed, if you don't make mistakes, you aren't trying hard enough. But as mistakes are necessary, so is a healthy organizational attitude toward them. First, risk taking must be encouraged. Second, mistakes must be seen as an integral part of the process, so that they are regarded as normal, not abnormal. Third, corrective action rather than censure must follow.

Aviator Brooke Knapp said, "There are two kinds of people: those who are paralyzed by fear, and those who are afraid but go ahead anyway. Life isn't about limitation, it's about options." A healthy organizational culture encourages the belief in options.

In this same area, as we've seen, and as Morgan McCall et al. also found, potential leaders learn as much, if not more, from difficult bosses as good bosses. But feedback is always more productive than confrontations, and honesty is always better, and more instructive, than meaningless pleasantries.

All organizations, especially those that are growing, walk a tightrope between stability and change, tradition and revision. Therefore they must have some means for reflecting on their own experiences and offering reflective structures to their employees.

MEANING = ENGAGEMENT

The executives surveyed by McCall and his colleagues said that while the notion of mentors was a nice idea, it didn't work very well, either because they didn't stay in one place in the organization long enough to benefit from such a relationship or because the so-called mentors were relatively ineffectual. But the organization itself should serve as a mentor. Its behavior, its tone, and its pace instruct, positively or negatively, and its values, both human and managerial, prevail. If its meaning, its vision, its purposes, its reason for being, is not clear, if it does not reward its employees in tangible and symbolic ways for work well done, then its reflective structures are inadequate, and in effect it's flying blind.

Corporate vision operates on three levels: strategic, which is the organization's overriding philosophy; tactical, which is that philosophy in action; and personal, which is that philosophy made manifest in the behavior of each employee. If you want to measure the effectiveness of, say, a retail operation, measure the attitude of any clerk in any store. If the clerk is rude, uninformed, helpless, chances are the top executives either are inept or lack a coherent vision. To enlarge on an Emerson statement mentioned earlier: the organization is only half itself; the other half is its expression.

Because reflection is vital—at every level, in every organization—and because burnout is a very real threat in today's hectic atmosphere, all executives should practice the new three R's: retreat, renewal, and return. Academia has long recognized the value of the sabbatical, and so should other organizations. Ken Olson, then CEO of Digital Equipment, took two weeks off every summer and spent them canoeing, far from phones or any other links with his office. Then Prosecutor Jamie Raskin said, "When I've finished all my work and talked to everyone I talk to, then come those moments when nothing's in the way, and I feel most intensely those things that are true in me." Those moments when nothing's in the way. It's in such moments that meaning begins to emerge, and understanding, and new questions, and fresh challenges.

John Sculley summed it up: "Organizations can do a lot to assure that they don't have good leaders. There are things in the organization, the roots of its culture, the bureaucracy of its processes, that make it very difficult for even talented people to rise and become strong leaders." But organizations can also do a lot to ensure the rise of their most talented people. Just as thought should precede action, reflection should follow it, on the organizational as well as the personal level.

LEARNING = LEADING

An organization should, by definition, function organically, which means that its purposes should determine its structure, rather than the other way around, and that it should function as a community rather than a hierarchy, and offer autonomy to its members, along with tests, opportunities, and rewards, because ultimately an organization is merely the means, not the end.

Since the release and full use of the individual's potential is the organization's true task, all organizations must provide for the growth and development of their members and find ways of offering them opportunities for such growth and development.

This is the one true mission of all organizations and the principal challenge to today's organizations.

10
Forging the Future

> In a time of drastic change, it is the learners
> who inherit the future. The learned find themselves
> equipped to live in a world that no longer exists.
>
> —ERIC HOFFER
> QUOTED IN
> *Vanguard Management*

I began this book with a chapter on mastering the context, and I'd like to end it the same way. I offered two stories, one of Ed, who surrendered to the context, and another of Norman Lear, who conquered it. You may recall that the board of directors that ultimately refused to promote Ed was looking for five qualities in a new leader: technical competence (which Ed had), people skills, conceptual skills, judgment and taste, and character. Those are all important qualities, and I think the board was moving in the right direction. But these are complicated times we live in, and even more will be required of tomorrow's leaders. As Abigail Adams wrote to her son John Quincy Adams, "These are the hard times in which a genius would wish to live. . . . Great necessities call out great virtues."

To master the competitive environment, the leader must first understand the challenges of the twenty-first century. Common Cause founder John Gardner once said that leaders are people who understand the prevailing culture, even though much of the culture is latent, existing only in people's minds and dreams, or in their unconscious. But understanding is only the first step. The leaders of the future will be those who take the next step—to change the culture. To reprise Kurt Lewin, it is through changing something that one truly comes to understand it.

Here and now, we need such leaders. We have lost our competitive edge. Adjusted for inflation, average American salaries have grown only 10 percent over the last 30 years. Our inventive genius remains peerless, but we've lost our ability to manufacture and, to a lesser extent, to successfully market new products. What we invent, China makes and sells—to us.

There are continuing crises in public education, health care, and government. Wall Street and Washington seem sometimes to have been overtaken by outlaws. Once an industrial giant, America's principal business now is service, but service has never been worse. Increasing numbers of homeless people wander the streets of this land of plenty, and no one seems to know what to do about them. Gangs blight neighborhoods in many of our cities. And the threat of international terrorism is now part of our reality.

If America is to regain its edge, and face and solve its myriad problems, leaders—the real thing, not copies—must show the way. Donald Alstadt, former CEO of the Lord Corporation, has said that the philosopher, not the tycoon or the mandarin, is king, because history proves that sooner or later ideas take root. Plato's republic is in existence, according to Alstadt, if not in the form Plato had imagined. Ideas, of course, are a leader's strong suit—the way the leader draws forth vision from chaos.

Chaos is all around us now, but the leader knows that chaos is the beginning, not the end. Chaos is the source of energy and momentum.

Rosabeth Moss Kanter described some of the attitudes mandated by the current chaotic environment in *When Giants Learn to Dance: Mastering the Challenge of Strategy, Management, and Careers in the 1990s:*

- Think strategically and invest in the future—but keep the numbers up.
- Be entrepreneurial and take risks—but don't cost the business anything by failing.
- Continue to do everything you're currently doing even better—and spend more time communicating with employees, serving on teams, and launching new projects.
- Know every detail of your business—but delegate more responsibility to others.
- Become passionately dedicated to "visions" and fanatically committed to carrying them out—but be flexible, responsive, and able to change direction quickly.
- Speak up, be a leader, set the direction—but be participative, listen well, cooperate.
- Throw yourself wholeheartedly into the entrepreneurial game and the long hours it takes—and stay fit.
- Succeed, succeed, succeed—and raise terrific children.

TEN FACTORS FOR THE FUTURE

How does a leader learn to transmute chaos? How does a leader learn not only to accept change and ambiguity, but to thrive on it? There are ten factors, ten personal and organizational

187

characteristics for coping with change, forging a new future, and creating learning organizations.

1. *Leaders manage the dream.* All leaders have the capacity to create a compelling vision, one that takes people to a new place, and then to translate that vision into reality. Not every leader I spoke with had all ten of the characteristics I'm about to describe, but they all had this one. Peter Drucker said that the first task of the leader is to define the mission. Max De Pree, in *Leadership Is an Art*, wrote, "The first responsibility of a leader is to define reality. The last is to say thank you. In between, the leader is a servant."

Managing the dream can be broken down into five parts. The first part is communicating the vision. Jung said, "A dream that is not understood remains a mere occurrence. Understood, it becomes a living experience." As CEO, Jim Burke spent 40 percent of his time communicating the Johnson & Johnson credo. There, managers still attend J&J challenge meetings, where they go through General Johnson's credo line by line to see what changes need to be made. Over the years some of those changes have been fundamental. And, like the United States Constitution, the credo itself endures.

The other basic parts of managing the dream are recruiting meticulously, rewarding, retraining, and reorganizing. All five parts are exemplified by Jan Carlzon, former CEO of SAS.

Carlzon's vision was to make SAS one of the five or six remaining international carriers (he thought many international airlines would go under, as they did, although he hadn't anticipated the rise, in recent years, of small, cut-rate carriers that now crisscross unified Europe). To accomplish this, he developed two goals. The first was to make SAS 1 percent better in a hundred different ways than its competitors. The second was to create a market niche. Carlzon chose the business traveler, because he believed that this was the most profitable niche—rather than college students, or travel agent deals, or any of the other choices. In order to attract business travelers, Carlzon had to make their every interaction with every SAS employee rewarding. He had to endow with purpose and relevance, courtesy and caring, every single interaction—and he estimated that there were 63,000 of these interactions per day between SAS employees and current or potential customers. He called these interactions "moments of truth."

Carlzon developed a marvelous cartoon book, *The Little Red Book*, to communicate the new SAS vision to employees. And he set up a corporate college in Copenhagen to train them. On top of that, he de-bureaucratized the whole organization. The organization chart no longer looks like a pyramid—it looks like a set of circles, a galaxy. In fact, Carlzon's book, which is called *Moments of Truth* in English, is titled *Destroying the Pyramids* in its original Swedish.

One of those circles, one organizational segment, is the Copenhagen–New York route. All the pilots, the navigators, the engineers, the flight attendants, the baggage handlers, the reservations agents—everybody who has to do with the Copenhagen–New York route—are involved in a self-managed, autonomous work group with a gain-sharing plan so that they all participate in whatever increment of profits that particular route brings in. There's also a Copenhagen–Frankfurt organizational segment. The whole corporation is structured in terms of these small, egalitarian groups.

Former General Electric CEO Jack Welch said, "Yesterday's idea of the boss, who became the boss because he or she knew one more fact than the person working for them, is yesterday's manager. Tomorrow's person leads through a vision, a shared set of values, a shared objective." Yeats said, "In dreams begins responsibility." Vision is a waking dream. For the leader, the responsibility is to transform the vision into reality. In doing so, leaders transform their dominions, whether that dominion is a motion picture, the computer industry, journalism, or America itself.

2. *Leaders embrace error*. Management consultant Donald Michael's elegant phrase sums up the experiences of those, like Barbara Corday, who are not afraid to make mistakes, and admit them when they do. Like Jim Burke, they create an atmosphere in which risk taking is encouraged. Like Sydney Pollack, they tell the people who work with them that the only mistake is to do nothing. Like Karl Wallenda in his prime, they walk the high wire with no fear of falling. As former UCLA basketball coach John Wooden put it, "Failure is not the crime. Low aim is."

3. *Leaders encourage reflective backtalk*. Norbert Wiener told me, "I never know what I say until I hear the response." Leaders know the importance of having someone in their lives who will unfailingly and fearlessly tell them the truth. One of the most intriguing discoveries I made in the original interviews for *Leaders* was that almost all of the CEOs were still married to their first spouse. I think the reason may be that the spouse—for both men and women—is the one person they can totally trust. The backtalk from the spouse, the trusted person, is reflective because it allows the leader to learn, to find out more about him- or herself.

4. *Leaders encourage dissent*. This is the organizational corollary of reflective backtalk. Leaders need people around them who have contrary views, who are devil's advocates, "variance

sensors" who can tell them the difference between what is expected and what is really going on.

Actually, leaders tend to come in two sizes: those who hire reflectors, clones who will mirror the leader's opinions and desires, and those who hire compensators, people who have complementary views of the organization and the society. John Sculley, who is a dreamer, hired a real manager to be his COO. But even when these compensators are on hand, it isn't easy to get them to speak up. Sam Goldwyn, after six consecutive box office flops, brought together his staff and said, "I want you to tell me exactly what's wrong with me and MGM. Even if it means losing your job." The people around a leader are all too aware of what they perceive as the dangers in speaking up. More than forty years ago, when Nikita Khruschev visited America, he gave a press conference at the Washington Press Club. The first question from the floor—handled through an interpreter—was: "Today you talked about the hideous rule of your predecessor, Stalin. You were one of his closest aides and colleagues during those years. What were you doing all that time?" Khruschev's face got red. "Who asked that?" he roared. All 500 faces turned down. "Who asked that?" he insisted. Silence. "*That's* what I was doing," he said. One of the tragedies of most organizations is that people will let the leaders make mistakes even when they themselves know better.

To counteract this tendency, leaders must be like former Herman Miller CEO Max De Pree, who abandoned himself to the wild ideas of others. Or like Barbara Corday, who encouraged dissent by blending with her staff. Seeing her sit in a room with them, you couldn't pick her out as the boss, unless you knew in advance.

D. Verne Morland argues that CEOs must have someone handpicked for the job of dissenter. In an article called, "Lear's Fool: Coping With Change Beyond Future Shock," he offers a position description for a Fool, who would report to the CEO. Here is the Fool's basic function: "To disturb with glimpses of confounding truths that elude rational formulation. To herald the advent of cosmic shifts and to apprehend their significance. To challenge by jest and conundrum all that is sacred and all that the savants have proved to be true and immutable." Every leader, like King Lear, needs at least one Fool.

5. *Leaders possess the Nobel Factor: optimism, faith, and hope.* One of the executives I interviewed for *Leaders* was certain he would have won the Nobel Prize if he had been a scientist, because he had the sense he could do anything. He communicates this optimism to the people around him. As President, Ronald Reagan was a good example of this boundless optimism. Richard Wirthlin, who was Reagan's pollster, tells the story of the time he had to let Reagan know, one year following the assassination attempt, when his approval rating had been at record highs, that his approval rating had fallen to a record low. Normally, Wirthlin didn't go in to see the President alone. This time, no one would go in with him. Reagan took one look at the lone Wirthlin and said, "Tell me the bad news." Wirthlin told him. Not only had his approval rating dived since the assassination attempt—it was the lowest approval rating of any president in his second year of office in the history of polls. "Dick, for God's sake, don't worry," Reagan told him. "I'll just go out there and try to get assassinated again."

Optimism and hope provide choices. The opposite of hope is despair, and when we despair, it is because we feel there are no choices. President Carter was done in by his "malaise" speech. He thought he was getting real, but we thought he was leaving us with no choice but despair. The leader's world view is always contagious. Carter depressed us; Reagan, whatever his other flaws, gave us hope.

Another example of the boundless optimism of those who possess the Nobel Factor was the late comedian George Burns, who said as he approached 100, "I can't die. I'm booked."

And an old Chinese proverb says, "That the birds of worry and care fly above your head, this you cannot change; but that they build nests in your hair, this you can prevent."

6. *Leaders understand the Pygmalion effect in management.* In George Bernard Shaw's *Pygmalion*, Eliza Doolittle married Freddy Eynsford-Hill because she knew that she would always be a cockney flower girl to Professor Henry Higgins. She knew that he could never accept the change in her, but would always see her as she used to be. As she told Freddy, "The difference between a lady and a flower girl is not how she behaves but how she's treated. I shall always be a flower girl to Professor Higgins because he always treats me as a flower girl and always will; but I know I can be a lady to you because you always treat me as a lady and always will."

J. Sterling Livingston applied the Pygmalion effect to management thusly:

- What managers expect of their subordinates and the way they treat them largely determine their performance and career progress.
- A unique characteristic of superior managers is the ability to create high performance expectations that subordinates fulfill.
- Less effective managers fail to develop similar expectations, and as a consequence, the productivity of their subordinates suffers.

• Subordinates, more often than not, appear to do what they believe they are expected to do.

Leaders expect the best of the people around them. Leaders know that the people around them change and grow. If you expect great things, your associates will give them to you. Jaime Escalante believed that students in a Los Angeles inner-city high school could learn calculus. And they did.

At the same time, leaders are realistic about expectations. Their motto is: stretch, don't strain. Pretend you're training for the Olympics, where easy does it. If you pull a muscle in today's game, you sit on the bench for tomorrow's.

Former Lucky Stores CEO Don Ritchey said, "One of the real responsibilities of a manager is to set standards for people, expectations. It's a heavy responsibility, because if you set them too low it's a waste, not only to the organization but for the individual, but if you set them so high that a person can't succeed, you destroy the person and the organization. So it doesn't mean that all of us shouldn't fall short once in a while, but if you structure something so that a person always fails, it's corrosive. . . . I guess the ideal would be, stretch the person a little, but don't let them fall short too many times."

7. *Leaders have what I think of as the Gretzky Factor, a certain "touch."* Wayne Gretzky, the best hockey player of his generation, said that it's not as important to know where the puck is now as to know where it will be. Leaders have that sense of where the culture is going to be, where the organization must be if it is to grow. If they don't have it as they start, they do when they arrive.

Elizabeth Drew described a similar phenomenon in politics, referring specifically to the 1988 presidential campaign: "A great many people wondered why Dukakis didn't haul off and let Bush have it in a way that everyone would understand for questioning his patriotism. This gets back to Dukakis's instincts. For a man who has been in politics for some time, he shows a curious lack of political instinct—of spontaneity, of knowing just what to do at the right moment, of feel. A President must have feel—but it's not clear that either candidate for President has it."

8. *Leaders see the long view.* They have patience. At 89, the late Armand Hammer said that he sets his long-range plans for only ten years in advance now, because he wants to be around to see them happen. In her 40s, Barbara Corday knew she had time to find a new job, or even a new career. The Japanese are patient almost beyond our conception—one company I know of has a 250-year plan.

Even Wall Street occasionally rewards a long-term perspective. In the late 1980s, Michael Eisner of Disney sent Robert Fitzpatrick to France to head up the new EuroDisney project, anticipating the realization of the European Union in 1992. Disney stock rose as a result of Eisner's ability to think ahead. CalFed, too, prepared for what may be the largest single market on the planet. CalFed opened a bank in England in the late 1980s and added others in Brussels, Barcelona, Paris, and Vienna, in anticipation of a single Europe.

9. *Leaders understand stakeholder symmetry.* They know that they must balance the competing claims of all the groups with a stake in the corporation. Jim O'Toole, in his book *Vanguard Management,* calls stakeholder symmetry the first of the principles followed by the best corporations. He quotes the late Thornton Bradshaw, former president of Arco:

Every decision at my desk is influenced by some, and at times many, of the following: the possible impact on public opinion;

the reaction of environmental groups; the possible impact on other action groups—consumers, tax reform, antinuclear, pro-desert, pro-recreational vehicles, etc; the constraints of government—DOE, EPA, OSHA, ICC, FTC, etc., etc.—and the states and the municipalities; the effect on inflation and on the government's anti-inflation program; labor union attitudes; the OPEC cartel. Oh yes, I almost forgot, the anticipated economic profit, the degree of risk, the problem of obtaining funds in a competitive market, the capability of our organization, and—when there is time—the competition.

Because they are conscious of stakeholder symmetry, leaders are wary of the Dick Ferris Syndrome (I'm resisting an urge to call it the Ferris Wheel). Ferris, who was the head of UAL, had vision—a kaleidoscopic vision of a full-service organization that not only flew people where they were going, but also owned the limos that met them at the airport and the hotels where they were staying. To this end, he even changed the name of the corporation. It would no longer be UAL, the old United Air Lines. The new name for the new venture was Allegis. It didn't mean anything, but it had style. But Ferris's vision was skewed. He forgot that there were other players in the game: the pilots' union and the board of directors, to name only two. He could see only the wonderful world outside the organization, not what was going on in his immediate vicinity. The pilots tried to buy the airlines, the board had a fit, and when the wheel came full circle, Ferris was out and the company was UAL again.

The reality of the world, the complexity of the immediate environment, the need for stakeholder symmetry, must not be lost in the colorful glories of the kaleidoscopic vision.

10. *Leaders create strategic alliances and partnerships.* They see the world globally, and they know it is no longer possible to hide. The shrewd leaders of the future are going to recognize the significance of creating alliances with other organizations whose fates are correlated with their own. So SAS forms partnerships with other airlines. The Norwegian counterpart of Federal Express—with more than 3,000 employees, one of the largest companies in Norway—formed a partnership with Federal Express. First Boston linked up with Credit Suisse, forming FBCS. GE set up a number of joint ventures with GE of Great Britain, meshing four product divisions. Despite the names, the companies hadn't been related. GE had considered buying its British namesake, but it ultimately chose alliance over acquisition. More and more nonprofit organizations recognize the value of strategic alliances and partnerships as well.

That's how this group of leaders thrives. That's how they forge the future. What about the upcoming leaders? The next generation of leaders will have certain things in common:

- Broad education.
- Boundless curiosity.
- Boundless enthusiasm.
- Contagious optimism.
- Belief in people and teamwork.
- Willingness to take risks.
- Devotion to long-term growth rather than short-term profit.
- Commitment to excellence.
- Adaptive capacity.
- Empathy.
- Authenticity.

- Integrity.
- Vision.

And as they express themselves, they will make new movies, new industries, and perhaps a new world.

If that sounds like an impossible dream to you, consider this: it's much easier to express yourself than to deny yourself. And much more rewarding, too.

Epilogue to the Twentieth-Anniversary Edition

by Warren Bennis

When I last revised *On Becoming a Leader* six years ago, the world was anxiously waiting to see if the United States would go to war with Iraq. Today we all know the tragic answer. The question that now torments the United States is when we will get out of Iraq, where we have been fighting longer than in World War II. That conflict has cost the lives of more than 4,000 American soldiers, left thousands more grievously wounded, and killed hundreds of thousands of Iraqi civilians. The war has also cost the United States almost a trillion dollars, money raised by borrowing from China and other nations because, for the first time in American history, we went to war without raising taxes to pay for it.

The United States was also suffering economically during the previous revision. In 2002 the nation was still reeling from a recession that saw the stock market tumble more than 40 percent. Today, as I write this, the country is in the midst of even deeper recession, one that is being compared to the Great Depression. In a pattern that has become distressingly familiar, the current economic downturn followed a bubble. This time around, houses, not tulips, were the object of the public's frenzied buying. After soaring to absurd heights, prices of American homes are now in free fall, with sale signs blighting entire neighborhoods. The prices of food and fuel have jumped, even as American jobs vanish by the hundreds of thousands. These problems were no act of God. They resulted from lack of leadership at every level, including failures by government officials and those heading the banking and financial services industries.

Crises reveal leadership as well as require it. The current financial mess elicited a relatively swift and concerted effort to address it. In the fall of 2008 lame-duck president George W. Bush urged Congress to pass a $700-billion rescue package. Action came after a false start or two, including treasury secretary Henry Paulson's initially using the toxic term *bailout* to describe the plan. Government intervention did not stop the stock market from going crazy in October, with the New York Stock Exchange plunging hundreds of points every day for a week, then surging a record 936 points in a single day. The market turbulence coincided with the end of the fiscal quarter, which meant millions of Americans received their 401(k) statements in the midst of it. Many were afraid to open them—with good reason, since the news inside the envelopes was dire. According to the Congressional Budget Office, Americans collectively lost $2 trillion in retirement money between July 31, 2007, and September 30, 2008. Many feared they would never be able to retire. Ever timely, *the New Yorker* spoke to the national mood with a pointed cartoon by Roz

Chast. It offered this among three "Thanksgiving Recipes from the U.S. Treasury Department":

> *Six sweet potatoes*
> *One can crushed pineapple*
> *Your retirement account*
>
> *Mix everything together.*
> *Bake until the account is completely melted.*

In the past, an economic catastrophe could usually be contained within the nation's borders. But this economic emergency was especially scary because we are now all citizens of an interconnected world with a linked global economy. The crisis had been triggered by the freezing up of credit markets; that had been caused by subprime mortgages that an underregulated financial industry bundled and sliced into complex new securities that plunged in value. The shaky new instruments were born in the United States. But when they suddenly lost value, investors in Brazil, Ireland, Bulgaria, South Africa, China, and Qatar also felt the pain.

The New York Times ran a map showing affected countries blotched with red under the headline "A Crash Heard Around the World." Tiny Iceland was hit especially hard. As it teetered on the edge of economic collapse, someone jokingly put the entire nation up for sale on eBay. In a column in the *New York Times*, Thomas L. Friedman asked: "Who knew that Iceland was just a hedge fund with glaciers?" The era when an economic event in one nation caused a far-off ripple was clearly over. As Friedman so persuasively argues in two recent bestsellers, today's world is flat and its institutions and interests so intertwined that what happens in Iowa can hit Shanghai like a tsunami. With the economic dominoes stretched around the globe, greed and wrongdoing in one quarter can cause trouble anywhere. And so, when unscrupulous manufacturers in China contaminated milk with an industrial plastic, the first, most tragic victims were Chinese babies whose kidneys were damaged. But because the tainted dairy products were distributed worldwide, chocolate bunnies tainted with melamine were soon being pulled from Easter baskets in Europe and the United States.

In recent decades, Americans have rarely had to face such grim evidence that their leadership had failed. We were shocked at the fragility of the economy and shaken in our confidence that our leaders could fix the problem. The economic mess alone would explain why most of 2008 was an unusually pessimistic time in the world and especially in the United States. In the months before the landmark 2008 presidential election, many had a growing sense that the so-called American Century was fast coming to an end. Thoughtful people were not troubled by some jingoistic fear that the United States was losing its status as the world's sole superpower. Rather, many had an uneasy feeling that the country's best days were behind it. Those feelings were understandable. The dollar had become so weak against the euro that many U.S. citizens were foregoing European travel. Once a badge of honor, a U.S. passport no longer guaranteed a friendly welcome almost anywhere. And Americans were battered by nonstop criticism from European and other allies, most of it directed at policies of the Bush administration, but distressing nonetheless. The criticism surged as our meltdown proved contagious. In an op-ed piece in the *New York Times*, British writer Andrew

O'Hagan wrote that "many a Londoner [is] seething at the subprime-mortgage disaster in America." To convey the quality of British anger at the Americans responsible, O'Hagan cited F. Scott Fitzgerald's description of the lethal disregard of *The Great Gatsby's* Tom and Daisy Buchanan: "They smashed up things and creatures and then retreated back into their money or their vast carelessness or whatever it was that kept them together, and let other people clean up the mess they made."

America's decline was evident on other fronts as well. Unimproved by the No Child Left Behind policy, our mediocre public schools have made the United States much less competitive, especially in math and science. A third of all American children and half of its minority children do not graduate from high school. And then there was the psychic wound of watching the city of New Orleans—the birthplace of that most American of art forms, jazz—all but destroyed by Hurricane Katrina and government incompetence. Even as this country grappled with uncharacteristic self-doubt, other nations were feeling newly empowered. No country is jacked up higher on its nascent sense of global clout than China. Every few weeks another of the highest skyscrapers in the world opens in Shanghai. China recently passed the United States in Internet users: 253 million Chinese are now on-line, compared to 220 million Americans. The point, of course, is not that China now holds the record for computer use, but that China is now embracing on a breathtaking scale the technology that defines our time. In a sense, the symbol of this shift away from American preeminence was the triumphant 2008 Olympic Games in Beijing. The most watched event in television history, the Beijing Olympics mesmerized 4.7 billion viewers worldwide.

Every decade or so I find myself writing that we need leaders now as never before. That seems especially true as I write this, observing the worried malaise that the country seems unable to shake off in the final months of the Bush administration. Others share my concern. A 2007 study of confidence in leadership found that 77 percent of participants felt the United States was in the midst of a leadership crisis. Slightly more (79 percent) thought the country would decline if it did not find better leaders. The 2008 survey, taken prior to the national election, showed results that were significantly worse. (The study was conducted by the Center for Public Leadership at Harvard's John F. Kennedy School of Government and *U.S. News & World Report*.)

A major reason for this downbeat view was the spectacular failure of the presidency of George W. Bush (although nobody was very happy with Congress either). When I wrote the introduction to the previous edition, the new president had recently delivered his most eloquent speech—his 2001 address to Congress in the wake of the awful terrorist attacks on the World Trade Center and the Pentagon on 9/11. That speech, which inspired hope about Bush's ability to lead in difficult times, was the high point of his administration.

Unfortunately for the nation, failure followed failure during Bush's two long terms in office. Invading Iraq on questionable grounds and failing to plan for the postinvasion were among the most egregious. Others included the shockingly inadequate response to Hurricane Katrina, the erosion of the nation's moral stature in the world, the assault on the rights of American citizens, the economic catastrophe—the list goes on and on. Unfortunately, in large part because of the administration's reflexive lack of transparency, we still know very little about the mechanics of these failures. That lack of transparency constitutes a serious problem in itself. Without knowing how things failed (in some cases, without knowing what things failed), the incoming administration will be seriously handicapped in its effort to change government for the better.

As president, Bush was an example of a particularly dangerous kind of leader—one with limited ability, great certainty, and enormous power. Indeed, no aspect of Bush's leadership was more striking than his assumption of unprecedented powers to the detriment of the legislative branch of government. A single example illustrates the imperial bent of the Bush presidency. While in office, Bush used so-called signing statements to change more than 1,100 sections of newly passed laws. In these signing statements Bush asserted that sections of the law should be ignored because they unconstitutionally constrained presidential power. How common is it for an American president to countermand the law of the land in this way? Rare indeed. According to the *New York Times*, all the previous presidents in U.S. history collectively made only 600 such changes.

Much of the credit or blame for the administration's extraordinary extension of presidential power goes to Bush's vice president, Dick Cheney. Francis Bacon wrote that "truth is the daughter of time." We will have to wait to know the actual role Cheney played in the Bush administration, but it appears that he quietly and assiduously transformed his office from one of legendary insignificance to a virtual shadow presidency. According to the U.S. Constitution, the vice president has only two responsibilities—to preside over the Senate and vote there in case of a tie, and to succeed the president should he or she die, become incapacitated, or be impeached and found guilty.

That modest brief prompted Ben Franklin to label the vice president "his superfluous excellency." But John Adams, who actually served in the office, had a much shrewder sense of the paradox of the American vice presidency when he observed: "I am nothing but I may be everything."

The numbers bear Adams out. During the twentieth century, one in three U.S. presidents died or became incapacitated in office (or in the case of Richard M. Nixon, resigned on the cusp of impeachment). All but Woodrow Wilson, who remained president despite a debilitating illness whose seriousness was not made public, were succeeded by their seconds in command. But Cheney upgraded his job description without waiting for a change at the top. Like the Wizard of Oz, he toiled out of public view, tirelessly influencing such momentous decisions as the nation's oil-centric energy policy, going to war with Iraq, and adoption of such controversial policies as the use of "enhanced interrogation" techniques such as water-boarding. Many observers believe Cheney was a major architect of the Bush administration's exceptional lack of transparency (which in no way lessens the president's responsibility for it).

As I noted earlier, it will be years before we know the full truth about the Bush presidency. There are too few investigative journalists to go around in these days of shrinking newspapers. But we already have some meaningful measures of its unprecedented lack of transparency. Consider writer Graeme Wood's important 2007 piece on the subject in the *Atlantic* magazine. Wood compared and contrasted the approaches taken by the William J. Clinton and George W. Bush administrations in making government information public. According to Wood, Clinton's basic approach was, "When in doubt, let it out." His successor's antithetical approach was, "When in doubt, classify." As a result of this profound philosophical difference, 20.6 million documents were classified under Bush in 2006, more than six times the number classified during the entire Clinton presidency. As someone who has advocated candor and transparency for at least a half century now, I am convinced that opacity in government is the organizational equivalent of hardening of the arteries. Opacity blocks the free flow of information, the *sine qua non* of informed decision making and organizational health. Without candor and transparency, organizations sicken and fail.

As we know from one-time insiders in the Bush White House, the president valued loyalty above candor. There are few absolutes in the study of leadership, but there is at least one: No leader becomes truly great unless he or she accepts, even embraces, candor. Candor performs many invaluable functions within an organization. It keeps the leader from disappearing into an isolation booth of sorts, built and guarded by yes men. It forces the leader to listen to unpleasant truths and thus helps ensure that he or she has all the data needed to make informed decisions. We have a tendency to admire leaders who act decisively on the basis of gut instinct. Sometimes gut reactions are a wise, efficient response that takes into account many insights and pieces of data that are hard to articulate but are relevant nonetheless. But gut reactions are often nothing more than hasty choices based on too little information. My guess is that Bush's well-known confidence in his gut will give instinctive leadership a bad name, at least for a time. That should benefit us all.

As to candor, it is important to remember that it should be reciprocal. It needs to operate both up and down because followers also have a need to know. Leaders sometimes try to confine important information to the executive suite. They treat it as an executive perk, like the company jet. But whenever possible, information should be shared throughout the organization, whether it is a workplace or a nation. Obviously certain trade and national secrets must be kept. But most information is not sensitive, and sharing it allows followers to make informed decisions and act accordingly. Those who are given information are brought closer to the heart of the organization. Morale improves, often boosting performance. Alternatively, lack of candor lowers morale. The worst possible scenario is one in which people are given false information. In my experience, the follower who discovers he has been lied to is never the same. Thus are enemies born.

A vivid case in point is Scott McClellan, one-time press spokesman for George W. Bush. McClellan was a faithful, even avid supporter of the president. And then he discovered his superiors had lied to him about White House involvement in the politically motivated outing of CIA agent Valerie Plame. Their lack of candor caused McClellan to mislead, however unintentionally, the White House press corps and other media covering the Plame affair. Even more devastating for McClellan was the president's belated admission that he had green-lighted the selective leaking of classified information, after McClellan had been assured Bush had not done so. Once a reliable agent of opacity for the administration, McClellan was transformed by the president's revelation. When he published his 2008 confessional *What Happened: Inside the Bush White House and Washington's Culture of Deception*, some former Republican colleagues acted as if McClellan had lost his senses. But the former press liaison behaved as one would expect of a person who felt he had been betrayed by those he once trusted and admired. McClellan became an eleventh-hour convert to candor, with all the convert's zealous commitment to his new faith. He didn't just praise candor and transparency. In his book he argued that the White House needed a new post, a deputy chief of staff in charge of candor whose job would be to "make sure the president is open, forthright and working to transcend partisanship and achieve unity." In McClellan's plan the new deputy chief would have three assistants, including one whose sole mission was to promote and protect transparency. His or her responsibilities would include ensuring that information was classified for reasons that served the national interest, not simply "to protect the administration from revelations that are merely embarrassing or politically inconvenient."

Volumes will eventually be written on why and how the Bush presidency failed. But even now, it is important to scrutinize the former president, not to demonize him, but to learn from his negative example—to extract key lessons in how not to lead. One of Bush's major failings, I believe, was his overriding commitment to an ideology rather than to principled pragmatism. In foreign affairs, for example, Bush acted in the fervently held belief that democracy is universally desired and desirable and will ultimately triumph. That ideology proved particularly ill-adapted to the realities of the Middle East. Elections in Iraq resulted in a Shia government at odds with the country's once-powerful Sunni minority and our Sunni allies in the Middle East. Free elections in Gaza empowered Hamas, an anti-Western terrorist organization that seeks the destruction of Israel, our closest Middle Eastern ally. And, because of the administration's ideological disdain for government itself, one of the most destructive forces at work during the Bush years was the corrosive drip, drip, drip of privatization unchecked by effective oversight. It caused the outsourcing of much of the war in Iraq, inadequate oversight of the financial sector and other industries, and the stealthy semiprivatization of Medicare and other government programs. The administration's overt partisanship also harmed the Justice Department and other traditionally apolitical government departments that had proud histories of striving to be meritocracies. Moreover, by acting less like the president of the nation than of the conservative wing of the Republican Party, Bush further polarized an already badly divided country. There is a lesson here that transcends any single administration, Republican or Democratic. Ideologically charged approaches rarely solve complex problems. Great leaders do not try to impose an ideological template, right- or left-leaning, on problems. First-rate leaders know that every problem is thorny in its own way and inclusively and collaboratively find solutions that reflect the unique realities at hand.

In short, between my last introduction to *On Becoming a Leader* and this epilogue, the context that I urge every reader to master has changed dramatically. Optimism has been tested by a protracted war, economic pain, and a polarized citizenry. Given this new context, it is not surprising that the U.S. presidential election of 2008 was a riveting cliff-hanger. You didn't have to be a student of leadership to be fascinated by the race. It was as important a contest as any in American history. And it was addictive. As the seemingly endless campaign approached the election on November 4, the media ran stories on election junkies who spent so much time reading political blogs that their work suffered and relationships frayed. Candidates began to pop up in the dreams of those who watched too much political coverage on-line or on TV.

In many ways, the campaign was a microcosm of the most important cultural changes of the past decade. One major development has been the technology-driven emergence of alternative media that have transformed American society, including the electoral process. The most popular on-line newspapers, such as the Huffington Post, have as much clout as venerable opinion-shapers such as the *New York Times* and the *Wall Street Journal.* Cable television has edged out network TV as the go-to source for information, even though, or perhaps because, many cable TV personalities wear their politics on their sleeves. The pace of campaigning (like the pace of everything else) has also sped up to the point where the lag time between a candidate's remark and the appearance of a slick television ad countering it is a matter of hours. Thanks to Google, most of what the candidates have said in the past can be accessed in a nanosecond. In a sense, there is no past in the blogosphere. Anything that happens in front of a camera (and almost every cell phone is a camera) can be stored forever and retrieved and disseminated in an instant. As a result, what the candidates are saying on the campaign trail is paralleled by another campaign going on in the blogosphere. In this Internet campaign, truth and lies are mixed in unpredictable ways and may be hard to tell apart; Stephen Colbert's *truthiness* is the perfect coinage for this new reality. In contrast to the public campaign, the candidates don't necessarily control this shadow campaign, although they can influence it. And whether it is fact-based or steeped in bias or worse, this shadow campaign shapes attitudes and has a real though unpredictable affect on the outcome of the election.

Given the seriousness and complexity of the problems roiling the nation, it is no surprise that voters followed the 2008 presidential race with a nerve-wracking awareness that the stakes have rarely been higher. With no sitting president or vice president in contention, all the cards were in the air. The election season began unusually early in 2007 and was marked by the emergence of history-making rivals for the Democratic presidential nomination. New York senator and former first lady Hillary Rodham Clinton was the first woman to have a real shot at the Democratic nomination. She proved a formidable competitor in what quickly became a contest between her and the first serious African American contender, Illinois senator Barack Obama. First hailed as presidential material by Oprah Winfrey, Obama gave a reputation-making speech at the 2004 Democratic convention and distinguished himself from most Democratic political figures by his prescient opposition to the war in Iraq.

Obama was a phenomenon as well as a candidate, able to fill Yankee Stadium with his supporters, many of them voting for the first time. A sea of 100,000 people stretched before him at a campaign rally in St. Louis. When Obama went abroad to meet with world leaders, presidents and sheiks grinned like teenagers as they shook his hand. Perpetually poised and unflappable, Obama was endorsed early by Ted and Caroline Kennedy and later by former secretary of state Colin Powell. At the annual benefit dinner named for Al Smith, the first Catholic nominee for the presidency, Obama made fun of his cult-like following: "Contrary to the rumors you've heard, I wasn't born in a manger," he joked. For many, Obama embodied the promise of a postracial America in which candidates were judged "not by the color of their skin, but by the content of their character." But at the same benefit, Obama alluded with a light touch to the unknown effect on his chances of his

Swahili and Arabic names, unprecedented for someone seeking the country's highest office. "I got my middle name [Hussein]," he explained, "from someone who obviously didn't think I'd ever run for president."

After a series of bruising debates, Clinton won an unprecedented 18 million votes in the 2008 primaries but ultimately lost the nomination to Obama. Although Clinton distinguished herself in the numerous Democratic debates, particularly in her mastery of the issues, Obama chose as his running mate Delaware senator Joseph Biden, who had also sought the presidential nomination.

The contest for the Democratic nomination was sometimes so contentious it seemed to call for net and trident. In contrast, the Republican contest was as dull as an infomercial. The Republican candidates were all mature white men, including 9/11 New York City mayor Rudolph Giuliani and former Massachusetts governor Mitt Romney. And their primary strategy seemed to consist of distancing themselves from President Bush without actually uttering his name and reminding voters that they were members of the president's party. Despite being counted out early in the contest, Vietnam War hero and Arizona senator John McCain eventually emerged as the Republican presidential candidate. A self-proclaimed maverick, McCain overcame such major obstacles as his unpopularity among hard-core conservatives and his age. If elected, he would become, at seventy-two, the oldest person to assume the office.

But the Republican campaign suddenly caught fire in the last days of August 2008 when McCain made the stunning announcement that his vice-presidential pick was not Democrat-turned-Independent Joe Lieberman or another of the relative moderates McCain was thought to favor. Instead McCain chose forty-four-year-old Sarah Palin, the young governor of Alaska little known outside of party circles. A former small-town mayor, beauty queen, and self-styled "hockey mom" of five, including an infant with Down Syndrome, Palin introduced herself to the nation in a mesmerizing speech that drew as many television viewers as Obama's convention address. In that speech, Palin—the first woman on the Republican ticket and thus a maker of history in her own right—made a bid for Hillary Clinton's many women supporters with a promise to assail the glass ceiling Clinton had cracked. As an opponent of abortion even in cases of rape and incest who believes creationism should be taught in the schools alongside evolution, Palin appealed strongly to evangelical Christians who helped elect President Bush and had little enthusiasm for McCain.

Initially the media fell hard for Palin, much as it had for Obama. Both were hailed as celebrities and rock stars, terms the Republicans had previously used to demean Obama. Palin proved to be a gifted campaigner with a sharp edge and a populist pitch (she often mentioned "Joe Six-Pack," apparently to capitalize on the belief that Bush had won, in part, because voters would rather have had a beer with him than with Al Gore or John Kerry). Palin had a folksy touch, smiling readily, winking, and dropping her final g's, but she also served as her party's attack dog. Without apparent qualms, she often roiled up conservative crowds by accusing Obama of "palling around with terrorists." Despite her initial appeal, she had a serious downside. With her paper-thin resume, she undermined McCain's contention that Obama lacked the experience to be president. In my view, that had been a losing argument all along. History has shown over and over again that experience per se is no substitute for good judgment in determining the quality of a leader.

To an unusual degree, the lives of the four contenders were the stuff of biopics. As so often happens in our culture, where even brands of toothpaste are marketed via their own carefully honed "stories," the race became a battle of competing narratives. McCain, who took as his campaign slogan "Country First," embodied a tale of courage and patriotic sacrifice as a former navy pilot shot down over Vietnam who was tortured while a prisoner of war in the notorious Hanoi Hilton. Since then, he has earned a reputation as a maverick for bucking his party on such matters as immigration and cutting taxes for the wealthiest Americans (positions he later reversed). Born in 1961, Obama had a more exotic, more contemporary story, one that emphasized his ties with the rest of the world. He is the son of a black Kenyan father and a white mother from Kansas, who had struggled to raise him in Hawaii and Indonesia. All but abandoned by his father and briefly on food stamps as a child, Obama became the first African American editor of the *Harvard Law Review*. Instead of joining a four-star law firm after Harvard, he had begun his public life as a community organizer in Chicago. Obama, who acknowledged that he didn't look like the other men on American currency, ran on the promise of change.

Like McCain and Obama, Biden had experienced a life-changing event, a crucible that shaped his character and his leadership. Biden was twenty-nine in 1972 when he was elected to the Senate, the second youngest person in history to win the office. He was in Washington, getting ready to move into his new office, when a phone call revealed that his wife and infant daughter had died in an auto accident back in Delaware.

Gravely injured, his two young sons were not expected to survive. The boys recovered; Biden was sworn in at their bedside. A popular senator and devoted single father, Biden remarried and is now the father of an adult daughter as well as a grandfather. A foreign-policy expert who opposed the appointment of conservative judge Robert Bork to the Supreme Court, Biden is also known for verbal gaffes and for taking the long train ride home to Delaware each night to be with his family.

Perhaps because Palin's was initially the least familiar tale, her narrative got the most media play. Her photogenic face appeared on one newsmagazine cover after another, often accompanying text that made her sound like a cross between Annie Oakley and Wonder Woman, able to shoot and dress a moose as well as change a diaper and do the state's business. Opponents saw her selection as a cynical bid to appease the Republican base and attract women (detractors dubbed her "Caribou Barbie"). The Republican campaign hailed her as a maverick in the McCain mold, who had fearlessly taken on her own party in Alaska. In a piece in *Newsweek*, Jeffrey Barthelot and Karen Breslau described how Palin fit into a time-honored American tale. They wrote: "Palin's personal story taps one of the great American myths—the hardy woman of the frontier, God-fearing and determined to succeed against the odds. Her story could be a Capra film, or a chick flick. But as with most political biographies (or Hollywood films), the rougher edges have been burnished. To her critics, she's also shallow, opportunistic and even corrupt herself." The last was an allusion to a bipartisan investigation by the Alaska legislature into whether Palin improperly fired a state official. In October, the investigative body determined that the governor Palin had violated state ethics laws and misused her power but had the legal right to replace the official.

The election season underscored the fact that ours is a culture in which entertainment and news have been transmogrified into a third category that marries the two, for better or for worse, often called *infotainment*. When polled, young voters routinely said they get their news from "The Daily Show with Jon Stewart" or "The Colbert Report," which are cable comedy shows, not news sources, to those who rely on the mainstream media. John McCain declared his intention to run for president on "Late Night with David Letterman" and returned to the show to ask Letterman's forgiveness after abruptly canceling an appearance. Cable TV pundits reported regularly on where the women of "The View" stood on the candidates. But the campaign became downright surrealistic after writer and performer Tina Fey began playing Sarah Palin on "Saturday Night Live." Sporting the candidate's signature glasses and often quoting her verbatim, Fey brilliantly caught Palin's *Fargo* accent, down-home mannerisms, and serpentine syntax. Palin later made her own appearance on the show, passing Fey in the studio and replacing her on the podium.

Like Palin, who trained for a career in television, Obama is richly endowed with charisma, the personal magnetism that allows an individual to captivate and sway audiences. It is the same kind of star power that allows certain actors to own a stage or a screen. Politics, too, is a performance art, as Orson Welles made clear when he first met President Franklin Delano Roosevelt. FDR graciously said to the already-legendary actor/director: "You know, Mr. Welles, you are the greatest actor in America." And Welles replied: "Oh, no, Mr. President. You are." Except for those rare occasions when candidates share the same physical space as those they hope to lead, they must have powerful enough rhetorical and acting skills to transcend the distorting effect of television and other media. They must be good enough performers to persuade the audience that they share the same dreams and interests. Such leaders have the ability to turn a crowd into a community—or a mob. Charisma is no small gift. FDR had it, JFK had it, Reagan had it, Clinton had it. Tragically, so did Hitler. But it is always part of the political equation, whether we like it or not.

More than ever since the advent of television, physical attractiveness is a constituent of charisma, albeit a controversial one. It has been noted so often it has become a cliché: virtually everyone who heard the landmark 1960 debate between Nixon and Kennedy on radio thought Nixon had won. It was only those who saw the close-up visuals—a frowning Nixon, with his five o'clock shadow, mopping flop sweat from his brow, versus a youthful, athletic-looking Kennedy, comfortable in his skin and flashing a ready smile—who knew that the victory belonged to JFK. Beauty is more than symmetrical features. It can be enhanced by behavior and our knowledge of the individual. But it is routinely a factor in the leaders we choose. Some leaders are so powerful they can rise above the way they look. Lincoln used humor to mock his strange appearance, once remarking to a rival who called him "two-faced": "Do you think if I had another face, I'd appear in public in this one?" But appearance matters to voters as well as prospective dates. An unkind but astute observer once remarked that Nixon had a face like a foot. Did that contribute to his disastrous debate? Likely it did. Certainly Sarah Palin's good looks are part of her appeal, as Republican conventioneers from Indiana crudely acknowledged with T-shirts that read: HOOSIERS FOR THE HOT CHICK. And it is a fair bet that Obama's athletic grace and easy smile attracted more voters than his Harvard law degree or his tax policy.

It is no secret that ours is a celebrity culture, and that routinely means that issues get short shrift in our public discourse. In the first weeks following Palin's debut, in the grip of Palimania, Americans heard about her seventeen-year-old daughter's untimely pregnancy and Palin's installation of a tanning bed in the governor's residence (an act hailed as a blow to the "the sun-scare industry" by the tanning lobby). In what could be called the *People* magazine phase of the race, the incidental drove out the substantial, in part, because the McCain campaign kept Palin, who performed best when scripted, away from traditional media. Cable TV filled its gaping news hole with such inconsequential questions as whether McCain looked less like the presidential candidate than Palin's second banana.

All that changed when giant investment banker Lehman Brothers announced it would seek bankruptcy protection on September 15; the Dow plummeted, and people began pulling their cash out of their banks. Suddenly the campaign focused with laser-like intensity on the battered economy and the pain it was causing voters. The resonant personal stories carefully constructed by the candidates and their handlers were put aside, and the public was able to compare and contrast the candidates' very different positions on matters of real weight. For a time, the carnival-like process of choosing a president and vice president was relinked to the next phase in the process—the one of paramount importance: how the president we choose will lead and, thus, shape our lives and those of our children and grandchildren. But just as the debate seemed finally to settle on the economy, with all its gravity, the politics of distraction reemerged. In the last of the three presidential debates, McCain repeatedly cited a voter in Toledo, Ohio, whom he called Joe the Plumber. Before the debate was over,

Joe the Plumber was being alternately hailed and vilified in the blogosphere. He was a household name by the following day.

In the final weeks, the presidential race turned really ugly. At her rallies Palin continued to accuse Obama of terrorist associations, focusing on rehabilitated Weatherman Bill Ayers. Chants of "Kill him" directed at Obama were heard from some of the angry crowds. McCain bristled when civil rights leader John Lewis accused him of allowing a dangerous undercurrent of violence to develop at his campaign events. But anti-Obama innuendo, slurs, and distortions continued to mark the McCain campaign. Automated "robocalls" from the Republican Party warned anyone who picked up the phone away from Obama with charges of terrorist associations, involvement in voter fraud, and nefarious plans to redistribute the nation's wealth. Race was rarely mentioned during the campaign (until the Colin Powell endorsement was dismissed by some as an act of racial solidarity), but race was always close to the surface. Democrats feared the possible effect of an active on-line campaign that falsely but graphically presented Obama as a Moslem with ties to al-Qaeda. Supporters feared for Obama's life in a nation that has seen more than its share of politically and racially motivated assassinations. So did the U.S. government, which had assigned Obama Secret Service protection before any other candidate.

By mid-October Irish bookmakers were already paying off bettors who had put their money on Obama to win. But his supporters worried that polls that showed him ahead of McCain might be distorted by the Bradley Effect. That phenomenon was named for the late Tom Bradley, the first black mayor of Los Angeles, who ran for governor of California in the 1980s against George Deukmejian. Overwhelmingly, the polls showed Bradley in the lead. But he lost the election because, political scientists conjectured, voters feared being thought racist if they told pollsters they did not plan to vote for Bradley. Race was not the only emotionally charged issue in the 2008 campaign. Age was another. Obama, who fully exploited the Internet to raise funds, organize his supporters, and get out the vote, was the clear favorite of young, technologically hip voters. Obama even advertised on popular video games in the last weeks of the campaign. Although McCain argued that his age was evidence of his experience, many potential voters, including older ones, thought he was too old to serve as president. Their fears about his age were exacerbated by his history of malignant melanoma and by his choice of so green and controversial a running mate. McCain supporters accused the Obama campaign of exploiting such fears when they called McCain "erratic" in frequently changing his positions and tactics.

We now know who Americans wanted as their president. But it is interesting to look back at what qualities Americans *said* they were seeking in a president before the election. The national study on confidence in leadership that I alluded to earlier asked that question. Five qualities or traits were identified as extremely important by half or more of the respondents. The single most important trait was honesty and integrity, named by 66 percent. Next most important—intelligence. Ability to communicate was next, followed by willingness to work with people in both political parties and the ability to bring the American people together. The least important trait was having served in the military, which just 13 percent thought extremely important. Being likeable was the next lowest in importance (21 percent). Only 23 percent believed experience in Washington was extremely important. Two other responses are noteworthy. A strong belief in God was extremely important to 38 percent of those who responded. Having new ideas was extremely important to almost the same number (37 percent).

Those top five traits were perceived as extremely important across political or ideological lines. But the study reported significant differences between Republicans and Democrats on the value of other traits. Decisiveness, a strong belief in God, and military service were more important (in that order) to Republicans than Democrats. Democrats thought experience in foreign policy, having new ideas, understanding and sympathizing with others, experience in Washington, and being likeable were more important than Republicans did. The biggest gap between the parties was this: 14 percent or more Democrats than Republicans thought the following were extremely or very important—having new ideas, understanding and sympathy with other others, and being likable.

The study was published in November 2007, and it is fascinating to see which candidates were ascendant at that time. The top choice was Hillary Rodham Clinton—33 percent of respondents said they had a great deal of confidence she would be a good president. Barack Obama was second, with 22 percent reporting a great deal of confidence in his ability to lead. Next was Rudy Giuliani, chosen by 18 percent. John Edwards followed at 13 percent. Twelve percent said they had a great deal of confidence that John McCain would be a good president. Also worth noting is that 26 percent of respondents said they had no confidence ("none at all") that Clinton would make a good president. That was the largest no-confidence rating in the study. Nineteen percent had no confidence in Barack Obama, and 20 percent had no confidence in John McCain.

When retired general Colin Powell endorsed Barack Obama on "Meet the Press" on October 19, Powell described Obama as a "transformational figure" who was the right president for this moment in time. The long, contentious campaign had been a "final exam" for McCain and Obama, in Powell's view. Obama emerged as his choice because "he has both style and substance." The former Bush secretary of state said he thought the new president should address both the American people and the world at large to describe how his policies will be different from those of the past eight years. One of the most pressing challenges the new president will face, Powell said, is "to fix the reputation we've left with the rest of the world."

In the run-up to the election, historian Doris Kearns Goodwin noted that an even temperament characterized many of our best presidents. No matter what crisis Lincoln and FDR faced, they dealt with it in a calm, deliberative way. And great leaders are often able to rise above personal disappointments and hurts, even tragedies. Lincoln's political genius included his ability to assemble a brain trust of his former political opponents into a brilliant "team of rivals." "You can't let resentments poison you," Goodwin said.

It is clear that the new president will have to restore not just the broken economy, but the confidence of the nation. He will have to give the country its optimism back. The very fact of his election is a giant first step in that process. As Colin Powell predicted, Obama's election was a matter of pride not just for African Americans, but for all Americans. My guess is that Obama will conduct his new presidency with Lincoln, FDR and John F. Kennedy in mind (we know he read Doris Kearns Goodwin's *Team of Rivals: The Political Genius of Abraham Lincoln* during the campaign). There is a time-tested pattern for inspiring American citizens. Our greatest leaders have reminded us that we are all in this together, and that we will have to make hard choices, even sacrifices.

In the months ahead, the new administration will also have to begin discovering and undoing the worst machinations of the Bush years. None of that will be possible until the reflexive, even obsessive opacity of the previous administration is reversed and more transparent government restored.

Obama must also reach out to the rest of the world. It, too, needs reassuring. He will have to overcome the isolation of the United States that Bush's policies created. Many other nations seem eager to work with the new president. More than any president in our history, Obama looks like the rest of the world. That is an asset of incalculable value. Obama wasn't just the choice of American voters. He was the world's preferred candidate, in a campaign that was followed overseas as avidly as the world soccer finals. Just as international cooperation helped save far-flung banks and other financial institutions in 2008, we will need ongoing international collaboration to solve such enormous, shared problems as global warming, nuclear containment, and potentially explosive economic disparity throughout the world.

A classic purveyor of hope, Obama was able to energize young voters as never before. His appeal was even more palpable than John Kennedy's. Millions of older voters who had grown cynical about government and the electoral process were also galvanized. Those voters, young and old, whose passion was reignited now constitute a precious pool of talent excited by the possibilities of public service, including government. As a nation we pay a terrible price when we stop believing in the possibility of good government. In our disdain, we cede our country to the ideologues and the hacks. Those who worked for Obama's election know the joy of struggling for and achieving significant change. Now, while the crackle is still in the air, is the time to create twenty-first-century versions of the Peace Corps and dozens of other organizations that tap American energy and idealism.

In 2008, all eyes were on the men and the woman who sought the highest office in the land. But it is a mistake to focus only on leaders. Even if we rise to become president of the United States, we spend most of our lives as followers, not leaders. In the past we have tended to think of the distinction between the two hierarchically. But, in fact, as our workplaces and other organizations become flatter and more collegial, the terms become less and less meaningful. Leadership is a temporary assignment among Google engineers, who serve for a time, then pass the crown to another member of their small working groups. Even in more traditional organizations, a reciprocal relationship exists between leaders and followers. Leader and follower are partners in the same dance. It is our most important obligation as followers to speak truth to power. As hundreds of unemployed whistle blowers can tell you, candor is a more dangerous job than silence. Speaking truth to power always requires courage, and when the stakes are high enough, it demands true heroism. But the follower who boldly points out the elephant in the room or the flaw in the boss's preferred plan is transformed into what can only be called a leader—someone who assumes responsibility and acts in the best interest of the group. And it's not only the whistle blowers or the dissenters who need to be listened to, to be heard. We all do. A story about FDR comes to mind: crowded, grieving masses surged along Constitution Avenue in April 1945, waiting for his funeral cortege to pass by. As his hearse neared, a well-dressed, middle-aged man standing in the throng fell to his knees, sobbing desperately until finally regaining his composure. A stranger by his side asked, "Did you *know* the President?" The man could barely reply. "No. . .but he knew me."

As someone who remembers the Great Depression, I can assure you that the financial crisis of 2008 was an order of magnitude less serious. But it was a genuine crisis nonetheless, and they are always crucibles of leadership. Becoming a leader is not an orderly path. It is a fitful, often painful process that involves wrong turns and dead ends before great strides are made. Usually some transformative event or experience is central to finding one's voice, learning how to engage others through shared meaning, and acquiring the other skills of leadership. FDR's lifetime struggle with polio was most certainly his crucible of leadership. Instead of simply enduring hard times, we have to seize every opportunity for transformation they afford. In recent weeks, as the stock market rocked and rolled, I thought often of what Abigail Adams had written to John Quincy Adams in the turbulent days of 1780: "These are the hard times in which a genius would wish to live. . . . Great necessities call forth great leaders."

It is significant, I think, that Adams chose the plural, *leaders*. Especially now that the United States has an exciting new president, it is easy to forget that we need more than one gifted leader at a time. At the founding of the United States, when our population was less than 4 million, we had six towering leaders: Washington, Jefferson, Hamilton, Madison, Franklin, and Adams. Now that we number more than 304 million people, we are surely capable of yielding at least 600 world-class leaders in this country alone.

Will you be one of them?

Biographies

Herb Alpert and Gil Friesen

Alpert and Friesen were two-thirds of the remarkable triumvirate that, with Jerry Moss, headed the A&M record label. They sold the company to Polygram for more than $500 million in 1990. As a performer, Alpert and his Tijuana Brass were an important part of the popular music scene of the 1960s. In addition to accumulating platinum records and Grammy Awards, Alpert is an inventive business leader, artist, and head of the Herb Alpert Foundation. Friesen, who started as general manager of A&M, became president in 1977. After broadening A&M's musical mix, Friesen established A&M Films. The sensitive study of adolescence, *The Breakfast Club*, was among the operation's box-office successes. Friesen left the company in 1997 and was a founding partner of Classic Sports, a cable network sold to ESPN in 1997. In 2000, Alpert and Moss sold Rondor, their music publishing company, to Universal Music Group for an estimated $400 million. In 2002, they stood to make more than $200 million on the deal, thanks to a contract that required Universal and, later, Vivendi to compensate them if the parent company's stock plummeted. Alpert and Moss were inducted into the Rock and Roll Hall of Fame in 2007. They received the President's Merit Award at the 2008 Grammy Awards.

Gloria Anderson

A graduate of the University of Texas School of Journalism with an MA from the University of Wisconsin, Anderson has been a reporter for the Associated Press, an editor at the *Cincinnati Enquirer* and the *Charlotte Observer*, managing editor of the Knight-Ridder news wire, and managing editor of the *Miami News*. She was founding editor and co-publisher of *Miami Today* and editor and publisher of the *Kendall Gazette* in suburban Miami. Formerly head of *The New York Times* Syndicate, she is now vice president for international and editorial development in the News Services Division of the *Times*. She has served as a Pulitzer Prize juror and as president of the World Editors Forum.

Anne L. Bryant

Born in 1949 in the Boston area, Bryant has a BA in English from Simmons College and a doctorate in education from the University of Massachusetts. She was vice president of the professional education division of P. M. Haeger & Associates, a Chicago-based association management firm, from 1974 to 1986. She then became executive director of the American Association of University Women, a national organization that promotes equity for women and girls in education and other arenas. She is now executive director of the National School Boards Association, which represents the concerns of more

228

than 14,500 school districts nationwide. She also serves as the vice chair of the Schools & Libraries Committee of the Universal Service Administrative Company, the not-for-profit corporation chosen by the FCC to administer the Universal Service Fund.

James Burke

Born in Rutland, Vermont, in 1925, and a graduate of Holy Cross College, Burke has an MBA from Harvard Business School. He joined Johnson & Johnson as a product director in 1953, was named director of new products in 1955, president in 1973, and chairman and CEO in 1973. During his tenure at the pharmaceutical giant, he was best known for his leadership during the Tylenol-tampering crisis in 1982. Burke retired from Johnson & Johnson in 1989 to become chairman of the board of Partnership for a Drug-Free America. For his work with the Partnership, he was awarded the Presidential Medal of Freedom by Bill Clinton in 2000, and in 2002, became chairman emeritus of the anti-drug group.

Barbara Corday

A native of New York City, Corday was born into a theatrical family. Her first job in show business was with a small theatrical agency. She became a publicist and then a screenwriter, with partner Barbara Avedon. In eight years together, they wrote numerous TV scripts and series pilots and served as executive story consultants on several series. After a stint as an ABC-TV executive, she joined Columbia Pictures Television as an independent producer and president of her own company, Can't Sing, Can't Dance Productions. In 1984, she became president of Columbia Pictures Television, and then president and CEO of Columbia/Embassy Television, overseeing every aspect of production. She later became CBS's executive vice president for prime-time programming. She was a co-founder of the Holly-wood Women's Political Committee. Corday now teaches at the University of Southern California, where she is chair of the division of film and TV production in its School of Cinema-Television.

Horace B. Deets

Deets came up through the ranks of the American Association of Retired Persons, now AARP, and was elected executive di-rector by the board at the age of 50. Under his leadership, the organization became increasingly visible, helping give voice to the burgeoning group of Americans over 50. Prior to joining AARP, Deets worked for the Equal Employment Opportunity Commission. Once a teacher and school administrator in Ala-bama, he has a BA from St. Bernard College in Alabama and a master's degree from Catholic University in Washington, D.C. After thirteen years as executive director of AARP, Deets re-tired in 2002 to become a senior advisor to its new leadership. He is now the chair of HelpAge International America, a global not-for-profit organization working to improve the lives of disadvantaged older people. He is also a research fellow at MIT's Age Lab, as well as a visiting research fellow at the Uni-versity of Oxford's Institute of Ageing.

Robert R. Dockson

A native of Illinois, Dockson took both a master's degree and a doctorate at the University of Southern California. After four years in the Navy in World War II, he taught at Rutgers Univer-sity, then spent six years as a financial economist. In 1954, he was named professor and chairman of the Department of Marketing at the University of Southern California. In 1960, he established the undergraduate School of Business and the Graduate School of Business Administration at USC. He served as dean of the school for ten years. He joined CalFed (later absorbed by Citigroup), the holding company of California Federal Savings and Loan in 1969, became president in 1970, CEO in 1973, and chairman in 1977. Since he retired from CalFed in 1988, he has been active in academic, civic, and philanthropic affairs, including the John Randolph Haynes and Dora Haynes Foundation, devoted to studying and solving social problems in the Los Angeles area.

Richard Ferry

Ferry is co-founder and former president and director of Korn/Ferry International, the world's leading executive search firm. Since its founding in 1969, Korn/Ferry has become a major force in shaping the leadership of corporations and organizations and has helped shape the field with its emphasis on industry specialization and professional consulting practices. Since Ferry's retirement in 1995, he has been active in educational, civic, and charitable activities in southern California. He has also served as a director of Avery Dennison, Dole Food Company, Mrs. Fields' Famous Brands, and Pacific Mutual Holding Company, the parent company of Pacific Life.

Betty Friedan

Author and feminist leader Friedan graduated first in her class from Smith College in 1942 and did graduate work at the University of California at Berkeley. Fired from her newspaper job when she became pregnant (she is the mother of three), she began looking into the lives of her fellow Smith College alumnae and, inspired by that research, wrote her feminist classic, *The Feminine Mystique*. She co-founded the National Organization for Women, the National Women's Political Caucus, the International Feminist Congress, and the First Women's Bank, an economic think tank for women. In 1993, she published her pioneering book on aging, *The Fountain of Age*. She was a visiting professor at numerous universities, including USC, and she continued to study, write and speak out on gender equality, aging, and other social and political issues until her death in 2006.

Alfred Gottschalk

Born in Germany in 1930, Gottschalk came to America in 1939, earned his BA at Brooklyn College, his master's, doctorate, and law degrees at the University of Southern California, and his bachelor of literature degree at Hebrew Union College. After becoming a rabbi, he continued to teach at Hebrew Union and became president there in 1971. Now president emeritus, he is active in civic, philanthropic, educational, and religious affairs, serving as both a trustee of the Museum of Jewish Heritage and a director of the National Underground Railroad Freedom Center.

Roger Gould

With a medical degree from Northwestern University School of Medicine, and a second degree in public health, Gould interned at Los Angeles County Hospital and completed his psychiatric residency at the University of California/Los Angeles. An associate clinical professor of psychiatry at UCLA, he is a practicing psychiatrist and innovator in the use of computers in psychiatry and the psychology of weight control. He is the author of *Transformations: Growth and Change in Adult Life* (Simon & Schuster, 1978) and *Shrink Yourself* (John Wiley & Sons, 2007).

Frances Hesselbein

A native of Pennsylvania, Hesselbein was the first Girl Scout chief executive to come up through the ranks. Starting as a volunteer scout leader, she became CEO of the Girl Scouts of the United States of America in 1976 and served in that capacity until 1990. Her leadership of the Girl Scouts earned her *Fortune* magazine's recognition as "best nonprofit manager in America." She is a winner of the nation's highest civilian honor, the Presidential Medal of Freedom, and founding president of the Peter F. Drucker Foundation for Nonprofit Management, now the Leader to Leader Institute. Her books include the 2002 best-seller, *Hesselbein on Leadership*, and *Be, Know, Do: Leadership the Army Way*.

Shirley Hufstedler

Born in 1925 in Denver, Colorado, Hufstedler earned her law degree at Stanford University and established a private practice in Los Angeles in 1950. She was appointed a judge of the Los Angeles County Superior Court in 1961 and in 1966, associate justice of the California Court of Appeal. In 1968, she was named to the U.S. Court of Appeals for the Ninth District by President Johnson, and in 1979 was appointed secretary of education by President Carter. Since leaving that post in 1981, she has taught and practiced law, most recently as senior counselor at the law firm of Morrison & Foerster in Los Angeles.

Edward C. Johnson III

After graduating from Harvard in 1954, Johnson joined Fidelity Investments in 1957 as a research analyst and then became the portfolio manager of the Fidelity Trend Fund. He is now chairman of the board and CEO of Fidelity Investments.

Martin Kaplan

Born in Newark, New Jersey, in 1950, Kaplan has a bachelor's degree from Harvard University in molecular biology and a doctorate in modern thought and literature from Stanford University. He also took a First in English from Cambridge University. He was a White House speechwriter, a journalist, a deputy presidential campaign manager, and a vice president and writer-producer during twelve years at Disney. He wrote and executive produced the Eddie Murphy film *The Distinguished Gentleman*. He is now a research professor and holds the Norman Lear Chair in Entertainment, Media, and Society at the USC Annenberg School for Communication, as well as being a regular commentator on National Public Radio and contributor to the Huffington Post.

Brooke Knapp

Knapp is a world-renowned pilot who has set more than 120 speed records in the air. She founded and operated Jet Airways, an air charter company. A former chair of the California Commission on Aviation and Airports and a winner of the Federal Aviation Administration Award for Extraordinary Service, she has been an entrepreneur in southern California real estate and other enterprises. She has served as a president of the Hollywood Chamber of Commerce and as a commissioner on the California Coastal Commission. She is currently on the board of My Jets, Inc., a firm that advises corporations and other organizations about their aviation needs.

Mathilde Krim

Krim received a doctorate from the University of Geneva, Switzerland, and did research on cytogenetics and cancer-causing viruses at the Weizmann Institute of Science in Israel. There, she was on the team that developed the first test for the prenatal detection of gender. She has also been on the research staff at the Cornell University Medical School and Sloan-Kettering Institute for Cancer Research, where she was head of the Interferon laboratory. She was founding chair and chair of the board of directors of the American Foundation for AIDS Research (AmFAR). She has received more than a dozen honorary degrees and numerous awards for her pioneering work in raising public consciousness about AIDS, including, in 2000, the Presidential Medal of Honor, the nation's highest civilian honor.

Norman Lear

A producer, screenwriter, and director and co-founder of People for the American Way, a 300,000-member civil-rights organization, Lear was born in 1922 in New Haven, Connecticut. He was educated at Emerson College and served in the Air Force during World War II. In 1945, he entered the new field of television as a comedy writer. As a writer-producer, he broke new ground with such innovative shows as "All in the Family," "Maude," and "Mary Hartman, Mary Hartman." A media entrepreneur, he is also active in liberal politics, advising political leaders, and speaking out on civil-liberties issues. In 1984, Lear was one of the first group of inductees into the Academy of

Television Arts & Sciences Hall of Fame. In 1999, he was awarded the National Medal of Arts. In 2000, he and Internet entrepreneur David Hayden bought the original copy of the Declaration of Independence for $8.1 million. They then put the founding document on tour, because, Lear said: "I want to take it where Americans can see it."

Michael B. McGee

An All-American tackle at Duke University, McGee received a bachelor's degree in business, before being drafted by the St. Louis Cardinals. He became an assistant coach at Duke when an injury ended his career as a player. Head coach at 29, he earned a doctorate and became an athletics administrator. In 1984 he moved to the University of Southern California as athletic director. McGee was inducted into the College Football Hall of Fame in 1990 for his leadership both on and off the field. He served as athletic director at the University of South Carolina for 12 years before retiring in 2005.

Sydney Pollack

Pollack was born in 1934 in Lafayette, Indiana. He studied acting in New York with legendary teacher Sanford Meisner. He began directing in the new medium of television during its Golden Age. He directed and produced more than twenty films, including *They Shoot Horses, Don't They?*, *The Way We Were*, *Three Days of the Condor*, *Out of Africa*, *Tootsie*, and *The Firm*. His films have received more than forty Academy Award nominations, including four for best picture. Pollack himself was nominated three times. *Out of Africa* won seven Oscars, including Best Picture, Best Director, and Best Screenplay. He won the New York Film Critics' Award for the highly acclaimed *Tootsie*. He continued to produce, direct, and act in a stream of critically and commercially successful films until his death in 2008.

Jamin B. (Jamie) Raskin

After graduating from both Harvard University and Harvard Law School, Raskin served as an assistant attorney general in Massachusetts and as general counsel to the National Rainbow Coalition. In 1990, Raskin joined the faculty of American University's Washington College of Law in the nation's capitol, a position he still holds today. There he founded and directed the Marshall-Brennan Fellowship Program, a competitive program that selects second- and third-year law students to teach high school courses on the Constitution and citizenship and now directs the Law and Government Program. In 2006, he won a landslide victory in a bid for a seat in the Maryland state senate.

S. Donley Ritchey

Retired CEO of Lucky Stores, Inc., Ritchey spent thirty-two years with the company, starting as a part-time clerk while attending college. A graduate of San Diego State University, he has taught courses in management and marketing and lectured at the University of California at Berkeley, Stanford University, USC, and elsewhere. He is a director of several corporations and active in Danville, California, politics and civic and philanthropic work. After retiring from the board of directors of AT&T in 2007, Ritchey was appointed to the board at San Diego State University's College of Business Administration.

Richard Schubert

Born in Trenton, New Jersey, Schubert attended Eastern Nazarene College in Quincy, Massachusetts, and graduated from Yale Law School in 1961. He immediately joined the legal staff of Bethlehem Steel. In 1971, he was named solicitor for the Department of Labor, and subsequently became under secretary of labor. In 1975 he returned to Bethlehem Steel and became president four years later. He resigned in June 1982 and became president of the American Red Cross the following year. He headed the international aid organization until 1989, and is credited with bringing it into the computer age. He was president and CEO of the Points of Light Foundation from 1990 until 1995. He is currently senior vice president of the Executive Coaching Network and a founding member of the Management & Training Corp.

John Sculley

Born in 1939 in New York City, Sculley studied at the Rhode Island School of Design, graduated from Brown University, and took an MBA at the University of Pennsylvania's Wharton School. Rising through the marketing department at Pepsico, he became president and CEO in 1974. Wooed away from Pepsi by Apple co-founder Steve Jobs, Sculley became president and CEO of the computer company in 1977. During his ten years at Apple, he was celebrated for his marketing campaigns, especially the 1984 Macintosh launch. An author and popular speaker on the future, he is now a partner in the venture-capital firm of Rho Ventures.

Gloria Steinem

Born in Toledo, Ohio, Steinem graduated from Smith College in 1956, spent two years in India on a Chester Bowles fellowship, and then became a writer and journalist in New York. A founding editor of both *New York* and *Ms* magazines, she is one of the most respected and visible champions of women's rights, equal justice, and other moral and political causes. A co-founder of the National Women's Political Caucus, she is a much sought-after speaker and author of several best-selling books, including *Outrageous Acts and Everyday Rebellions, Revolution from Within*, and *Moving Beyond Words*.

Clifton R. Wharton, Jr.

Wharton was born in Boston, entered Harvard at 16, and received a BA in history. While an undergraduate at Harvard, he was a founder and national secretary of the U.S. National Student Association. He has a master's degree in international affairs from the Johns Hopkins University School of Advanced International Studies, a doctorate in economics from the University of Chicago, and dozens of honorary degrees. He was president of Michigan State University and chancellor of the State University of New York system. From 1987 to 1993, he was chairman and CEO of Teachers Insurance and Annuity Association of America and the College Retirement Equities Fund—the world's largest pension plan. As such, he was the first African American to head a Fortune 500 service company.

Larry Wilson

Born in Louisville, Kentucky, Wilson grew up in Minnesota and graduated from the University of Minnesota with a teaching certificate. After a year as a teacher, he became an insurance salesman and, at 29, became the youngest lifetime member of the industry's Million Dollar Round Table. In 1965, he founded the Wilson Learning Corporation, now a multinational corporate training and research firm. After selling Wilson Learning to John Wiley & Sons, Wilson founded the

Wilson Learning Interactive Technology Group in Santa Fe, New Mexico, in partnership with Wiley. He is also the founder of the Alliance for Learning, a consortium of major corporations dedicated to advancing adult learning, and a much sought-after organizational consultant.

Renn Zaphiropoulos

Born in Greece, the son of a sea captain, Zaphiropoulos was raised in Egypt. He has bachelor's and master's degrees in physics from Lehigh University and is the holder of dozens of patents. His work as assistant director for research and development at Chromatic Television Laboratories led to the development of Trinitron. A pioneer in electrostatic printing, in 1969, he co-founded Versatec, the world's leading manufacturer of electrostatic printers and plotters, which merged with Xerox in 1979. Now retired from Xerox, he is a frequent lecturer at universities and in other forums, a consultant, author, sailor, breeder of Shire horses, and chef.

References

Introduction to the Revised Edition, 2003

xi Thomas L. Friedman, *The Lexus and the Olive Tree: Understanding Globalization*, Anchor (2000).

xiii Bethany McLean, "Where's the Loot Coming From?," *Fortune*, September 7, 1998; "CEO Pay Tomorrow: Same as Today," *BusinessWeek* Online, August 21, 2002.

xvi Warren G. Bennis and Robert J. Thomas, *Geeks & Geezers: How Eras, Values, & Defining Moments Shape Leaders*, Harvard Business School Press (2002).

xvii Jeffrey Zaslow, "Tricks of the Trade: Whistleblower's Warning," *Wall Street Journal*, October 30, 2002.

xix Warren Bennis and Patricia Ward Biederman, *Organizing Genius: The Secrets of Creative Collaboration*, Perseus Publishing (1998).

xxii David McCullough on Harry S. Truman, in *Character Above All*, ed. by Robert A. Wilson, Simon & Schuster (1996).

xxii Karl Weick, "Legitimization of Doubt," in *The Future of Leadership*, ed. by Warren Bennis, Gretchen Schweitzer, and Thomas Cummings, Jossey-Bass (2001).

xxiii Robert M. Sapolsky, *A Primate's Memoir: A Neuroscientist's Unconventional Life Among the Baboons*, Scribner (2001).

xxiv William James, *Letters of William James*, Vol. I (1878).

Introduction to the Original Edition, 1989

xxvii Ralph Waldo Emerson, "The Poet," *Essays: Second Series* (1844).

xxvii Harlan Cleveland, *The Knowledge Executive*, E. P. Dutton (1985).

xxviii Georges Braque, *Pensées sur l'Art*.

xxx Thomas Carlyle, *Sartor Resartes* (1837).

Chapter 1: Mastering the Context

1 *Time*, November 9, 1987.

8 Warren Bennis, Daniel Coleman, and James O'Toole with Patricia Ward Biederman, *Transparency*, Jossey-Bass (2008).

10 Quoted by William Bridges in "Getting Them Through the Wilderness: A Leader's Guide to Transition," in *New Management*, Fall 1988.

13 James Madison, *The Federalist*, #10 (1787).

14 Robert N. Bellah, Richard Madsen, William Sullivan, Ann Swidler, and Steven Tipton, *Habits of the Heart*, Harper & Row (1985).

19 Wallace Stevens, "Six Significant Landscapes," *Collected Poems of Wallace Stevens*, Knopf (1978).

Chapter 2: Understanding the Basics

37 Henry Kissinger, in an interview broadcast on KCET, Los Angeles, November 14, 1988.

46 Abraham Zaleznik, "Managers and Leaders: Are They Different?" *Harvard Business Review*, May–June 1977.

47 Sonya Friedman, "An Interview With Sonya Friedman," *Q Magazine*, March 1987.

Chapter 3: Knowing Yourself

49 William James, *Letters of William James*, Vol. I (1878).

52 Gib Akin, "Varieties of Managerial Learning," *Organizational Dynamics*.

58 David Riesman with Nathan Glazer and Reuel Denney, *The Lonely Crowd*, Yale University Press (1950).

59 Boris Pasternak, *Doctor Zhivago*. Pantheon (1958).

60 William James, *Principles of Psychology* (1890).

60 Erik Erikson, *Life Cycle Completed*, Norton (1982).

Chapter 4: Knowing the World

68 James W. Botkin, Mahdi Elmandjra, and Mircea Malitza, *No Limits to Learning*, Pergamon Books (1979).

73 Victor Goertzel and Mildred Goertzel, *Cradles of Eminence*, Little, Brown (1962).

75 Richard Wilbur, *Ceremony and Other Poems*, Harcourt Brace (1950).

75 Allan Bloom, *The Closing of the American Mind*, Simon & Schuster (1987).

75 E. D. Hirsch, Jr., *Cultural Literacy: What Every American Needs to Know*, Houghton Mifflin (1987).

References

75 Diane Ravitch and Chester E. Finn, Jr., *What Do Our 17-Year-Olds Know?* Harper & Row (1987).

76 Lynne Cheney, "My Turn," *Newsweek*, August 11, 1986.

77 Roger Smith, *Educating Managers*, Jossey-Bass (1986).

78 Frank Stanton, *Chronicle of Higher Education*, September 1986.

78 Ray Bradbury, "Management From Within," *New Management*, Vol. I, No. 4, 1984.

84 Joseph Campbell with Bill Moyers, *Power of Myth* (1988).

88 J. Robert Oppenheimer, *Science and the Common Understanding*, Simon & Schuster (1957).

88 John Cleese, "No More Mistakes and You're Through," *Forbes*, May 1988.

Chapter 5: Operating on Instinct

96 Carl Sagan, *The Dragons of Eden*, Random House (1977).

105 Wallace Stevens, *Necessary Angel*, Vintage (1942).

106 Henry James, *Notebooks of Henry James*, edited by F. O. Matthiessen and Kenneth B. Murdock, Oxford University Press (1961).

Chapter 6:
Deploying Yourself: Strike Hard, Try Everything

125 Mark Salzman, "Wushu: Meditation in Motion," *New York Times Magazine*, March, 1987.

126 George Leonard, *Esquire*, March 1986.

130 Carlos Fuentes, as quoted in *Elle*.

Chapter 7: Moving Through Chaos

137 Jacob Bronowski, *Ascent of Man*, Little, Brown (1973).

139 Morgan McCall and Michael Lombardo, study cited in "Learning the Lessons of Successful Leadership," *Success*, April 1984.

140 John Keats, letter to his brothers, George and Thomas (1817).

140 John Gardner, "Leadership Papers," Leadership Studies Program, Independent Sector (1987).

145 Lynn Harrell, *Ovation*.

146 Frank Rich, "The Father Figure," *New York Times Magazine*, September 30, 2001; "Person of the Year 2001: Rudy Giuliani," *Time*, December 31, 2001-January 7, 2002; "Setting a New Standard for Leadership: Mayor Rudy Giuliani," *People*, December 31, 2001.

References

Chapter 8: Getting People on Your Side

153 Max De Pree, *Leadership Is an Art*, University of Michigan Press (1988).

156 M. Cash Mathews, *Strategic Intervention in Organizations: Resolving Ethical Dilemmas*, Sage (1988).

156 William Frederick and James Weber, study, University of Pittsburgh (1988).

Chapter 9: Organizations Can Help—or Hinder

167 Bennis et al., *Transparency*.

169 U.S. Census 2000; "Data Points: Changing U.S. Demographics, Getting Older and More Diverse," *U.S. News & World Report*, www.usnews.com, November 9, 2008.

171 Tom Peters, personal communication.

176 Tom Peters, *Thriving on Chaos*, Knopf (1987).

177 Albert Einstein, letter.

178 Morgan McCall, Jr., Michael Lombardo, and Ann Morrison, *The Lessons of Experience*, Lexington Books (1988).

179 Lyman W. Porter and Lawrence E. McKibbon, *Management Education and Development: Drift or Thrust into the 21st Century*, McGraw-Hill (1988).

Chapter 10: Forging the Future

186 Paul Krugman, "The End of Middle-Class America (and the Triumph of the Plutocrats)," *New York Times Magazine*, October 20, 2002.

187 Rosabeth Moss Kanter, *When Giants Learn to Dance*, Simon & Schuster (1989).

188 Max De Pree, *Leadership Is an Art*, University of Michigan Press (1988).

192 D. Verne Morland, "Lear's Fool: Coping With Change Beyond Future Shock," *New Management*, Vol. II, No. 2.

193 J. Sterling Livingston, "Pygmalion in Management," *Harvard Business Review*, September–October 1988.

194 Elizabeth Drew, "Letter From Washington," *The New Yorker*, October 10, 1988.

195 James O'Toole, *Vanguard Management*, Doubleday (1985).

Index

245

Index

246

Index

Index

Index

Hurricane Katrina, 7, 203, 204
Hussein, Saddam, 15, 39
Huxley, T. H., 74

Iacocca, Lee, xvi–xvii
Iceland, 201
Ideology, 209–210
Imagination, 97
Imaging technology, 168
Imperial leader, xvi–xvii
Impulse, trusting, 91, 98, 99
Income gap, xvii, 14
Individual rights, common good *vs.*, 13
Individuality, ambiguous attitude toward, 44
Infotainment, 217
Inner voice. *See* Instinct
Innovation, 97–98
Innovative learning, 70–73
Instinct, operating on, 29, 95–106
  luck and, 102
  reliance on, 99–102
  right-brain characteristics and, 102–103
Integrity, xxvi, xviii, 152
  as desirable quality of American president, 221
  of institutions, 5
  parts of, 34–35
  trust and, 35, 155–159
Intellectual capital, New Economy and, xvi
Internet
  beginnings of, xiii, xv
  political campaigns and, 211
  See also World Wide Web
Intuition, 97
Iraq War, 199, 204, 210
Islamic fundamentalism, 11–12

Jackson, Andrew, xxvi
James, Henry, 106
James, William, xxxiv, xxvviii, 49, 60, 64
Japan, 11, 18, 168
Jefferson, Thomas, 12, 84, 226
Job rotation, 181–182
Jobs, Steve, 81, 238
Joe the Plumber, 219–220
Johnson, Edward C., III, 66, 234
Johnson, Lyndon, 37–38, 46
Johnson, Magic, 125

Johnson & Johnson, 90–91, 102, 142–145, 161–162
Jung, Carl, xxxv, 188

Kanter, Rosabeth Moss, 187
Kaplan, Martin (Marty), 53–55, 56, 234
  on the big questions, 75
  changes in career of, 163
  on competence, 124–125
  on empathy, 148
  on point of view, 115
  on reflection, 57
Kay, Alan, 87
Keats, John, 140
Kennedy, Caroline, 212
Kennedy, John F., 36, 37, 38, 88, 218, 223, 224
Kennedy, Ted, 212
Kerry, John, 214
Khruschev, Nikita, 191
King, Martin Luther, Jr., 2, 85, 125
Kissinger, Henry, 37
Knapp, Brooke, 50, 85, 182, 234–235
  on desire to achieve, 122, 123–124
  on overcoming fear, 122
Knowing the world, 67–93
Knowledge Executive, The (Cleveland), xxxi–xxxii
Koch, Howard, Jr., 103–104
Kozlowski, Dennis, xx
Krim, Mathilde, 31, 66, 118–119, 143, 235
  on instinct, 101
  on requirements of growth, 98
  on self-knowledge, 45

Lack of leadership, 2–4
Latinos, 9, 170–171
Leaders
  cyclical attitudes toward, xx
  essential competencies of, xxv–xviii
  importance of, 5
  managers *vs.*, 41–46, 132
Leaders (Bennis & Nanus), xxix–xxx, 143, 190, 192
Leadership
  capacity for, xxxvi, xxxii–xxxiii
  defined, 132
  demonstration of, xxxiii
  lack of, 1
Leadership development, 36, 178–182

Index

Index

Index

Index

Index